Windows NT

A Practical Guide

Windows NT
A Practical Guide

Arthur D.Tennick

BUTTERWORTH
HEINEMANN

Butterworth-Heinemann Ltd
Linacre House, Jordan Hill, Oxford OX2 8DP

ℛ A member of the Reed Elsevier group

OXFORD LONDON BOSTON
MUNICH NEW DELHI SINGAPORE SYDNEY
TOKYO TORONTO WELLINGTON

First published 1994

NOTICE
The author and publisher have used their best efforts to prepare this book, including the
computer examples contained in it. The computer examples have all been tested. The author
and the publisher make no warranty, implicit or explicit, about the documentation. The author
and the publisher will not be liable under any circumstances for any direct or indirect damages
arising from any use, direct or indirect, of the documentation or computer examples contained
in this book.

TRADEMARKS/REGISTERED TRADEMARKS
Computer hardware and software brand names mentioned in this book are protected by their
respective trademarks and are acknowledged.

British Library Cataloguing in Publication Data
Tennick, Arthur D.
  Windows NT
  I. Title
  005.369

ISBN 0 7506 0852 8

Typeset by Arthur D.Tennick
Printed and bound in Great Britain

Contents

Part One – For users new to Windows

Contents

Part Two – For all users

Contents

Contents

Conventions

Given the release of both Windows NT and Windows for Workgroups, the generic term Windows no longer conveys a specific enough meaning. Throughout this book, Windows refers to the whole family of Windows products. Where differentiation is required then the terms Windows NT (or just NT), Windows for Workgroups, and Windows for DOS are employed. Windows for DOS refers to Windows 3.0 and Windows 3.1 running under DOS. Thus Windows for DOS indicates those versions of Windows that have been traditionally called just Windows. Windows for DOS is a more explicit reference and avoids confusion with Windows NT, Windows for Workgroups, and the generic phrase Windows.

Starting and quitting Windows NT

Starting Windows NT

The exact method of starting a Windows NT session (see FIG. I.1) depends upon a number of circumstances – whether NT's the sole bootable operating system on the computer or not, and whether you're working on a single- or multi-user machine. Let's begin by looking at the simplest case – where you're working on a single-account, single-user computer and NT is the only operating system available. If you want to get started straight-away then jump to the steps at the end of this section.

If NT is your sole operating system then you're thrown straight into NT when you switch on the computer. The first action that's required on your part is to press **Ctrl-Alt-Del** when you see the small Welcome panel (see FIG. I.2) on screen. If you've come straight from DOS, or Windows for

Introduction

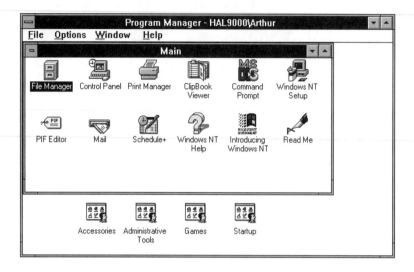

FIG. I.1

DOS, you might be slightly surprised at this key combination – after all, **Ctrl-Alt-Del** is normally used to reboot the computer (or to terminate a recalcitrant application under Windows 3.1 for DOS). Things are rather different under Windows NT. Here **Ctrl-Alt-Del** serves two purposes, which have nothing to do with rebooting or escaping from errant programs. First, the key combination is used to log on to your system. Second, once you are logged on, **Ctrl-Alt-Del** calls the Windows NT Security dialog. The latter enables you to log off, or change your password, or lock your workstation, and one or two other things. The choice of key combination for logging on is deliberate, as it helps ensure that 'Trojan horses' don't pick up on your username and password. A Trojan horse is a piece of software maliciously introduced to your system that can trap your username and password. The information elicited is then employed to gain unauthorised access to your computer (and possibly to others if you're on a network). **Ctrl-Alt-Del** effectively flushes out any Trojan horse so your username and especially your password do not fall into the hands of hackers.

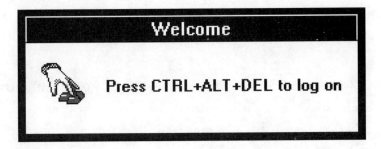

FIG. I.2

After pressing **Ctrl-Alt-Del** you are presented with the Welcome dialog box (see FIG. I.3). This is the last barrier to starting up Windows NT, and

Welcome

Username:	administrator
From:	BILBO
Password:	*********

OK   Help

FIG. I.3

Introduction

is where you enter your username, your computer name, and your password. When you've completed these entries correctly, and clicked OK, you go into NT (if someone else has added you as an authorised user you may be asked to redefine your original password). You know you have made a successful entry once NT accepts your data in the Welcome dialog and starts up Program Manager.

The first time you start NT on a single-user machine then the username, computer name, and password entered are the ones you established as you installed NT. If Windows NT was installed for you then you need to get those details from the installer. Once you're in NT you can change any of the details if you wish, provided you have the necessary authority.

When you share the computer with a colleague it's possible that they logged off but left NT running. In that case, there's no call to switch the computer off and then back on. If your colleague logged off correctly, then you should see the Welcome panel asking you to press **Ctrl-Alt-Del**. However, your colleague may have pressed this combination already for you, so the Welcome dialog is displayed, ready for you to type in your password. That's very kind of them – to save you pressing **Ctrl-Alt-Del** – but it's misplaced help. What you should do in those circumstances is to press the key combination again. That way you can be sure that it really *is* the Welcome dialog and not a Trojan horse masquerading as such.

Alternatively, a colleague may have shutdown NT but left the computer switched on. This time you see a small dialog telling you it's safe to switch off. This dialog is entitled Shutdown Computer and contains a Restart push button. Here you have two choices. One, you can switch off, wait a few seconds, and turn the computer back on. Two, click the Restart button. Either way you get back to the Welcome panel, though Restart is safe and much quicker.

The above discussion may have prompted a question, especially if you are from a single-user DOS, or Windows for DOS, environment. What's the difference between logging off from and shutting down Windows NT? When you log off, you effectively leave NT running but another user (or yourself) must log on again to actually use NT. In other words, NT is locked – you can explicitly lock NT as well, but that denies access to most other users (apart from yourself and a system administrator). If, by contrast, you shutdown NT then anyone requiring access must reload the operating system before they can attempt a log on. Both logging off and shutdown are equally secure with regard to keeping out unauthorised users. Shutdown, however, correctly closes down any NT services and should always be used before powering off the computer – it's generally not advisable to turn off your machine after merely logging off. Although logging off does prompt you to save any unsaved data in application data files, it may not terminate some NT functions satisfactorily. The differing procedures for logging off and shutdown are explained presently.

Again on a multi-user workstation the previous user may have locked NT. This means that only that user, or someone with administrative rights, can unlock it. To lock NT you press **Ctrl-Alt-Del** after gaining access and clicking the Lock Workstation button in the ensuing dialog. This is a handy security measure if you need to leave your desk and don't want to log off. Logging off allows other authorised users to get into NT – locking NT keeps everyone out (including other authorised users but excluding users with administrative rights).

Introduction

Many NT installers arrange for NT to coexist with a previous operating such as DOS. Here, there may be an added consideration before you can successfully log on. You might have to explicitly opt for Windows NT as the operating system as the computer boots. Typically, the boot sequence might display a choice of Windows NT and DOS as the operating system. One of these will be the default operating system, though you are normally given a few seconds to override the default. To do this, you press the **Up** or **Down** keys to move the default highlight. Of course, if Windows NT is the default, you don't have to do anything to get to the Welcome log on screen. Though there may be occasions where the other operating system is the default, and you are given no time in which to change the default. This situation can arise if the someone has set the timeout for choosing operating systems to zero seconds. For instructions of how to get into Windows NT in that circumstance, see the next section: *If you ever get locked out.*

To summarise the way to start Windows NT:

1   Switch on the computer. Usually this step takes you straight into NT. If the computer has a dual operating system make sure that the choice is defaulting to NT. You can then press **Enter** or wait for the timeout to expire.

2   At the Welcome panel (see FIG. I.2) press **Ctrl-Alt-Del** to initiate the log on process.

3   At the Welcome dialog (see FIG. I.3) enter your username, computer name, and password. On a single-user machine you may only have to enter your password as the other entries are

ready filled in. On a network you select your domain rather than the computer name. A successful logon results in the display of Program Manager. If this is your first logon and you installed alongside Windows for DOS or Windows for Workgroups you are given the opportunity to migrate some of your existing Windows settings, such as Program Manager groups, to Windows NT – this assumes you're not logging on as Administrator.

If you ever get locked out

You only need to refer to this section if you're ever denied access to NT. However, you may want to read it now so you are prepared for the possibility of being locked out of Windows NT.

There's a number of reasons why you may not be able to get into Windows NT. These include a forgotten or inappropriate password, the system defaulting to another operating system with no timeout, unwise changes to the NT setup, or even corrupt system files.

If you forget your password you won't be able to log on. Without the right password you can't log back on as the same user. This means you lose most of your changes to the NT environment, such as personal groups in Program Manager and desktop configurations. You could get back in as the Administrator user and reset the password for your usual username, or ask a member of the Administrators group to do it for you. You change passwords with the User Manager program in the Administrative Tools group. This is covered in due course. By default you can always log on as a guest user, this one requires no password. But here you don't have

Introduction

enough rights to go into User Manager and alter your own personal password.

A forgotten password is not the only potential cause of a lock-out. Some of the changes you make can cause Windows NT not to function correctly, or at least not to display on screen. The latter may happen if you swap to an inappropriate display through Windows NT Setup. You have two options here, short of a complete reinstallation. One, try starting Windows NT again but hold down the **Spacebar** as NT loads. That causes NT to use its last-known good configuration. If that doesn't fix the problem then you have to have your Emergency repair disk to hand. You should have created this disk when you installed Windows NT for the first time. The Repair disk is also vital for repairing any NT system files that may become corrupted and keep you out of NT. To use the Repair disk insert Disk 1 from the installation disk set in your A: drive and turn on the computer. When you see the initial Setup screen press **r**. You'll be asked to insert the Repair disk and maybe some of the other installation disks. When you've followed all the prompts on screen, reboot and all should be well.

The final observation in this section concerns the possibility of the system booting straight into another operating system, and giving you no time to select Windows NT from the boot loader. This can only happen if you have a dual-boot computer and someone has changed the boot setting. The latter is set through the System icon in Control Panel. If you are being thrown straight into another operating system with no timeout then the timeout has been changed to zero seconds, and the other operating system has been selected as the default. That results in a Catch-22 – you have to alter the System settings to get into NT, but you have to get into NT to make the alteration. Fortunately, there is a way out if your other operating system has a utility for editing text files – in Windows for DOS you can use Notepad or try Edit in DOS. The NT System settings for booting are held in a read-only text file in your root directory called BOOT.INI. This file includes a line that specifies the timeout for changing the boot operating system. All you have to do is to change the line **timeout=0** in the [boot loader] section to something like**timeout=10**. This gives you ten seconds in which to select NT as the boot operating system. BOOT.INI is read-only so to make the changes you must remove the read-only attribute. You can do this in DOS by entering **attrib -r BOOT.INI**, or in Windows for DOS File Manager through File, Properties. Remember to reset its read-only setting after fixing the timeout line – in DOS enter **attrib +r BOOT.INI**. Normally, you should not try and edit this file manually – it's far better to write changes to it by going through the System program in Control Panel.

Quitting Windows NT

How you quit Windows NT depends on whether you want to log off or to shutdown Windows NT completely. Should you want to try shutdown or logging off then you can jump straight to the steps at the end of this section. If you, or another user, are likely to require Windows NT the same working day, then logging off is probably sufficient. If it's the end of the working day then a full shutdown is advisable. Alternatively, you might want to return to the computer but to deny access to all other users (apart from administrators) in the meantime. That way you can ensure that you can continue working and aren't delayed by someone who's nipped in to borrow your machine. To keep other non-admin users away you lock your workstation. As already mentioned, you lock the computer by pressing **Ctrl-Alt-Del** and clicking the Lock Workstation button in the

Introduction

Windows NT Security dialog. To open it again you must enter your password – anyone with administrator privileges can do the same. Incidentally, setting up a password-protected screen saver through the Desktop icon in Control Panel has the same effect. But there the system does not lock up until after the delay you specify when you enable the screen saver. You should only lock the workstation or allow a password-protected screen saver to be invoked if you plan to return to your machine that day, and you don't want anyone else to use it.

Before logging off and shutting down you may want to back up your data. On a single-user machine where only a few data files get altered in the course of a day it's a simple matter to copy the changed files to floppy disk. The easiest way to do this is through File Manager. But with lots of files and users it makes sense to adopt a more rigorous policy. You, or a system administrator, might consider using the Backup program in the Administrative Tools group. In order to do so there must be a tape attached to your computer or elsewhere on a network. Both File Manager and Backup are discussed at greater length later.

To shutdown Windows NT:

1   Click File, Shutdown in Program Manager. Alternatively, press **Ctrl-Alt-Del** and click the Shutdown button in the Windows NT Security dialog.

2   The Shutdown Computer dialog (see FIG. I.4) appears. This dialog contains a check box which enables you to restart NT immediately on shutdown. Click OK whether you turn on this check box or not. A small dialog informs that unsaved data is

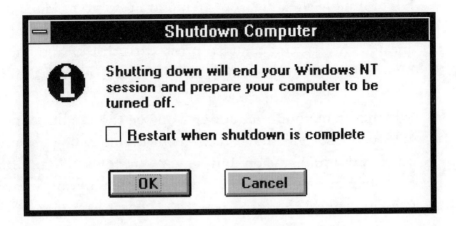

FIG. I.4

being written to disk and a second Shutdown Computer dialog takes its place. If you enabled an automatic restart you don't get to see this particular dialog and your whole system reboots itself so you're ready to log on again.

3   If you see the second Shutdown Computer dialog you then have two choices. As the dialog suggests, it is safe to switch off your computer or you can restart NT by clicking the Restart button. If you want to end this session then simply turn off the computer. To safeguard all your data and system files it's essential that you never switch off until you see this dialog. It's not good practice just to log off before powering down.

To log off from Windows NT:

Introduction

1   Click File, Logoff in Program Manager. Alternatively press **Alt-F4**, or double click the Control menu in Program Manager, or select Close from the Control menu. If these don't present enough choices you can also press **Ctrl-Alt-Del** and click the Logoff button in the ensuing Windows NT Security dialog.

2   Whichever method you adopt, you see the Logoff Windows NT dialog (see FIG. I.5). Clicking OK in this dialog terminates your individual session, but leaves Windows NT running so any other authorised user can begin work without restarting. Clicking Cancel aborts the log off and you can continue working without interruption.

Once you're in

A successful log on results in Program Manager starting. The main window (see FIG. I.1) carries the name Program Manager in its title bar. In addition, the title bar displays the name of your computer or workgroup

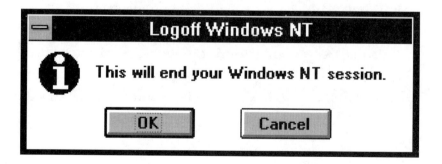

FIG. I.5

and your username. Inside the main window you see the Program Manager groups.

The default groups are personal groups and are called Main, Accessories, Administrative Tools, Startup, and Games. You may also have another group called Applications if you let Windows NT search for existing applications on your hard disk during installation. You may have different groups if you've already migrated existing Windows for DOS groups or NT was installed by a system administrator. For readers with no previous knowledge of either Windows for DOS or Windows for Workgroups a full introduction to Program Manager comes later. Even if you are familiar with Windows for DOS or Windows for Workgroups then some of the group names and the icons they contain are going to be new. Again these are covered fully in the course of the book.

Before you begin to configure Program Manager to reflect your own way of working there are a few things you ought to consider (note that if you're a user in a workgroup then your system administrator may have restricted your freedom to configure Program Manager). To begin with, you may want to take a look at an overview of Windows NT – this concentrates on topics relating to workgroups and networks, though it does show how to log on, which is of benefit to all users. To see the overview double click the Introducing Windows NT icon in your Main group. You might want to configure the appearance and behaviour of your desktop – for example, changing the colour scheme or adding sound events.

If you didn't specify a printer during installation you must do so before you can print out – though the printer may already be set up for networked

Introduction

users. Again if you omitted to do so during installation, you might have to set up your network connections and join a workgroup or domain. If you're an administrator you should set up the users and groups allowed to work on the computer (see Chapter 18 on *User Manager*). In addition, you may want to establish security measures and perhaps alter your initial password. Finally, you might like to see how the Windows NT Help system works – double click the Windows NT Help icon in your Main group.

Essentials

ESSENTIALS

■   How to work with windows and menus

■   How to use a mouse

■   How to use keyboard alternatives

■   Lots of hands-on exercises

Initial screen

Once Windows NT has started it displays the initial screen. If you have had Windows NT installed for a while then your initial screen may be quite a bit different from the example screenshot shown (see FIG. 1.1). You will need to adapt the exercises to match your display. Even if you have not used Windows NT yet, then some of the elements of the window may be different. What you might see is a window called Program Manager, containing a smaller window entitled Main. Underneath this second window, but still within the first window, you will notice some small rectangles. These are named Accessories, Administrative Tools, Startup, and Games. In addition, you may see a rectangle called Applications. These rectangles are windows too, albeit very small ones.

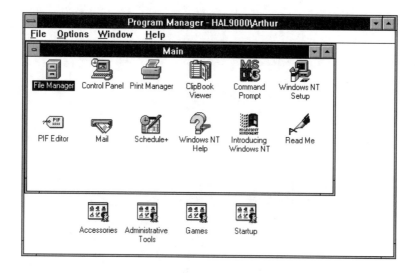

FIG. 1.1

Essentials

When a window is shrunk to its smallest possible size it does not look much like an ordinary window, and is known as an icon.

Components of a window

All windows look more or less identical. This applies to Windows NT itself and Windows-based applications. A window is merely an area on screen that has distinct boundaries. A window may be as large as the screen, shrunk to an icon, or any size between. It is possible to have two or more windows showing at once. If you refer to your initial screen you will notice that there are two windows, one inside the other. There are also some smaller windows in the form of icons. The two windows are called Program Manager and Main. If we take a trip around the Program Manager window we can identify its features. At the top left of the window is the Control menu box. Clicking this pulls down a menu. To remove the menu you click once anywhere outside the menu.

This menu appears in most windows and is used to carry out a variety of tasks. To the right of this is the title bar. This contains the name of the window and in applications indicates the name of the data file on which you are working. At the top right are two buttons. The one on the left contains a downward pointing arrowhead and is called the Minimize button. The next one contains an upward pointing arrowhead and is the Maximize button.. Do not worry if you sometimes notice two arrowheads on this button. Above this top row of Control menu, title bar, Minimize and Maximize buttons is a thin band. The band extends around the whole perimeter of the window and is called the border. At each corner of the window the border is partitioned by two small lines. This area of the border is referred to as a window corner. Beneath the top row of the window is a second row containing the words File, Options, Window and Help. These are all used to access pull-down (or drop-down menus) and the row is called the menu bar. The area of the window enclosed by the menu bar and the left, right, and bottom border is the workspace. Some windows have extra features like scroll bars, but you may not see them in the initial Program Manager window.

The second window, Main, is very similar in structure to the Program Manager window, except it does not have a menu bar. Windows with menu bars are usually application windows, those without are document windows.

Icons

Icons are minimized windows. There are two major categories of icons. Application icons are used to start (or restore) application windows. Document icons are for opening document windows. In the Main window the icon labelled File Manager is an application icon while the icon at the bottom of the Program Manager window, labelled Accessories, is a document icon.

Mouse actions

There are five mouse actions normally carried out while working with Windows NT and Windows-based applications. Four are used all the time and the fifth, known as right clicking is used less frequently. The other four are referred to as moving, clicking, double clicking and dragging. It is important to keep practising these actions until you feel quite comfortable with the mouse. Many people take to the mouse straight away, a minority requires that extra bit of patience.

Make sure you have an area of your desktop free to manoeuvre the mouse. To begin with, have as large an area as possible to the right (if you're right-handed) or in front of the keyboard, at least a square foot. As you become more proficient you should find this area can be as small as about six inches by four inches. Always work with the mouse tail pointing away from you, towards the top of the desk. Rest your right hand gently on the mouse with the index finger lightly on the left hand mouse button. Of course the left-handed reader should reverse these positions. The difficulty here, for left-handed users, arises because your index finger is naturally on the right-hand button. You really need to have your index finger on the left-hand button because first, the index finger is the most natural finger to use for clicking and second, the left-hand button is pressed most of the time. The solution is to swap functions of left and right mouse buttons. This can be accomplished by configuring the mouse through the Control Panel (see the entry on Mouse in Chapter 11 on *Control Panel*). Should your mouse have three buttons you can ignore the middle button.

Moving the mouse across the desktop results in a corresponding movement of mouse pointer on screen. Try to move the mouse with your hand still resting on top and your thumb and little (or second finger) lightly gripping the flanks of the mouse. Do not move the mouse by holding it between your thumb and index finger in a pincer fashion. A small amount of downward pressure may be necessary. Any failure of the pointer to keep track with the mouse indicates an unsuitable surface for the mouse. Some laminated desk tops are just too smooth, and a sheet of coarse paper under the mouse will help. Better still is a mouse mat. You may discover that you run out of room on your desk before the mouse reaches the edges of the screen. Just pick up the mouse and place it in a more central position. Picking up the mouse has no effect on its pointer location.

Clicking, or single clicking, is the action of pressing the left button once and letting it go quickly. Depending upon the make of mouse there should ideally be a single audible click and some tactile feedback as the button is pressed. It is important not to push the mouse away as you press the button, this may give unexpected and undesired results.

Double clicking is simply single clicking twice rapidly. Beginners often double click either too quickly or too slowly, and a few people can never quite manage it comfortably. Once again it is essential that you keep the mouse totally still as you double click. You can adjust the speed required for double clicking through the Mouse icon in Control Panel.

Dragging the mouse requires that you press and hold down the left-hand mouse button, during which time you move the mouse across the desk top. It is better here to keep the button down until you are entirely satisfied with the location of the pointer. Your action has no effect until you let go of the button. Letting go too soon might have surprising results.

Right clicking, which is only occasionally used, involves pressing the right-hand button with the middle finger and immediately letting go. You may have reason to right click, say, in Paintbrush to alter background colours.

Other mouse techniques you might come across are right dragging, right double clicking, shift and control clicking. However to begin productive work it is sufficient to be able to move, click, double click and drag the mouse. Keyboard users should note that there are alternatives to these actions that do not require the mouse.

Mouse and keyboard practice

If you are new to Windows and mouse, it is vital to practice basic mouse actions in this section. If you are new to Windows and do not have a mouse you need to understand keyboard alternatives that follow each step below.

1   Move the mouse until the tip of the pointer is over the word File in the menu bar of the Program Manager window. Practice will show how accurate you must be, there is some degree of leeway allowed in positioning the pointer.

2   Click the mouse and a pull-down menu (see FIG. 1.2) appears. To make a choice from the menu you click the choice. For now we will back out of the action.

   Keyboard – Press **Alt-F**. The **Alt** key with the underlined letter in a menu option is the standard procedure for accessing the menu.

3   Click anywhere apart from the menu to remove it. You might find it convenient merely to click File again.

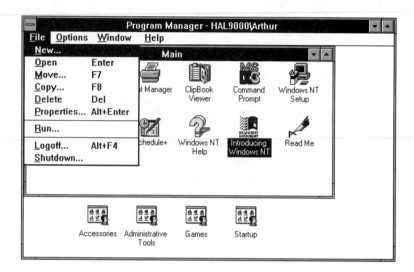

FIG. 1.2

Keyboard – Press **Esc**. The word File will be highlighted. Pressing **Esc** a second time removes the highlight.

4   Double click the Control menu. If you are successful in double clicking the Logoff Windows NT dialog appears. Click Cancel to back out of your action. If you did not double click fast enough, or indeed too rapidly, Windows will interpret your action as a single click and display a pull-down menu. Should this happen click anywhere outside this pull-down menu to remove it and try again. Clicking in the original position also removes the menu.

Keyboard – Press **Alt-Spacebar** (see FIG. 1.3) then **L** then **Esc**. Pressing **L** chooses Logoff. You do not use **Alt-underlined letter** within menus, only to access menus. Instead of pressing

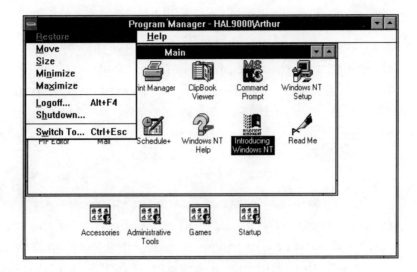

FIG. 1.3

L you could move to Logoff with the direction keys and press **Enter**.

It is possible a slow double click combined with an unwanted movement of the mouse causes unexpected things to happen. You might see a dialog box pop up on screen, or a four headed arrow, or Program Manager leaps to fill the screen, or even seems to disappear altogether. What has occurred is that Windows NT has interpreted the slow double click to be two quite distinct single clicks. The first single click opened the menu, the involuntary movement of the mouse positioned the pointer over a menu option and the second single click chose the option. To get rid of any dialog box, click the Cancel button in the dialog box. If you have summoned a four headed arrow, click anywhere on screen to restore the normal mouse pointer.

A larger than normal Program Manager means an inadvertent choice of maximizing. In this case locate the up and down arrow heads on the button at the extreme top right of the screen and click this button. This is actually the maximize button, which changes to being a restore button whenever a window is maximized.

A disappearing Program Manager suggests an accidental minimizing, it will be an icon at the bottom of the screen. To restore the icon to a window double click the icon. The fact that you are in this situation is a result of faulty double clicking. It is possible that your second attempt at double clicking does not work either. Should you now see a menu that has popped up from the icon click Restore in the menu. If nothing at all happens, first click the icon then click Restore in the resulting menu. Go back to step 4 until you get it working.

5   Click the maximize button in the Program Manager window (not the Main window). Program Manager expands to fill the whole display and the maximize button has changed slightly – there is an extra arrowhead. It is now a restore button.

Keyboard – Press **Alt-Spacebar** then **X**. Such a sequence of keystrokes is represented by **Alt-Spacebar**, **X** from here on.

6   Click the restore button to revert to the original size of Program Manager.

Keyboard – **Alt-Spacebar**, **R**.

7 Click the minimize button to shrink the window to an icon. Note the Main window goes. This is because Main is a subsidiary document (or child) window within the Program Manager window.

Keyboard – **Alt-Spacebar**, **N**.

8 Move the mouse pointer to the Program Manager icon and drag the mouse. The icon moves with the mouse across the screen. Stop dragging the mouse to anchor the icon in its new position.

Keyboard – **Alt-Spacebar**, **M**. Then use the direction keys and press **Enter** to anchor the icon in position.

9 Drag the icon back to approximately its original position.

Keyboard – Repeat the actions for step 8.

10 Double click the icon to restore the window. Note the Main window is back inside the Program Manager window. If you are experiencing problems with double clicking try single clicking the icon, and clicking Restore in the ensuing menu.

Keyboard – **Alt-Spacebar**, **R**.

11 Click the minimize button in the Main window (*not* Program Manager this time). The Main window becomes a document icon in the Program Manager window.

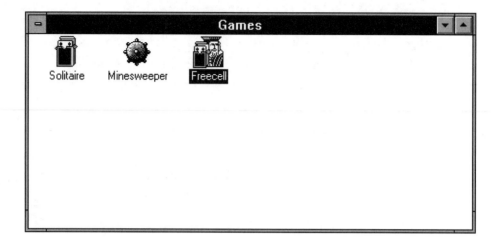

FIG. 1.4

Keyboard – **Alt-Hyphen, N**. Note that **Alt-Spacebar** accesses the Control Menu in application windows, **Alt-Hyphen** is used in document windows.

12 Double click the Games document icon. Or try clicking and choosing Restore. There is now a document window for Games (see FIG. 1.4). Inside there are application icons for Solitaire (Patience), Freecell, and Minesweeper.

Keyboard – **Alt-W, 4. Alt-W** pulls down the Window menu. Each document icon and window has an associated underlined number. It is possible that Games is not number 4, in which case press the relevant number key.

13   Double click the Solitaire icon and take a break. Or single click to highlight the name Solitaire and press **Enter**.

Keyboard – Use direction keys to move between application icons in the Games window. When Solitaire is highlighted press **Enter**. Solitaire is much easier to play if you have a mouse, though you can move cards with the keyboard. Experiment with **Tab** and direction keys, and the **Spacebar**. To get keyboard help press **Alt-H**, **C** and **Tab** to the entry for Play Solitaire by Using the Keyboard, and press **Enter**. To exit help press **Alt-F**, **X**.

14   When you have finally won at Solitaire double click its Control menu to close it down, back to an application icon.

Keyboard – **Alt-Spacebar, C**.

Indiscriminate clicking may have minimized Solitaire to an icon beneath Program Manager. You may well be staring at two identical icons for Solitaire. The one in the Games window starts the application. The one at the foot of the screen represents a program already started and still running. You can close it down by double clicking the icon and double clicking the Control menu in the restored window. Such icons retain any data present in the application. Minimizing applications in this manner is a good way of tidying up the screen without recourse to saving data and closing applications. Should you see a pack of Solitaire icons (a pack of packs of cards, so to speak) at the bottom of the display you have started Solitaire more than

FIG. 1.5

once. Close each occurrence of the program by first double clicking its icon (or click once followed by Close) – though not the one in the Games window, this only starts up more games.

15 Minimize the Games window with its minimize button.

Keyboard – **Alt-Hyphen, N**.

16 Open the Accessories window (see FIG. 1.5) by double clicking its document icon. Remember you can click and press **Enter** if you prefer.

Keyboard – **Alt-W, 1**. Check that 1 is the number next to Accessories in the Window pull-down menu. Your number could well be different.

In the Accessories window there are quite a few applications icons. You start these just the same as Solitaire.

17   Double click the icon for Paintbrush in the Accessories window. Unnecessary movement of the mouse at this point could well dislodge the icon from its original position. This shifting of icons results in untidy group windows and you could eventually lose icons past the edge of the window. Of course you can easily get them back, but for now I recommend you reposition dislodged icons by dragging them back into place.

Keyboard – Use direction keys to move to Paintbrush and press **Enter**.

Paintbrush opens in its own window and partly, or completely, obscures the Program Manager window which now lies underneath.

18   Minimize Paintbrush by clicking the minimize button in the Paintbrush window.

Keyboard – **Alt-Spacebar, N**.

19   In the Accessories group window in the Program Manager window double click the icon for Notepad.

Keyboard – Use the direction keys to move to Notepad and press **Enter**.

20 Minimize Notepad too.

Keyboard – **Alt-Spacebar**, **N**.

21 Minimize Program Manager itself, be careful to use the minimize button for Program Manager and not for the Accessories window.

Keyboard – **Alt-Spacebar**, **N**.

You should now see three icons at the foot of the display. Paintbrush and Notepad are actually running applications, and the icons contain any work you carried out in those applications. This is one of the many ways of working with multiple applications in Windows. As you temporarily finish one application you minimize it, and begin work on another application. When you wish to return to the first application you minimize the current application and restore the first by double clicking its icon.

22 Restore Program Manager, Paintbrush and Notepad by double clicking their respective icons.

Keyboard – Press **Alt-Tab** until the Program Manager icon is reached and let go of both keys. Repeat **Alt-Tab** for Paintbrush and Notepad.

23 The Notepad window should be at the front. Do not worry if you restored the applications in a different order from here, all we are going to do is to maximize all the applications. Maximize Notepad or the front window.

Keyboard – **Alt-Spacebar, X**.

The other two windows disappear behind the maximized window. We want to bring them to the front, in other words to make them current windows. The following actions are very important and fundamental to working with multiple applications. They involve switching the current application when some or all the other applications are in hidden windows. There are various methods of doing this and you will need to experiment until you discover the one that suits you. Some involve combination key strokes – **Ctrl-Esc**, **Alt-Tab** and **Alt-Esc**. If part of a hidden window is visible then clicking the visible portion brings that window to the front.

24 Press **Esc** while holding down the **Ctrl** key (if your keyboard has two **Ctrl** keys then either will do). You could click the Control menu (of any application) followed by the Switch To option instead.

Keyboard – **Ctrl-Esc**.

The **Ctrl-Esc** combinations summons the small Task List window (see FIG. 1.6). In the list box in this window you will see the currently open applications: Program Manager, Paintbrush and Notepad. An alternative is to double click the background area (wallpaper) if it is not obscured.

FIG. 1.6

25   In the list box click Paintbrush to highlight its entry then click the Switch To button. Or simply double click the entry.

Keyboard – Use the direction keys to highlight the entry for Paintbrush and press **Enter**.

Task List disappears and the Paintbrush window is brought to the front.

26   Maximize Paintbrush.

Keyboard – **Alt-Spacebar, X**.

27   Use **Ctrl-Esc** again to see the Task list.

Keyboard – **Ctrl-Esc**.

28   Select Program Manager in the list and click Switch To.

Keyboard – Highlight Program Manager in the list and press **Enter**.

29   Maximize the Program Manager window.

Keyboard – **Alt-Spacebar**, **X**.

Instead of three icons representing open applications we now have three maximized windows. Obviously only one is visible, the other two are in the background. To switch from one maximized window to another you can use **Ctrl-Esc** to see the Task List. A quicker method, however, is through the **Alt-Tab** combination (**Alt-Esc** is similar in its operation).

30   Press and hold down the **Alt** key. Press the **Tab** key a few times with **Alt** kept down. You will cycle through the three applications. Try and end up with the Program Manager window current.

Keyboard – **Alt**(held down)-**Tab**.

Alt-Tab is normally quicker than **Ctrl-Esc** unless you have a lot of applications running, in which case the cycling may take some time. There is a nice variation of the **Alt-Tab** combination

which is ideal if most of your work involves repeatedly moving
between just two of the applications.

31 Press and hold down the **Alt** key. While it is depressed press the
Tab key repeatedly until you cycle to Notepad and then let go
of both keys. Repeat this step for Paintbrush.

Keyboard – **Alt**(held down)**-Tab**.

32 Press and hold the **Alt** key down and then press the **Tab** key
and let go of both immediately. You will cycle from Paintbrush
to Notepad (or vice versa).

Keyboard – **Alt-Tab**.

33 Repeat step 32 to see Paintbrush again (or Notepad). You can
repeat step 32 as many times as you like, but you will notice
that Program Manager has been dropped from the sequence.
To reintroduce Program Manager to the sequence you will
need to use **Alt-Tab** as in step 30.

Keyboard – **Alt-Tab**.

Alt-Tab (let go of **Tab** only) cycles through all open applications.
Alt-Tab (let go of both) cycles between the last two applications
only. You can alter the default two applications by using
Alt-Tab until you find one of the applications you want and
then letting go of **Tab**. Repeat this for the second application

you wish to work on. These are the new defaults and you can utilize **Alt-Tab** (let go of both) to cycle between these two only.

So far we have looked at multiple applications as icons and as full windows. There are yet more alternatives, for example having two or more windows moved and sized in such a manner that you have two or more windows completely visible at the same time. This is called tiling. Or you might prefer to have overlapping windows with a portion of each window just showing behind the ones on top. This is referred to as cascading. Tiling and cascading of open application windows can be done through the Task List (by clicking Tile and Cascade respectively in the Task List window). We are going to do it manually, as this will involve practice in moving and sizing windows.

To summarise – the modes of working include icons, full windows, tiling and cascading. And of course you can combine any or all of these at the same time. The exact mode you eventually adopt is entirely down to personal preference and the demands of the current session.

Working with multiple applications has great benefits. The more memory in your computer the more applications you can have open, though there is no reason why you should not work with one application at a time if you wish. Perhaps the greatest single benefit of working with multiple applications is that while one application is tied up in printing (or lengthy processing) you can switch to another application and continue working.

One popular method of working is to tile two applications horizontally, clicking the window of the other application when you want to switch. This is also a useful arrangement when you wish to transfer data from one of the applications to the other. This data transfer between applications is known as clipboarding.

34 Make Paintbrush current with **Alt-Tab** and click the restore button to reduce it from its full window. You should see Notepad, or possibly Program Manager, behind the Paintbrush window.

Keyboard – **Alt-Tab, Alt-Spacebar, R**.

35 Repeat step 34 with Notepad.

Keyboard – **Alt-Tab, Alt-Spacebar, R**.

36 Make Program Manager current with **Alt-Tab** (or you can just click its window if you can see it), restore it first *and* then minimize it. We are tucking Program Manager away as an icon just to make the display less cluttered.

Keyboard – **Alt-Tab, Alt-Spacebar, N**.

37 Make Paintbrush current with **Alt-Tab** (or click the Paintbrush window if you can see it).

Keyboard – **Alt-Tab**.

38   Place the mouse pointer on the title bar of Paintbrush and drag the mouse. You should detect a corresponding movement of the Paintbrush window on screen. Continue dragging until the Paintbrush title bar is flush with the top of the screen.

Keyboard – **Alt-Spacebar**, **M**, **Up**, **Enter**. Use the **Up** key until the title bar is in position and press **Enter** to anchor this position.

39   Place the mouse pointer on the lower border of Paintbrush. The pointer will change into a double-headed arrow. When you see this double-headed arrow drag the mouse up or down until the border is about half way down the screen.

Keyboard– **Alt-Spacebar**, **S**, **Down**, **Up**, **Enter**. Here the **Down** key is used to select which border to move in order to resize the window. **Down** selects the border at the bottom. The second direction key, in this example **Up**, indicates the direction in which you wish to move the selected border. Once again **Enter** is for anchoring the final position of the border.

40   Place the mouse pointer on the left border and drag the mouse to the left until the left border is flush with the left edge of your display. If the left border is actually off the screen you will first have to drag the whole window to the right. You do so by dragging on the title bar of the Paintbrush window.

Keyboard – **Alt-Spacebar**, **S**, **Left**, **Left**, **Enter**.

41 Adapt step 40 to align the right border of Paintbrush with the right of the screen. Hopefully Paintbrush is nicely positioned in the top half of your display.

Keyboard – **Alt-Spacebar, S, Right, Right, Enter**.

42 Click Notepad to bring it to the front (or use **Alt-Tab** if it happens to be hidden behind Paintbrush).

Keyboard – **Alt-Tab**.

43 Place the mouse pointer on the lower border of the Notepad window and drag the border up so that the height of the Notepad window is slightly less than half the height of your screen.

Keyboard – **Alt-Spacebar, S, Down, Up** (or **Down**), **Enter**.

44 Place the pointer on the title bar of Notepad and drag its window until the top border is immediately below the lower border of Paintbrush. The lower border of Notepad should be just above the bottom of the screen.

Keyboard – **Alt-Spacebar, M, Down, Enter**.

45 Drag the left border of Notepad so that it aligns with the left of the screen.

Keyboard – **Alt-Spacebar, S, Left, Left, Enter**.

46   Drag the right border of Notepad to the right of the screen.

Keyboard – **Alt-Spacebar, S, Right, Right, Enter**.

Notepad and Paintbrush are now tiled horizontally. If, say, you are waiting for a Paintbrush graphic to print you could click Notepad and type in some text.

Practice moving and sizing the two windows until they a little smaller than full-screen yet slightly offset so they overlap. The two applications are now cascaded. Switching from front to hidden window is simply a matter of clicking the visible section of the partially hidden window.

47   Switch to Paintbrush by clicking its window or using **Alt-Tab**.

Keyboard – **Alt-Tab**.

48   Maximize Paintbrush by clicking its maximize button. Take a break and create a masterpiece in Paintbrush.

Keyboard – **Alt-Spacebar, X**. You will find Paintbrush is not so easy to use without the mouse. If you can't wait to paint a picture try **Alt-H, C** to get help.

Incidentally Paintbrush and Solitaire are excellent for practising standard Windows techniques. Minesweeper is just plain infuriating and Freecell should carry a health warning.

49 Close both Paintbrush and Notepad by double clicking their Control menus. If you are asked if you want to save your work, click No. I am glibly assuming you have not actually created a masterpiece in Paintbrush yet.

Keyboard – **Alt-Spacebar**, **C**.

50 Restore the Program Manager icon to a window by double clicking. If it's maximized click the restore button to get back to the original size.

Keyboard – **Alt-Spacebar**, **R**. Press **Alt-Spacebar**, **R** again if it's maximized.

51 In Program Manager close the Accessories window by double clicking its Control menu.

Keyboard – **Alt-Hyphen**, **N**.

In future you might like to try double clicking title bars to maximize and restore windows.

Menus, lists, and dialog boxes

The following set of exercises is designed to make you acquainted with most of the remaining Windows techniques, actions and conventions. In particular you will be looking at pull-down menus, lists, and dialog boxes.

Essentials

1   In Program Manager double click the Accessories group icon to restore it to a window.

Keyboard – **Ctrl-F6** to highlight Accessories, then press **Enter**. Or you could try **Alt-W**, **1**, though you might require a different number from 1.

2   Double click the application icon for Notepad to open a window for Notepad.

Keyboard – Move to the Notepad icon with the direction keys and press **Enter**.

3   Maximize Notepad by clicking its maximize button.

Keyboard – **Alt-Spacebar**, **X**.

4   Click File in the Notepad menu bar to access the File pull-down menu.

Keyboard – **Alt-F**.

There are a number of entries in this menu. In particular note the option called Open. This has three dots after it, the term for the dots is *ellipsis*. An ellipsis in a menu choice indicates further information must be provided by the user before the command is implemented, in this case opening a file. The extra information is entered in the subsequent dialog box.

5   Click the Edit option in the menu bar and take a look at the choices in the Edit pull-down menu.

Keyboard – **Alt-E**.

You should see that Undo and a few other options are in faint type. Such entries are said to be grayed, disabled, or dimmed and are not available for selection. Some other action must be carried out first before they become enabled. Undo, for example, lets you undo your previous activity in the workspace. However, there has been no activity yet and Undo is therefore not yet available. Next to the option for Time/Date is an entry **F5**. This is a keyboard shortcut. These shortcuts are especially appropriate when your hands are on the keyboard, perhaps you are typing in text or numeric data. Simply hitting the **F5** function key inserts system date and time at the current location of the cursor (this does not work if the menu is visible). Otherwise you would have to reach for the mouse and click Edit followed by Time/Date.

If you click the final choice in this menu for Word Wrap the whole menu disappears. Clicking Edit once more shows a tick (check mark) next to Word Wrap. Clicking Word Wrap a second time removes the check mark. This type of menu selection is called a toggle. Toggles are clicked to turn them on and off. Word Wrap, by the way, causes the text to wrap at the right side of the screen instead of continuing off the edge. The final type of menu entry, which you will encounter less often, has a black triangle next to it. This is the mark of a cascading (or pull-right) menu. A menu option that cascades summons an additional menu to the side.

6   Click File then click Open in the File pull-down menu. As Open is followed by an ellipsis, clicking Open leads to a dialog box where you can provide additional information.

Keyboard – **Alt-F, O**.

The Open dialog box (see FIG. 1.7) partially overlays the Notepad window. It has its own Control menu. This contains two options, for closing or moving the dialog. With the mouse it is easier to close a dialog box by clicking Cancel. Cancel leaves the previous default settings intact. To move the dialog box with the mouse you drag it by its title bar. Clicking OK in

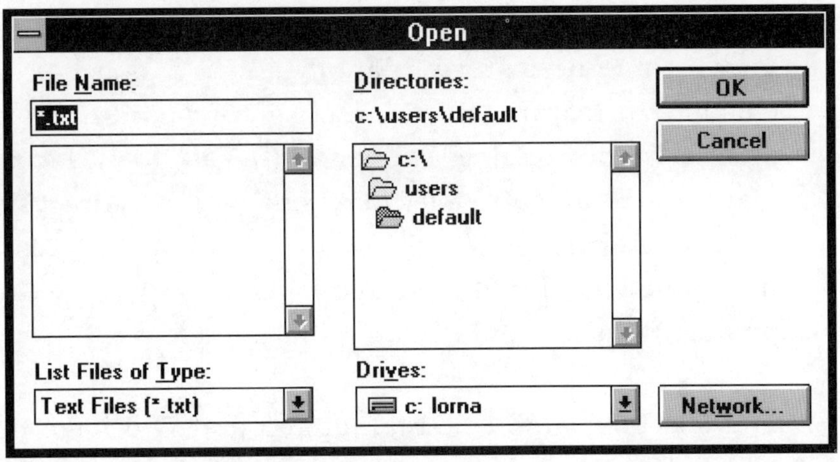

FIG. 1.7

a dialog box also closes the dialog but registers any changes you may have made to the contents. Most dialog boxes observe the same conventions. This dialog box also includes a number of standard Windows features. There are a couple of additional features not shown in this Open dialog, but these will be covered shortly.

The dialog contains a text box, labelled File Name. Text boxes allow you to type in text, here you might want to type in the name of a file you wish to open. There are two list boxes. List boxes, as the name suggests, contain lists, from which you can choose the list entry you require. OK and Cancel are examples of command buttons. In addition there is an information line, labelled Directories. This tells you the name of the current directory. Your dialog box might have another feature, this will depend upon the number of directories on the current drive and the number of files in the current directory. This additional feature is a scroll bar, or perhaps two of them. To move from one feature to another in a dialog box involves clicking the feature with the mouse. Keyboard users have the alternative of pressing **Tab**, or **Shift-Tab**, to cycle round the features – **Shift-Tab** cycles in reverse. A more direct keyboard method is to press and hold down **Alt** while pressing the underlined letter of the desired label, though some command push buttons do not have an underlined letter.

The text box should be highlighted and will have the entry *.TXT. This tells Notepad to display all files with a TXT extension, found in the current directory, in the list box below.

If you want to see all the files with a BAT extension you type **.BAT**. *.BAT will only directly replace *.TXT if *.TXT is highlighted. You can highlight text in a text box, if the highlight is not already there, by dragging the mouse across the text. Or you can position the cursor in the text box by clicking it and changing the current entry with **Backspace** and **Delete** keys, then typing the replacement. If you experiment make sure the entry is put back to *.TXT. You can also try the List Files of Type drop-down list box, where the template *.* means all files. With the keyboard you cycle to a text box with **Tab** or **Shift-Tab** or jump directly with **Alt-underlined letter**.

The list box to the left is the one containing all the files in the current directory that match the filename, or filename template, in the text box. Something like MYFILE.TXT is a filename and *.TXT is a template. The current directory is shown on the information line. You use a list box to choose alternatives; here it is used to stipulate a file to open. Choosing with a mouse involves clicking the filename then clicking OK, or you can simply double click the filename. Choosing with the keyboard, after cycling or jumping to the list box, is done by moving the highlight to the choice with the direction keys (**Up** and **Down**) then pressing **Enter**. Quite often lists are too long to fit in the space for the list box. Then you see vertical scroll bars at the side of the list box. With the keyboard you use direction keys to scroll hidden entries into view. With the mouse you click the up or down arrows at the top and bottom of the scroll bar. If *.TXT is still in the text box you see all files with a TXT extension in the current directory. It's likely there are no TXT files in the current directory. It is important that you know how to change the current directory, especially when searching for files to open. The list box on the right is designed to allow you to do just that.

This second list box follows exactly the same conventions as the list box on the left. You may have a scroll bar to the side, this depends upon the number of drives and directories you have. You access the Drives drop-down list to switch drives. Drop-down lists are discussed shortly. Once you are logged onto the correct drive you can move around directories on that drive. Directories actually listed are subdirectories of the current directory on the current drive. You move into a subdirectory by choosing it. Often you may want to switch to a directory at the same level as the current directory. In order to do this it is necessary to back through the directory tree to the next highest level and come down the required branch. Backing through a directory tree is done by double clicking the parent directory. If you choose this one repeatedly you end up in the root directory of the current drive. You can move straight to the root by double clicking it as well.

Command buttons in this dialog are for OK and Cancel. Cancel always backs you out of a dialog and leaves original settings intact, useful if you call one up accidentally. OK accepts settings in the dialog. Choosing a command button with the mouse is done by clicking. From the keyboard you can cycle to the relevant button with **Tab** and press **Enter**. If the command contains an underlined letter, it is possible to jump straight to the command by pressing **Alt-underlined letter**. A command button with a heavier outline than others is currently selected and can be activated simply by pressing **Enter**. A button with an ellipsis (...) opens another separate dialog box. A button with a double chevron (>>) expands the current dialog. A keyboard shortcut for choosing a Cancel button is to press **Esc**.

7   Place your Windows NT Disk 4 in your floppy drive. Click to open the Drives drop-down list and select A:. You should see a list of TXT files. Select SETUP.TXT and click OK. If you can't find SETUP.TXT then substitute any other TXT file in the following steps.

      Keyboard – Press **Tab** to jump to the Drives drop-down list. Press **Alt-Down** to open the list. Use **Up** and **Down** to select A: and press **Enter**. Press **Tab** to jump to the list box, then **Down** to select SETUP.TXT and finally press **Enter**.

8   Click Search on the Notepad menu bar then click Find. This displays the Find dialog (see FIG. 1.8).

      Keyboard – **Alt-S**, **F**.

9   Type **to** in the text box.

      Keyboard – Type **to**.

      Underneath this you see a check box labelled Match Case. The check box should be empty, that is it is not selected. When selected a check box displays a cross in the box. This particular check box helps to narrow the criteria of the search. When

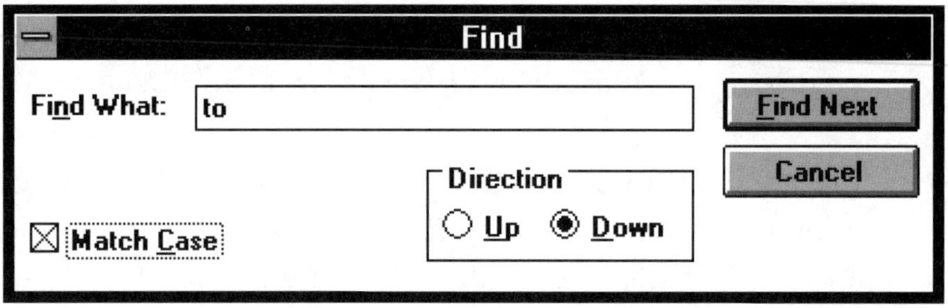

FIG. 1.8

selected it performs a case sensitive search for the entry in the text box. To select a check box with the mouse you click the box. Repeat this to turn off the check box. With the keyboard first cycle or jump to the check box then press **Spacebar** to turn the box on or off.

10   Turn on the check box for Match Case.

Keyboard – Press **Alt-C**. As this check box is not part of a group there's no need to press **Spacebar** to toggle it on and off.

Next to the check box are two circular buttons called option buttons. In some applications' manuals they are referred to as radio buttons. They differ from check boxes in that they are normally mutually exclusive, you can not choose two option buttons in the same group. Multiple check boxes in a group are not subject to this restriction, you can turn on as many as you wish. The option buttons in question instruct Notepad to search either forwards or backwards through the text, from the current cursor location: it can not search forwards and backwards at the same time. We want to search forwards in this example, the cursor being at the start of the document. Default setting is forwards though it is worth having a go with the option buttons. Once again you simply click with the mouse to turn option buttons on and off. From the keyboard you cycle to the option button group and use the direction keys to turn on and off. A keyboard shortcut is **Alt-underlined letter**.

11   Turn on the Up button.

Keyboard – **Alt-U**.

12   Turn on the Down button.

Keyboard – **Alt-D**.

13   Choose Find Next.

Keyboard – **Alt-F**.

14   Click Cancel.

Keyboard – Press **Esc**.

The word *to* in the second paragraph is now highlighted. Note the word *TO* in the first paragraph has been skipped over, a result of the Match Case check box being operative.

Notice the scroll bars at the foot and to the right of the Notepad window. They are there to help you move around the text (or graphic, database or spreadsheet, depending on the application). With the mouse you could click the desired cursor position, but this desired location may not be visible. At the end of each scroll bar is a scroll arrow. Clicking an arrow moves you by increments in the direction of the arrow. In each scroll bar there is a scroll box. Clicking the scroll bar outside the scroll box moves you vertically or horizontally, though by a much greater distance than the scroll arrows. Dragging a scroll box along a scroll bar allows you to reach a desired position quickly. For example dragging the box all the way down the vertical scroll bar takes you to the end of the document, dragging the box in the horizontal bar sweeps left and right.

Working with text

All Windows accessories and applications observe similar conventions when it comes to working with text.

There are conventions for moving around in text documents and for selecting text. Once text is selected it is manipulated in various ways. For example, it can be retrospectively formatted, or moved or copied. Text conventions generally apply to text entries in spreadsheets and databases, not only to text editors and word processors.

Essentials

To move the cursor position with the mouse you click the desired location. If the new location is not in the current screen, then use the scroll bars to scroll to the correct point. Some applications have a Goto option (through the menu bar) which enables you to jump to a specified page number.

Moving within text via the keyboard depends upon where you want to move to. The usual conventions are in the following table. If your hands are on the keyboard anyway, you might be typing, then even if you have a mouse the keyboard options are often more convenient.

When entering text the **Spacebar** forces a gap of one character width, **Enter** forces the cursor to begin a new line. Mistakes are rectified with the **Delete** and **Backspace** keys. Former deletes the character right of the cursor, latter the character to the left. Once text has been selected **Delete** removes all selected text. Many applications have an undo option on the edit menu which retrieves accidentally deleted text, as long as you do nothing else in between. The keyboard shortcut for undo is**Alt-Backspace**. To insert text in existing text, position the cursor and type. The existing text moves to the right and down to accommodate the new text. Most applications (though not Notepad) have an overtype facility. Overtype means new text actually overwrites existing text as you type. Overtype is turned on by pressing **Insert**. This key is a toggle and pressing it again turns off overtype, and restores the default insert mode.

New location	Keyboard method
Next character	**Right**
Previous character	**Left**
Next word	**Ctrl-Right**
Previous word	**Ctrl-Left**
Next line	**Down**
Previous line	**Up**
Next window of text (down)	**Page Down**
Previous window of text (up)	**Page Up**
Next window of text (right)	**Ctrl-Page Down**
Previous window of text (left)	**Ctrl-Page Up**
End of line	**End**
Start of line	**Home**
End of all text	**Ctrl-End**
Start of all text	**Ctrl-Home**

To select text with the mouse drag the mouse over the text. In many applications you can select a word by double clicking the word. One alternative to dragging is to click at the start or finish of selected text then to press the **Shift** key as you click at the opposite end. Windows word processors normally give you an extensive range of options for selecting text. Notepad is not really a word processor, it is more of a text editor, and its facilities for selecting text are limited. Write, a basic word processor bundled with Windows, has more options. To select a line in Write, for instance, you click to the left of it.

To select an area of text with the keyboard, position the cursor at the start or finish of the block of text. Then while holding down the **Shift** key use the direction keys to move to the other. The **Shift** key may be used with keyboard methods of moving through text, given in the table, to easily extend selection.

As already mentioned, selected text may then be formatted, moved or copied. Text can be moved or copied within the current document or to another document, and even into another application. To copy text try Edit then Copy, which copies the text to the Clipboard. Place the cursor at the destination point, this can be in a completely different application if you wish, and choose Edit followed by Paste. Moving text is an almost identical procedure, except you choose Cut rather than Copy. To deselect selected text click anywhere in the window.

Getting help

Accessories that accompany Windows NT, and the vast majority of Windows applications, have an extremely useful help feature. This is usually accessed by clicking Help or pressing **Alt-H** (a keyboard shortcut is **F1**). From the pull-down menu Contents provides a gateway to an onboard manual. And depending upon application you might well see other Help options. Depending upon the application, the **Shift-F1** key combination may give context sensitive help. Many Help pull-down menus have the Keyboard option which gives information specifically for users without a mouse.

While you are learning an accessory or other application, the Help window can be sized, moved and left running. That way you have immediate access to help, without impinging too much upon the workspace.

Once you are in Help there a couple of methods of moving through the documentation without returning to the Contents all the time. Back, for example retraces your steps and Browse (which you may or may not see) shows topics related to the current topic in the Help window.

1   If Notepad is still on your screen practice moving around the SETUP.TXT document. Try clicking Help, looking up information, then closing Help down. Practice selecting text. You might like to try Edit, Copy - Edit, Paste and Edit, Cut - Edit, Paste. Do not worry about messing up the text for we will not keep the alterations you make.

Keyboard – See the table earlier for keyboard methods of moving through text. Open Help with **Alt-H**, **C**. Close Help with **Alt-Spacebar**, **C**. Edit, Copy is **Alt-E**, **C** (or **Ctrl-C**). Edit, Cut is **Alt-E**, **T** (or **Ctrl-X**). Edit, Paste is **Alt-E**, **P** (or **Ctrl-V**).

2   Close Notepad by double clicking the Control menu. If you have made any changes at all Notepad asks if you wish to save your changes. Choose No to retain the original document and to lose your changes.

Keyboard – **Alt-Spacebar**, **C**. To retain the original document and lose your changes press **N** in the ensuing dialog. If you have made no alterations then Notepad closes without putting up a dialog.

We will be working largely from the Accessories group for a while so you may leave that group window open. There is however one more standard

Essentials

Windows NT attribute to consider and this involves opening Control Panel, which is in the Main group window. You are not obliged to keep these groups and their contents as they stand. Later you will see how to customize Program Manager.

Drop-down lists

1 Open the Main group window. There is no need to close the Accessories window first.

   Keyboard – **Alt-W, 5** (or the relevant number). If you prefer use the **Ctrl-F6** combination to highlight the Main icon and press **Enter**.

2 Start Control Panel (see FIG. 1.9) by double clicking its icon. In the Control Panel window is an icon labelled Color.

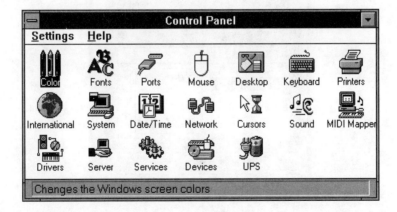

FIG. 1.9

Keyboard – Highlight the Control Panel icon by pressing the direction keys and press **Enter**.

3 Double click the Color icon and the Color dialog box (see FIG. 1.10) appears.

Keyboard – Highlight the Color icon, if necessary, by pressing the direction keys and press **Enter**.

This dialog is where you alter the colours of your windows. That is not the point of this exercise, however, which is to demonstrate use of drop-down list boxes. Most of the list boxes

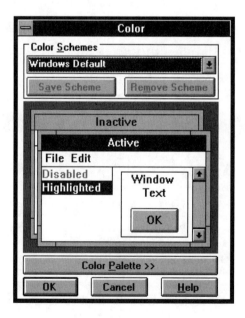

FIG. 1.10

we have met so far hold a maximum of six to ten entries. If there are more entries than the maximum available then Windows adds a scroll bar to the side, allowing you to scroll the hidden entries into view. In some dialog boxes, though, full list boxes are inappropriate, usually because of space limitations. Instead Windows NT has drop-down list boxes (you saw a couple in the Open dialog in Notepad). These initially display only one list item and to the right of this is an underlined down arrow.

To open the full list box click this underlined down arrow with the mouse. From the keyboard press **Alt-Down**. To see alternatives in the list one by one, press **Down** or **Up**. You can then make a choice from the list as normal. To hide a drop-down list, click the arrow again or press **Alt-Down** a second time. There may still be too many entries in a drop-down list, in which case use the scroll bar as usual to move through the list.

4   Open the drop-down list box for Color schemes and scroll through the list.

     Keyboard – **Alt-Down** (**Alt-Up** also works), and then **Down** and **Up** to scroll.

5   Close the drop-down list.

     Keyboard – **Alt-Down** (or **Alt-Up**).

6   Click Cancel to leave the dialog. Or click OK if you have a colour monitor and wish to alter the Windows NT colour

scheme. Fluorescent is worth trying, for a couple of minutes. The standard colour scheme is called Windows Default, as I am sure you will not want to keep Fluorescent, though some of the others are rather more restful!

Keyboard – Press **Esc**.

7   Close Control Panel by double clicking its Control menu.

Keyboard – **Alt-Spacebar**, **C**.

8   Minimize the Main group window to an icon, and restore the Accessories group, if necessary, to an open window. We will be looking at many of the accessories shortly.

Keyboard – **Alt-Hyphen**, **N** to minimize the Main group.

To avoid undue repetition of basic instructions in the rest of the book, it is assumed that you have learnt most of the essential skills. Should you encounter an action you are unable to carry out, refer back to this section on essential skills.

Cardfile, Paintbrush, and Write

CARDFILE, PAINTBRUSH, AND WRITE

■ An introduction to three popular accessories

■ How to work with data, graphics, and text

■ How to transfer data between applications

The accessories provide a range of applications suitable for many people. Their use is also an excellent introduction to learning Windows techniques and conventions. Should you ever outgrow the accessories (they may simply not be powerful or flexible enough to meet your needs), they can be replaced by separately bought Windows-based applications. This section provides a brief overview of Cardfile, Paintbrush, and Write using a fictitious company.

TypeCast plc is a busy desktop publishing agency. TypeCast has recently received a commission from another company, Rectangle and Circle plc, to design a company logo and print an in-house newsletter. Rectangle and Circle is a new client and has requested a breakdown of the costs and tasks involved, and to see a preview of the logo design.

To design the logo:

1   Open and maximize Paintbrush. The Paintbrush workspace is divided into four distinct sections. Down the left-hand side are the Toolbox icons (see FIG. 2.1) and beneath them is the Linesize area. Along the bottom is the Palette, the rest of the workspace being taken up by the drawing area. Keyboard users can move around these four areas with the **Tab** key.

It is worth mentioning some keyboard alternatives here. The direction and **Insert** keys replaces clicking when choosing options in the Toolbox, Linesize area and Palette. **F9** with **Insert** is the equivalent of double clicking (try it on the Brush tool) and the **Delete** (or **Del**) key is the alternative to right clicking. Right clicking is used in Paintbrush to select a

Cardfile, Paintbrush, and Write

background colour from the Palette. You can move around one of the sections with the direction keys. To choose the Filled Box (Rectangle) tool, for example, **Tab** to the Toolbox, move the pointer to the tool and press **Insert**. The equivalent to dragging the mouse is holding down the **Insert** key and moving with the direction keys. Note that **Shift-Page Up** is used instead of the normal **Ctrl-Page Up** to move one window to the right.

If Toolbox and Linesize ever disappear from the display, click View then Tools & Linesize. Clicking View then Palette recalls a missing Palette. If your drawing area ever changes into a series of small squares click View followed by Zoom Out. Small squares indicate that you have inadvertently zoomed in.

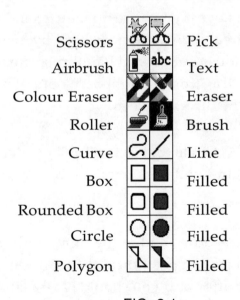

Scissors		Pick
Airbrush		Text
Colour Eraser		Eraser
Roller		Brush
Curve		Line
Box		Filled
Rounded Box		Filled
Circle		Filled
Polygon		Filled

FIG. 2.1

Zooming in (View, Zoom In) is very convenient for detailed editing work on your graphics.

At the left of the Palette is a small rectangle contained within a larger rectangle. The inner rectangle is the current foreground colour and the outer rectangle is the background colour. The default settings are solid black on white. We will work with the default settings, though to change the foreground colour later click (or press **Insert**) the desired colour in the Palette. Background colour is changed by right clicking (or by pressing **Delete**).

2   Click the Filled Box (Rectangle) tool.

3   Position the cursor at the left of the drawing area (use the **Tab** and direction keys if you have no mouse) and drag the mouse to form an area about one inch high by two inches across. Release the mouse button and Paintbrush creates a solid black rectangle. To drag from the keyboard hold down the **Insert** key while using the direction keys.

4   Click the Filled Circle tool in the Toolbox. Position the cursor at the top right-hand corner of the rectangle you have just drawn.

5   Drag the mouse down and to the right, until the cursor forms a square with its first position at the top right of the rectangle. Let go of the button and you should have a circle to the right of the rectangle.

It is not at all important to the exercises if your logo is a mess, all that matters is that you have drawn something. If you feel like starting again click File then New, and when asked if you wish to save the current image choose No. A quick way of beginning again is to double click the Eraser tool (or press **F9** with **Insert** with the pointer on the Eraser tool).

As the logo is used later it is vital that it is saved. To save the logo:

1   Click File then Save (Save As is for creating a copy of a file with a different name). File, Save is the method of saving data in all Windows accessories and applications.

The text *.BMP in the text box is highlighted. Typing in a filename will automatically overwrite the selected text. Before you do so check that the directory shown is the one where you wish to store your data. If necessary change the directory in the Directories list box, you might have a specific directory where you hold data files. Changing directory like this removes the highlight from *.BMP. You can rehighlight by dragging and overtype with the filename, or you will have to edit the text box contents manually with **Backspace** or **Delete**.

2   Type **LOGO** as the filename and click OK. All the examples of saved files in this book assume a FAT disk partition – hence the short filenames (maximum of eight characters) used. Of course, you can have much longer filenames in an NTFS partition. Remember where you save this and other files – they are used again in later exercises. It's likely (though not certain) that the

files you save go into C:\USERS\DEFAULT or your own home directory in C:\USERS.

A successful save results in the filename appearing in the title bar of Paintbrush: LOGO.BMP. BMP is the default file extension for Paintbrush files, there is no need to type in the extension yourself. Some Windows applications do not support the BMP format, in which case you might try PCX format, accessed through the Save File as Type drop-down list.

You might like a trial printout of the logo. This is achieved by clicking File then Print and accepting the defaults in the subsequent dialog by clicking OK. Nearly all Windows NT accessories and applications have the File, Print routine.

3   Close Paintbrush by double clicking the Control menu. If you have made any alterations to the graphic since saving it, Paintbrush asks if you wish to save the changes. Respond with Yes if you want to keep the changes, No if you do not.

The next set of exercises involves writing a TypeCast internal memo in Notepad. The contents of the memo are copied into Write as part of the letter to Rectangle and Circle.

1   Open and maximize Notepad.

2   Click Edit then Word Wrap.

3   Type the following:

To: John

From: Louise

**John, when you write to Rectangle and Circle, could you add something
to the effect:**

**As part of our fifth anniversary celebrations we are pleased to
announce a five percent discount to selected clients only. Please
deduct five percent accordingly from any prices quoted.**

4   Click File then Save.

5   Enter the name **MEMO** in the text box and click OK. The file is
        now called MEMO.TXT, Notepad adds the extension for you.

6   Close Notepad.

Another task which is quite likely to occur in such a business situation is
recording details of Rectangle and Circle in a client database. Cardfile is
the obvious choice for this task.

1   Open Cardfile.

2   Click Card then Add to see the Add dialog.

3   Type **RECTANGLE AND CIRCLE** in the text box and click OK.

You are now presented with an index card bearing the title RECTANGLE AND CIRCLE, with the cursor positioned on the first line of the card.

4   Type

Rectangle and Circle

Foundry Square

London

5   Click File then Save and call the file **CLIENTS**. This will be given a CRD extension. Click OK.

In normal usage there might well be dozens of index cards (each added with Card, Add) which are shown in an overlapping stack. You move through the cards by clicking titles of cards. The clicked card comes to the front where it is possible to see all details on the card. View, List shows the data in a list rather than in a stack of cards. Search, Go To is for jumping straight to a card that may not be visible in the window, simply type in the title. Search, Find will locate a card with specified text on the main body of the card. The latter is useful if you remember the name of an individual but not the company under which they are filed.

6   Close Cardfile.

Cardfile, Paintbrush, and Write

Let us now begin to put everything together in a letter from TypeCast to Rectangle and Circle.

1   Make the Accessories group window current. You can use **Ctrl-F6** if it is hidden or minimize a group window like Main to uncover it.

2   Open and maximize Write. The cursor will be ready at the top of the new document.

3   Type the following text:

TypeCast plc
Fleet Street
London

Dear Jane,

Thanks for your call earlier today. I hope this will answer most of your queries.

Yes, your company logo is finished and here it is!

The costs are as follows:

    Publication of newsletter   **£1000**

    Design of logo   **£8000**

TOTAL   £

Yours sincerely,

John Font

PS

The exact point for line breaks is unimportant, yours may be different. Though try using the **Tab** key to line-up the entries in the schedule.

So far Write, a word processor, seems little more exciting than Notepad, a text editor. Therefore we will experiment with just a few of the features of Write.

4   Drag the mouse over *TypeCast plc, Fleet Street, London* in order to select it. Just as a reminder, keyboard users should press **Shift** while pressing the direction keys to select text.

5   Click Paragraph then Centered.

6   With the same text still highlighted click Character followed by Bold.

7   And still with the same text selected click Character followed by Fonts. The Font dialog (see FIG. 2.2) appears with a Fonts list box to the left and a Sizes list box to the right.

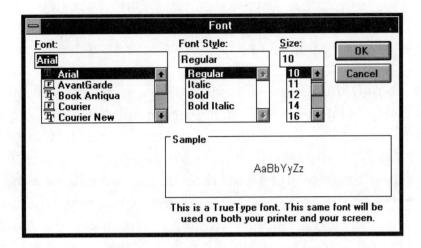

FIG. 2.2

8   Choose Arial or another font in the Fonts list.

9   Choose a point size of 14, or a similar size, from the Size list. You might have to scroll the list first. Click OK.

10   Select the word *TOTAL* in the letter.

11   Click Character then Bold.

12   Click File and then Save. Type **JANE** in the text box for the filename. Make sure none of the check boxes are on before clicking OK to save the letter. Write automatically appends the WRI extension.

There is obviously a lot more to Write than we have space to consider here. You are referred to Chapter 5 for more information.

The letter is not quite complete. It needs the logo pasting in, the name and address of Rectangle and Circle, a message about discounts, and a figure to represent the total cost of the job. The logo, name and address, and message have already been created and are saved in Paintbrush, Cardfile, and Notepad respectively. Those three applications have been closed down. In a normal working session there is no reason why you should not keep two or even more applications running simultaneously. This obviates the need to keep opening and closing. There is however a limit, and as you begin to run short on memory Windows NT slows down and occasionally displays warning dialogs. If this should ever happen then you have to shut one or more of the currently open applications. The figure for the total costs is to be worked out in Calculator and pasted into the letter. As you go through the next set of exercises I leave it up to you whether you close applications or not.

Now for some heavy mathematics:

1   **Alt-Tab** back to Program Manager and open Calculator.

2   Click **1** then **0** three times to put **1000** in the calculator. This step and the next two you might find are quicker if you use the keyboard, rather than the mouse. Simply press the key that corresponds to the key on the calculator.

3   Click the plus sign and enter **8000**, in the same way as in step 2.

4 Click the equals sign and the total of 9000 will show on the calculator.

5 Click Edit then Copy. You do not need to highlight calculator entries to place the total of 9000 on the Clipboard.

6 Close Calculator and make Write the current window.

7 Position the cursor just after the £ sign opposite the word *TOTAL*.

8 Click Edit then Paste.

The figure 9000 remains on the Clipboard until you leave Windows or copy or cut new data to it. If you want to check the current contents of Clipboard at any time, open it in ClipBook Viewer in the Main group. You may then close it back down. In normal day-to-day operations Clipboard functions quite happily in the background, there is no requirement to have it open to use it.

John Font, the writer of the letter from TypeCast to Rectangle and Circle, is too busy to type in the information about discounts. He decides to paste in the relevant parts of the memo from his MD, Louise. This was created in Notepad and was saved with the filename MEMO.TXT.

1 Open and maximize Notepad. Use **Ctrl-Esc** or **Alt-Tab** to switch to Program Manager first.

2 Click File then Open.

3 Open the file MEMO.TXT. You may have to change directories to find the file.

4 Drag the mouse over the section of the memo beginning *As part* and ending with *quoted.*

5 Click Edit followed by Copy.

6 Close Notepad if you want and return to the letter in Write.

7 Place the cursor immediately after PS at the end of the letter.

8 Click Edit then Paste. The information about the discount should now be in the letter.

The next stage is to copy the name and address of Rectangle and Circle into the letter. The name and address are held on an index card in Cardfile in a file called CLIENTS.CRD. By the way, the order in which we are carrying out all this copying and pasting is relatively unimportant. There is no reason why we could not have done the name and address earlier or later.

1 Open and maximize Cardfile from the Accessories group window. You might have to use **Alt-Tab** or **Ctrl-Esc** to return to Program Manager. And once in Program Manager recall that **Ctrl-F6** cycles through the document icons and windows.

2 Click File, Open and open the CLIENTS.CRD file.

Cardfile, Paintbrush, and Write

3   Click the title of the card for RECTANGLE AND CIRCLE to bring it to the front. There is quite possibly a blank card lying on top of it.

4   Drag the mouse over the text for the name and address on the main body of the card to highlight it.

5   Click Edit, Copy.

6   Close Cardfile if you want and return to Write.

7   Place the cursor in Write immediately above Dear Jane and click Edit, Paste.

The name and address of Rectangle and Circle appears flush with the left margin between the letterhead and the salutation. You might like to insert some blank lines to improve the appearance, press **Enter** to do so. You can get rid of blank lines with the **Backspace** key.

The final preparation before the letter is printed and mailed is to incorporate the logo. This is a Paintbrush file with the name LOGO.

1   Cycle to the Program Manager window and open and maximize Paintbrush from the Accessories group window.

2   In Paintbrush click File, Open and choose LOGO.BMP.

3   Click the Pick tool in the Toolbox: the pair of scissors with a dotted rectangle.

4 Place the cursor just to the top left of the logo and drag the mouse to the bottom right of the logo. With the keyboard you hold down the **Insert** key while using the direction keys. A dotted rectangle is drawn around the logo.

5 Click Edit, Copy and leave Paintbrush if you wish.

6 Return to Write and place the cursor immediately below *and here it is!*

7 Click Edit, Paste to add the logo to the letter.

8 Select the logo in the letter by clicking it. To do this from the keyboard place the cursor at the very top left of the logo and while holding down the **Shift** key press the **Down** key. Or you could try just the **Down** key – the latter works so long as the logo is against the left margin.

9 Click Edit, Move Picture and move (do not drag) the logo halfway between the left and right margins and click once. On the keyboard use the **Right** key and press **Enter** when it is in position.

10 To practice resizing the logo click Edit, Size Picture. Move the mouse until the proportions seem right and click once. If you are working from the keyboard then pressing **Right** first will enable you to stretch or compress the logo horizontally from the right. **Left** does the same from the left. You can not switch from the left to the right of the logo without going back through Edit, Size Picture.

11   Click File, Save to save the finished letter.

The only thing that remains to do is to print the letter ready for signing by John Font. It can then be mailed to Rectangle and Circle. To print the letter:

1   Click File then Print to see the Print dialog (see FIG. 2.3). This should indicate that only one copy is to be printed.

2   Click OK to proceed with printing.

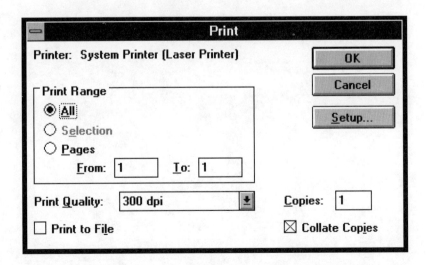

FIG. 2.3

To change the font and/or the font size:

1   Select the whole of the letter by holding down the **Ctrl** key as you click in the left margin. To do this from the keyboard press **Ctrl-Home** to go to the start of the letter and while holding down the **Shift** key press **Ctrl-End**.

2   Make any changes through Character, Fonts. Close Write and save your changes if you wish.

The changes, of course, affect all the text in the letter and you need to change the letterhead as we did at the beginning. Otherwise it will remain in the font and font size you have just selected.

More on Cardfile

MORE ON CARDFILE

■ How to enter and sort data

■ How to print data

■ Automatic telephone dialling

More on Cardfile

Cardfile is a flat-file database and is suitable for holding records in an index card manner. You can have as many index card files as you wish and open two or more at the same time. What you may not do is to easily relate the files together (for that a full-blown relational database like Access or Superbase is necessary). Nonetheless Cardfile is a valuable accessory and is ideal for storing lists of names and addresses, catalogs, and so on. The following exercise demonstrates some of the facilities available within Cardfile.

1   Open and maximize Cardfile. If you habitually open the same file in Cardfile you can instruct Cardfile to open the file automatically. There are many ways of doing so. One method is to use File, Properties in Program Manager and append the name of the file to the Command Line entry for Cardfile. Another involves creation of separate icons for the most popular Cardfile files, through File, New in Program Manager.

   A new file displays as a single blank index card. The cursor is positioned ready in the information area of the card. Above the information area is a double line and above that is the index line. Text entered in the index line is used as a basis for sorting the cards, you might like to think of it as the key field. The status line immediately below the menu bar indicates which view is current, whether Card View or List View. To the right of this are a couple of scroll arrows for moving through a stack of cards or a list – Cardfile does not have scroll bars. Finally there is a count of the total number of cards (records) in the file.

The initial step in creating a new file is to enter the data for each record. This is a two-stage process. First the index or key field is typed in the index line then the rest of the data (or fields) is typed into the information area.

2   Click Card followed by Add. For the first card only you can also click Edit followed by Index or double click the index line.

3   Type the key field data **RECTANGLE AND CIRCLE**, in the subsequent Add (or Index) dialog (see FIG. 3.1) and click OK.

Clicking OK puts the cursor back in the information area. You then have a choice. You can either enter all the data for that record or move on to the key field for the next cards. For the latter you repeat steps 2 and 3 for each card in turn then go back to type in the information area for every card.

4   Type the following in the information area:

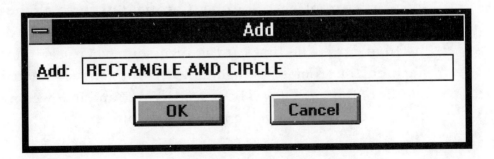

FIG. 3.1

Rectangle and Circle
Foundry Square
London

5   Repeat steps 2 to 4 for about twenty cards using different titles.

We do not want this to turn into a typing exercise so you could leave the information areas blank and simply enter one letter of the alphabet in the index line. Make this a different letter for each card and do not follow alphabetical order. Alternatively you might wish to record real data for your own name and address file, you can always delete Rectangle and Circle later.

Whatever your entries, they are displayed in alphabetical or numeric order. If you have both numeric and alphabetic index lines the numeric ones are sorted first. Should you be using two digit numbers make sure that you have 01 and not 1, similarly for three digit numbers, 001, 002 not 1, 2. If you want a particular card to be first in the stack, perhaps called NOTES, type a space before the name. The card first in the stack always shows at the front when you open Cardfile. Of course, although the cards always stay in order, it is possible to have any card as the front card. The first card is then somewhere else in the stack, but the order is still maintained. If you can see an A in the middle of the stack it will be preceded by Z and followed by a B then a C, assuming you entered these letters.

More on Cardfile

6 Make sure RECTANGLE AND CIRCLE is not at the front. If necessary click any other index line to bring that card to the front.

7 Bring RECTANGLE AND CIRCLE to the front, bring any other card to the front and once more get RECTANGLE AND CIRCLE. There are lots of ways of doing this and you might wish to try one or more of them. The list indicates the various options for moving through a stack of cards:

■ If you can see the card, click its index line.

■ If the card has disappeared off the top of the screen, click a card near the back to move the whole stack forward. Repeat this until the card comes into view then click its index line.

■ Click Search then Go To. Type one or more letters in the text box and click OK. You must type enough letters to distinguish the index line from any others. For example, if you had an R as well as RECTANGLE AND CIRCLE then you type **RE** (or **re** or **Re** or **rE**). Typing **R** brings the R card to the front and RECTANGLE AND CIRCLE is not far away.

■ Click Search then Find. Type **FOUNDRY** (or even **FO**) in the text box and click OK. Go To searches index lines while Find searches information areas. Find Next repeats the previous Find.

■ Click the scroll arrows on the status line until the card comes to the front.

■ Press **Page Up** and **Page Down** keys to scroll card by card backwards and forwards (**Ctrl-Home** gets the first card, **Ctrl-End** the final card).

■ Click View followed by List. In List View you may see scroll bars. Use the scroll bars to move through the list of cards and click *RECTANGLE AND CIRCLE*. Click View followed by Card.

■ Press **R** to bring the first *R* to the front in List View, then scroll card by card.

■ Press **Alt-V** then **L** to switch to List View. Use **Page Up** or **Page Down** keys to jump through the list. Press **Down** (or **Right**) to move one card forward. Backward is **Up** (or **Left**). Highlight *RECTANGLE AND CIRCLE* and press **Alt-V** then **C** to return to Card View.

8 Change the index entry for *RECTANGLE AND CIRCLE* to **WEIRD NON-EUCLIDEAN THINGS**. Bring the card to the front and double click its index line. Or you could try Edit, Index. If you are in List View double clicking has the same effect.

9 Change the data in the information area from *Rectangle and Circle* to **Weird Non-Euclidean Things**. Bring the card to the front and click the appropriate part of the information area. If text to be altered is on the first line then the cursor is in position.

By deleting and inserting text, change *Rectangle and Circle* to **Weird Non-Euclidean Things**. Remember the quickest way to delete a contiguous block of text is to select it by dragging and then press the **Delete** key or begin typing. The new company name *Weird Non-Euclidean Things* is just asking for a new logo – more on this later.

10 Print the card by clicking File then Print. If you want to print all the cards click Print All rather than Print.

11 Make a copy of the card by clicking Card, Duplicate. Change some of the text in the duplicate to make it slightly different from the original. Duplication is handy if two cards contain similar information.

Or you can try Edit, Copy to place selected text on the Clipboard and then Edit, Paste with another card at the front. Edit, Cut removes selected data from the current card. This followed by Edit, Paste on another card is the equivalent of moving, rather than copying, data from one card to another.

12 Delete the amended duplicate by clicking Card, Delete and answering OK to the warning message.

13 Make sure that the card for *WEIRD NON-EUCLIDEAN THINGS* is at the front and change the line for London to Tirana.

14 Click Edit then Restore to undo the change. Note that Edit, Restore goes back to the last saved version of a card, but it does not work if you bring any other card to the front in the meantime. Edit, Restore is suitable for undoing multiple changes to a card. Edit, Undo undoes the last change only. Edit, Undo is a toggle, and with it you may undo the previous undo.

15   Add an extra line to the information area. Type **071–111–1111** on this line.

16   Click Card followed by Autodial. Cardfile automatically places the first number it finds in the information area into the Autodial dialog (see FIG. 3.2). To avoid confusion with street numbers or numeric post codes, you must place the telephone number on the first line of a card's information area.

For the Autodial facility to work you need a Hayes-compatible modem connected to one of the serial ports on your computer, and a valid telephone number on the card. You could enter a

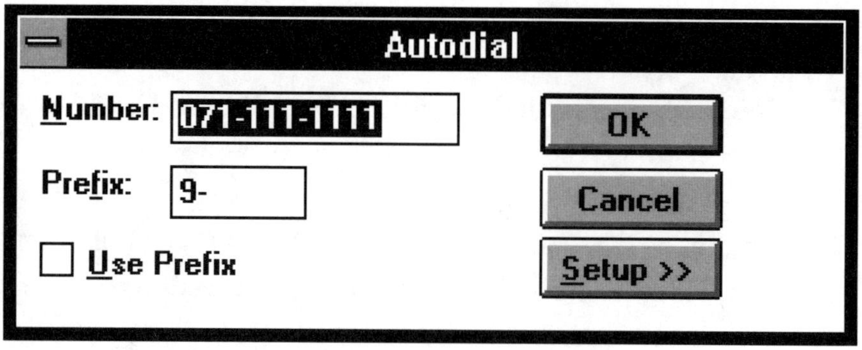

FIG. 3.2

commonly used prefix, for instance a 9 to access an outside line, in the Prefix text box. To incorporate the prefix turn on the Use Prefix check box. The Setup button expands the Autodial dialog. In the expanded dialog you can set the correct port for the modem, specify the baud rate and switch between tone and pulse telephone lines.

17 Click Cancel to exit the Autodial dialog. Clicking OK initiates the telephone call.

18 Click File then Save to keep the index file, it is needed in a later exercise. Enter **CUSTOMER** as the filename and click OK.

19 Close Cardfile.

The previous nineteen steps demonstrate most of the features of Cardfile. It is quite a versatile accessory and often gets overlooked by Windows users. Apart from some generic menu options, that is options appearing on most windows' menu bars, the only things not considered are the File, Merge option, and Picture and Text in the Edit menu. The latter two are covered in due course. File, Merge is for consolidating two or more index card files. One of the files must be open and the consolidated set adopts its name if you use File Save. File, Save As allows you to enter a new name for the merged files. The second file is left intact and you may wish to delete this file through File Manager. To add a third file you repeat the whole process, with the first merged file as the current file.

More on Paintbrush

MORE ON PAINTBRUSH

- How to use the toolbox

- How to work pixel-by-pixel

- Copying graphics to other applications

More on Paintbrush

The fact that Rectangle and Circle has changed its name to Weird Non-Euclidean Things is a perfect excuse for designing a new logo. The name would suggest some kind of free-form, stream-of-consciousness artwork. Probably the best way to learn Paintbrush is to experiment, the new logo is an ideal opportunity. This section mentions some of the options and it is up to you to try them out as you read. If you share my lack of artistic ability you may end up with a mess, but that is precisely what is required for the new logo.

To begin you open Paintbrush, of course, and to end choose File, Save and enter the filename **WEIRD**. In between, feel free to slap paint all over the place. Paintbrush saves files with a BMP extension by default.

When Paintbrush opens the Brush tool (see FIG. 4.1) is selected. Dragging the mouse across the drawing area leaves a streak of paint.

1   Try painting a few doodles.

There are various parameters that affect the appearance of your painting. The Linesize box can be utilized to work with a fatter or thinner brush. Just click the desired thickness. The foreground colour or pattern is the one used by the brush. Clicking Options followed by Brush Shapes allows you to change the type of brush. Some of the brush shapes result in delicate calligraphic effects, or not so delicate!

2   Paint a few more doodles, but work with differing linesizes, foreground colours and brush shapes.

3   The Airbrush tool is for spraying drops of paint. A light airbrushing can produce subtle shading effects. Heavy airbrushing, that is dragging repeatedly over the same area, gives a denser appearance. The airbrush really demands a variation on dragging, something I call wiggling the mouse. Wiggling involves holding down the mouse button and shaking the mouse from side to side. You will see what I mean when you try it. Spray a few lighter and denser patches of paint. Change the foreground colour and linesize to provide some variation.

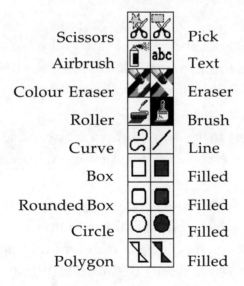

Scissors		Pick
Airbrush		Text
Colour Eraser		Eraser
Roller		Brush
Curve		Line
Box		Filled
Rounded Box		Filled
Circle		Filled
Polygon		Filled

FIG. 4.1

4 Go back to the Brush tool and paint an enclosed area, such as a wobbly polygon. The inside of the area is in the background colour and the outline in the current foreground colour.

5 Change the foreground colour in the Palette and click the Roller tool.

6 Place the tip of the paint roller inside the enclosed area and click. You may also roll paint over lines. Try clicking the tip of the roller on a line, and the line takes on the current foreground colour. If you miss the line, or an enclosed area for that matter, paint floods out until it meets the edges of the next enclosing area. Sometimes this means that you roll paint over the whole screen. If it is a garish colour you can always repeat the mistake with, say, white as the foreground colour.

7 Click the Text tool and click where you wish to begin typing. Your current foreground colour must be different from the background on which you propose to type.

8 Type**By Monet** in the drawing area. You can use the **Backspace** key to remove errors. Try the Text menu to vary the text.

9 Type some more text in varying fonts, sizes and styles. Pressing the **Enter** key takes you on to the next line. If you click another part of the screen or choose a different tool, text is converted into graphics. As a result the normal Windows text editing conventions no longer apply to the text, you must edit the text as a graphic.

More on Paintbrush

There are numerous ways of editing your work. You can try Edit, Undo; **Backspace**; the Eraser tools; the Scissors, and the Pick tool.

10 Paint a line with the Brush tool and click Edit, Undo (or press **Alt-Backspace**). This removes all of the previous action. Edit, Undo a second time restores the action.

11 Paint another line and press the **Backspace** key. A square appears in the drawing area. The size of the square is determined by the current linesize. Drag the square cursor over the line. This removes part of the last action.

12 Click the Eraser tool and drag the eraser over your painting. The eraser changes the foreground colours into the current background colour. If the background colour is white then the foreground colours disappear. The width of the eraser is determined by the current linesize. Double clicking the Eraser clears everything and you are asked if you want to save your picture. Double clicking the Eraser is the same as File, New.

13 Click the Color Eraser tool and drag over your work. If you just tried double clicking the Eraser you should paint something first in various colours. The Color Eraser changes only the current foreground colour into the current background colour. Double clicking the Color Eraser changes every occurrence of the current foreground colour into the current background colour.

14 Click the Line tool and drag a few lines across the screen. Holding down the **Shift** key constrains the line to certain directions only. If you do not like the line, click the right-hand mouse button before you stop dragging.

15 Click the Curve tool and drag the mouse to place a line in your painting.

16 Drag the mouse to one side of this line to produce a curve then click at the finish of the curve. You can draw an S-curve by not clicking at the finish, but dragging from the opposite side of the curve.

17 The bottom section of the Toolbox contains the Box, Rounded Box, Circle/Ellipse and the Polygon. These are shown in outline and the outline takes on the current foreground colour. To the right of each of these is the filled alternative. Filled shapes are filled in the current foreground colour and their outline is in the current background colour. Outline thicknesses depend upon the current linesize. Holding down the **Shift** key constrains boxes as squares, and circles/ellipses as perfect circles.

Choose Box, Rounded Box, Circle/Ellipse in turn and drag the mouse after choosing each one to produce some interesting geometric designs.

18 Repeat step 17 with the filled alternatives, even if we are getting a little Euclidean!

More on Paintbrush

19   Select either the Polygon or Filled Polygon tool. Drag the mouse to draw the first side of the polygon and let go of the mouse. Click in turn the remaining vertices of the polygon to draw additional sides. The last side is drawn automatically if you double click the position for the final vertex, or you could single click the first vertex.

The first two tools are the Scissors and the Pick tool. When chosen they let you select an area of the screen by dragging the mouse. Scissors is for selecting non-rectangular areas, Pick for rectangular areas. The selected area is called a cut-out. Once you have defined a cut-out you can cut it out, copy it and paste the copy somewhere else, all through the Edit menu. When a cut-out is defined the Pick option on the menu bar is enabled. Through the Pick option you can flip the cut-out horizontally and vertically, invert the colours, tilt it at an angle, enlarge it or shrink it. If you click Clear in the Pick menu the original is removed after any of these manipulations.

20   Click the Pick tool and drag over an area of your painting. Click Pick followed by Tilt. Position the cursor where you want a tilted copy and press and hold down the mouse button. Drag the mouse horizontally to produce a sheared rectangle and let go of the mouse button.

21   Practice flipping, shrinking and growing, and inverting a cut-out.

22 While the cut-out is still current, or after defining a new one, click Edit followed by Copy.

23 **Alt-Tab** back to Program Manager and start Cardfile.

24 In Cardfile choose File, Open and open the CUSTOMER file.

25 Bring the card for WEIRD NON-EUCLIDEAN THINGS to the front.

26 Click Edit in Cardfile followed by Picture.

27 Click Edit, Paste to place the cut-out from Paintbrush on the card in Cardfile.

28 Drag the cut-out into any position on the card then click Edit, Text. If the cut-out is a large one you may lose some of the graphics off the edge of the card. A small cut-out is better.

The index card now contains a company logo. This facility for pasting graphics onto cards is a convenient way to build up your own clipart library.

29 Close Cardfile and save your changes before **Alt-Tab**bing back to Paintbrush.

You will have noticed the scroll bars around the drawing area. The size of your painting can be larger than that shown on screen. You can move into the hidden areas with the scroll bars.

The size of the total drawing area is determined by Windows NT on the basis of your type of monitor. You may override the defaults through Options, Image Attributes. The Image Attributes dialog also enables you to work in black and white, if you have a colour monitor.

There are a number of methods of altering the amount of your picture showing on screen.

30   Click View, View Picture, or double click the Pick tool. This displays as much of the total picture area as possible on your monitor, though you can not edit in this mode. Click the picture once, or press **Esc**, to return to the default mode.

31   Click View then Zoom Out to see all of the picture area on screen. Your picture is scaled down to fit it in. Click View, Zoom In to return to the default mode.

You can hide the Tools and Linesize, and the Palette sections through View to give you more room. This means you have to redisplay them if you want to change tool, linesize or colour.

32   Click View then Zoom In. Place the resulting box over a part of your picture and click.

You will see a magnified image of the selected area where you may work on a pixel-by-pixel basis. This is valuable if you need to carry out detailed work. Clicking the left mouse button on a pixel paints in the current foreground colour, the right button the background colour.

33   Alter a few pixels and click View, Zoom Out to judge the results.

To print your picture you choose File, Print. The Print dialog has various options. You are able to specify a draft-quality or proof-quality printout, to set the number of copies, to scale the picture, to print the whole picture or part of it, and to adapt printer resolution. The latter may result in a better definition of printout but it may be slightly distorted.

34   Click File, Save and enter the name **WEIRD** before clicking OK.

35   Close Paintbrush.

More on Write

MORE ON WRITE

■ Character formatting

■ Paragraph formatting

■ How to print documents

If you worked through earlier exercises you will have already used some of the features available in Write. This section is designed to give guidance on most of the remaining features.

1   Open and maximize Write.

2   Click File then Open.

3   Double click JANE.WRI (which was saved from an earlier exercise). You may have to change directory to see JANE.WRI in the list box.

4   Select the whole document by holding down the **Ctrl** key while you click in the selection area to the left of the text.

The mouse pointer changes to an arrow when you are in the selection area. You may like to refer back to essential skills for information on selecting text. The keyboard equivalent for selecting all the text in a document is to press **Ctrl-Home** to take the cursor to the start of the document then, while holding down the **Shift** key press **Ctrl-End** to go to the end of the document.

All formatting options are available through the menu bar, whether accessed with a mouse or from the keyboard. A more convenient alternative for many of the options is to use the Ruler, although this requires a mouse.

More on Write

5 Turn on the Ruler (see FIG. 5.1), if you have a mouse, by clicking Document followed by Ruler On.

6 Change the line spacing of your text to one and a half, then to two and back to single spacing. On the ruler this is carried out by clicking the appropriate line spacing icon. Otherwise you will have to click Paragraph and click 1½ Space (and Double Space and Single Space).

Many of the formatting options, like line spacing, can be set before typing or retrospectively, after typing. If they are set retrospectively, as we have just done, they apply to the selected text only. Remember you can select one word, one line, one

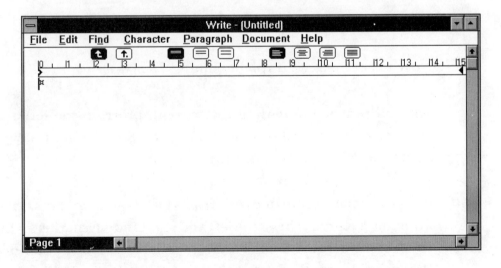

FIG. 5.1

sentence, a paragraph, or the whole text. You can also drag the mouse to select any area of text.

7   Change the justification of the whole text to centred, right aligned, fully justified and back to left aligned. On the ruler this is accomplished by clicking the relevant icon. From the menu bar click Paragraph then Centred (and Right, Justified, and Left).

The Paragraph, Normal option always returns the selected text to left alignment with single line spacing.

You will notice that the previously centred letter head is now left aligned. This is because all the text was selected during the last step.

8   Drag the mouse over the letter head and centre it.

9   Now select the paragraph beginning *Thanks for your call*.

We will practice indenting this paragraph from the left and right margins. To do so you can use the Ruler, if you have a mouse, or Paragraph, Indents.

10   Indent the paragraph one inch from the left and right margins. From the Ruler you drag the left and right indent markers – the small black arrow heads. To drag the left-hand one you must first drag the small dot out the way. This dot is the first line indent marker. Position the left and right markers one inch further in from their original positions. Then go back to the small dot and drag it half an inch to the left of the left indent marker. This creates a paragraph of hanging indented text, after a first line of full width.

If you habitually use indentation then you could set the Ruler markers before you begin to type, rather than working retrospectively as here. Should you not have a mouse choose Paragraph then Indents. In the Indents dialog (see FIG. 5.2) set Left and Right Indent at one inch and First Line at minus half an inch (-0.5), before pressing the **Enter** key.

Default margins in Write are one inch for top and bottom, and 1.25 inches for left and right. These again may be altered before you start typing or adjusted afterwards. They can also be given different settings on different pages. You might wish to experiment. If you set the left and right margins too narrow and/or your printer is set up for wide paper the text may scroll

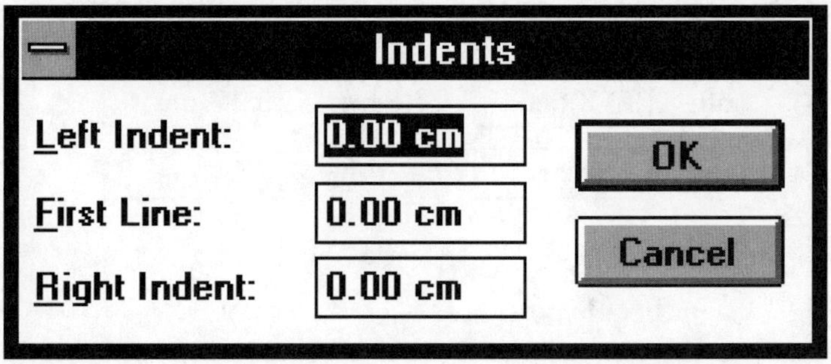

FIG. 5.2

off the right-hand edge of the screen. To see the hidden text use the horizontal scroll bar. Access to margin settings (see FIG. 5.3) is through Document, Page Layout.

11 Select an individual word in the text, any word will do. This word is used to practise character formatting. With the word selected click Character and try choosing Bold, Italic, Underline, Superscript and Subscript in turn. You might like to choose two at the same time to see the effect. You might find it useful to click away from the word to remove the highlight in order to see the effects of format changes fully. Do not forget to reselect the text before changing format again. It is obviously not possible to have superscript and subscript at the same time.

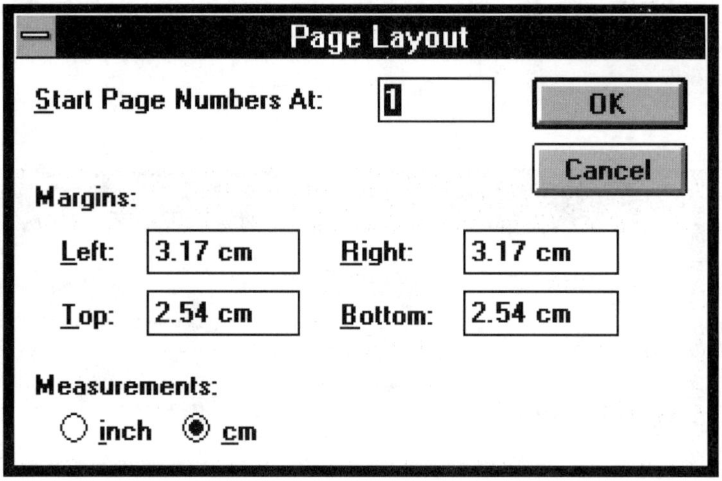

FIG. 5.3

The Regular option removes any format changes from the word.

12 With the word selected, click Character once more and try the Fonts item. While trying out some of the fonts take a look at Edit, Undo (Formatting) and see its effect on the selected word.

As you type Write inserts page breaks according to your paper size, and automatically suppresses widows and orphans. Widows and orphans are single lines of text at the bottom or top of a page. To see page breaks choose File, Repaginate. To insert forced page breaks press **Ctrl-Enter**. In a long document you can jump directly to a specified page with Find, Go To Page.

The Find menu also includes Find, Repeat Last Find and Replace. Find jumps straight to the first occurrence, after the cursor position, of a specified entry. Replace goes to the defined text and replaces it with any alternative text you enter in the Replace dialog. Repeat Last Find repeats the last Find or Replace carried out.

Write offers the facility to include headers and footers in your document. Both headers and footers can be configured to automatically paginate your text. They are defined through Document, Header or Document, Footer.

Write has default tabs, that is left tabs, set at every half an inch. If you wish you can create your own, whether left or decimal tabs. Any user-defined setting overrides the default settings, which are not shown anywhere. With the Ruler you click the icon for left or decimal tabs and then click at the required position immediately below the Ruler. Once in place, tab markers are easily dragged from side to side. To remove a tab drag it off the bottom of the Ruler. Without the Ruler it is necessary to go through Document, Tabs. In the subsequent Tabs dialog the position of each tab has to be typed in. The Decimal check box is for defining a decimal rather than a left tab. Note that the Write default tab positions do not appear in this dialog. Any entries you make take precedence over the hidden default settings. Individual tabs are adjusted by editing their entry in the Positions box. All the user-defined tabs can be removed by clicking Clear All.

13 Experiment as much as you like with JANE.WRI. Try and incorporate some features covered in previous steps. When you are reasonably happy that you understand how to access the facilities in Write, print the document to see the results of your editing. To print, click File, Print, OK.

The Print dialog that appears, before you click OK, contains a couple of parameters. You are able to print one or more copies, print all or a range of pages, or print selected text only.

Program Manager (1)

PROGRAM MANAGER (1)

■ The first of two chapters on Program Manager

■ How to create groups

■ How to create application icons

■ Moving and copying icons

So far you've been working with the default Program Manager and groups. There's no reason why you should not customize Program Manager to your own tastes. For example you might want to remove an icon. If you use Notepad and File Manager a lot, you might like to keep them in the same group window. You might want to have your application icons for separately purchased applications in the same group as Paintbrush. Solitaire might prove so much of a distraction that you get no work done, and want to remove the Games group. You might not like the name *Main* for a group, or want to change the name Paintbrush to Graphics, or you might wish to rearrange the layout of icons within a group window. All of this and more can be configured from Program Manager.

It is important to realise that exercises in this section can alter the way Windows NT looks. Should this not be what you want then read the section as a reference, and do not follow through the practical steps. Though if you are going to use Windows NT on a day-to-day basis you will invariably want to customize Program Manager. This section looks at some of the options available.

To rename a group:

1   Minimize the Main group, if it is a window, into an icon. Select the icon by clicking or with **Ctrl-F6**.

2   Click File then Properties (see FIG. 6.1).

3   Type **Utilities** to replace Main in the Description text box of the Personal Program Group Properties dialog and click OK.

Program Manager (1)

```
┌─────────────────────────────────────────────────┐
│ ═  │   Personal Program Group Properties         │
├─────────────────────────────────────────────────┤
│                                   ┌───────────┐  │
│  Description:                     │    OK     │  │
│  ┌─────────────────────────────┐  └───────────┘  │
│  │Main                         │  ┌───────────┐  │
│  └─────────────────────────────┘  │  Cancel   │  │
│                                   └───────────┘  │
│                                   ┌───────────┐  │
│                                   │   Help    │  │
│                                   └───────────┘  │
└─────────────────────────────────────────────────┘
```

FIG. 6.1

To create a brand new group:

1   Click File then New to summon the New Program Object
          dialog (see FIG. 6.2).

2   In this dialog choose the Personal Program Group option
          button and click OK. The next dialog is called Personal Program
          Group Properties.

3   In the text box labelled Description type **Mine** and click OK.

The new group window is the same as the ones we have been working
with up till now. It may be minimized, moved and sized. It does not yet
contain any icons, we will see how to place icons into group windows
shortly.

To delete a group:

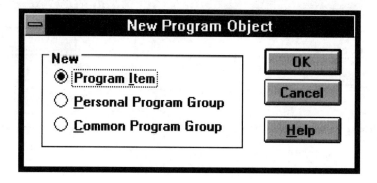

FIG. 6.2

1   Make the Mine group current as an icon or window and click File, Delete.

2   Respond in the affirmative to the warning message. If the group contains application icons then you should minimize the group first, otherwise the deletion applies only to the currently highlighted program icon and not to the group as a whole.

To place a brand new application icon in a group:

1   Make the Utilities group current.

2   Click File then New.

Program Manager (1)

3   In the New Program Object dialog choose the option button for Program Item and click OK.

4   The Program Item Properties dialog appears (see FIG. 6.3). In the Description text box type **Second Paintbrush**.

5   Press the **Tab** key or click to move to the Command Line text box and type **PBRUSH**.

You must enter the name of the main program file in the Command Line box. If the program is not in a directory on your path, or in the Windows directory, you must enter its full pathname – for example **C:\WINDOWS\SYSTEM32\PBRUSH**. If you follow the program name by a space and then the filename for a data file, associated with that program, the icon starts the program with the data file already loaded.

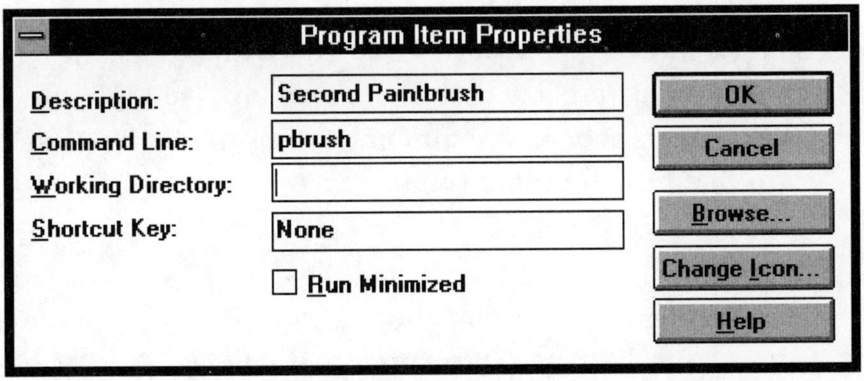

Program Item Properties		
Description:	Second Paintbrush	OK
Command Line:	pbrush	Cancel
Working Directory:		
Shortcut Key:	None	Browse...
	☐ Run Minimized	Change Icon...
		Help

FIG. 6.3

6   Click OK and restore the Utilities window, if necessary, to see the icon for Second Paintbrush.

To delete an application icon:

1   Make sure that the Utilities window is open and the Second Paintbrush icon is selected.

2   Click File then Delete and click Yes in the warning message.

The above method for adding an application icon is the one to adopt for adding brand new application icons (you can also use Windows NT Setup from the Main (Utilities) group, or drag a filename from File Manager into Program Manager). If an icon is already there, in another group, it is easier to drag the icon from one group to another. As you drag you will either copy or move the icon. You can in fact make copies of the same icon in the same group. To copy, rather than move, hold down the **Ctrl** key as you drag the icon. To move an icon:

1   Have both the Accessories and the Utilities group windows open. Move and size both these windows so that you can see the contents of both. Maximizing Program Manager itself gives you that little bit more room.

2   Drag the File Manager from the Utilities group into the Accessories group and let go of the mouse button. The keyboard alternative is to highlight the icon, choose File, Move, and select the name of the destination group.

Program Manager (1)

To get back to your original settings:

1 Drag File Manager back into Utilities.

2 Rename Utilities back to Main. To rename a group it should be minimized and highlighted. Use File, Properties for the renaming.

It is possible to have an application start automatically with Windows NT and bypass the double click required in Program Manager. You simply drag an existing application icon into the Startup group window from another window – either as a copy or move operation. Alternatively, create the application icon from scratch through File, New.

Maximizing groups in Program Manager

If you maximize a group or document window it takes over the whole of the Program Manager window. It will not maximize to full-screen, as an application window would, unless Program Manager itself is running full-screen. However it will overlay other group windows and icons. You can cycle hidden group windows with the **Ctrl-F6** (or **Ctrl-Tab** if you prefer) key combination. This works in the same way as **Alt-Tab** does for application windows and icons. You can also restore the maximized group window to its original size by clicking its restore button – the one containing the double arrow heads. It is directly below the maximize/restore button for Program Manager itself and is at the end of the Program Manager menu bar. **Ctrl-F6** is the Windows convention for cycling document windows and icons. **Alt-Tab** is the convention for cycling application windows and icons. An alternative to **Ctrl-F6** is to use the Window option on the Program Manager menu bar.

File Manager (1)

FILE MANAGER (1)

■   The first of two chapters on File Manager

■   Displaying files and directories

■   Copying, moving, and deleting files

■   How to select multiple files and directories

File Manager (1)

File Manager is the housekeeping application and is one of the most convenient applications bundled with Windows NT. It requires a little patience to learn but is well worth the effort. Once you have used it a few times, say, for copying or deleting files, groups of files, and whole directories, you will begin to wonder why you ever used the DOS prompt for housekeeping. File Manager is originally in the Main group and is also used for sharing and connecting to directories.

File Manager is exactly the same as all other Windows NT applications in that you can leave it running while working on something else, and switch quickly around applications with **Alt-Tab**. This is probably a good idea if your work involves a lot of housekeeping, for it saves continually opening and closing File Manager. Applications may also be started from File Manager by simply double clicking their names. To start File Manager:

1   In the Main group window double click the File Manager icon.

2   Maximize File Manager (see FIG. 7.1) by clicking its maximize button. This step is optional though it does give you more room to work in.

A word of warning is in order at this point. File Manager is deceptively powerful. It can show and delete all files, including hidden and system files. It can delete whole directories and subdirectories with all their files in one fell swoop, and can be configured to give no warning at all. Such actions are potentially quite dangerous and traumatic for the user when much valuable work is irretrievably deleted. Until you are completely familiar with File Manager do not alter any settings through Options, Confirmation. Doing so could well result in the suppression of all warning

File Manager (1)

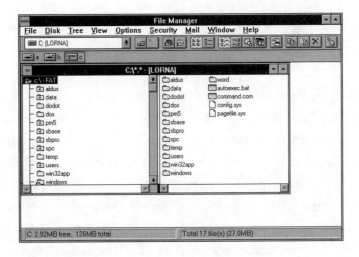

FIG. 7.1

messages, which means you have no opportunity of backing out of accidental actions.

The opening File Manager window has a row of icons along the top representing disk drives on your system. The highlighted icon is the current drive. Your display should have *A:* for your floppy disk drive, and *C:* for the hard disk. In addition you might see *B:* for a second floppy drive and *D:* if your hard disk is partitioned. Those of you who are logged onto a network may see even more drives for, say, *F:* or *G:* and even *X:*, *Y:* and *Z:*. Drive icons representing CD-ROMs are also be displayed if you have them. We are going to concentrate on *A:* and *C:*.

To log on to a different drive simply click the icon for the required drive. If you try to select a floppy drive and no disk is in the drive you receive an error message. Place a disk in the drive and Retry. The keyboard alternative for logging on to a drive is to type the letter for the drive while holding down the **Ctrl** key, or try Disk, Select Drive.

The Disk menu option allows you to format, copy or label a disk. The format option will only work with floppy disks so there is no danger of accidentally formatting your hard disk. The copy option is especially useful for making backup copies of valuable application software disks. Please note that the original (source) and the copy (destination) disks must have the same capacity for this to work. If they do not, you will need to copy the files through File, Copy or with the mouse. The latter method is covered shortly. You can copy a disk even if you have one floppy disk drive, all you do is follow the instructions on screen about when to switch the source and destination disks in the drive.

The File menu has a range of options. The Copy and Move options are essential if you do not have a mouse. With a mouse it is much easier to copy and move files simply by clicking and dragging. The Delete and Rename selections do just as they indicate, deleting and renaming files. Delete also works on whole directories and disks. Search is useful if you can not remember where you stored a file and wish to retrieve it. Create Directory does just that.

There is also a choice called Open. This is used to open an application once you have selected its main program file in the File Manager window; or you can double click the filename or press **Enter** on the file. Applications will also start if you double click an associated data file. For example, double clicking JANE.WRI starts Write, with the letter to Jane at Rectangle and Circle already loaded. Windows NT and Windows applications automatically provide these associations between data file extensions

File Manager (1)

and particular applications. As you become more experienced in Windows NT you can create your own associations through File, Associate. File Manager is an alternative to Program Manager for starting applications, only the pretty icons and convenient group windows are missing.

File Manager is an application window with a Control Menu. As you open directories, to examine or work with their contents, they are displayed in document windows. These document windows have a control menu too, but it is accessed from the keyboard with **Alt-Hyphen** rather than **Alt-Spacebar**. Mouse users do not have to worry about such niceties. And remember to cycle document windows with **Ctrl-F6** rather than **Alt-Tab**. The first document window is open and displays the directories on the current drive. The ensuing exercises assume you are logged onto the relevant partition of your hard disk to find the directory in which you saved the files earlier (possibly C:\USERS\DEFAULT). You should be seeing a list of directories for the current drive, or the root directory only, in the first document window.

To show the root directory only:

1   Double click the root directory if you can see its subdirectories. From the keyboard use Tree, Collapse Branch on the menu bar.

Click Tree, Indicate Expandable Branches to see a plus sign in directories that have subdirectories. This may not work on a directory if it has the share symbol (a hand) on the folder.

2   Double click the root to see its subdirectories. From the keyboard use Tree, Expand One Level.

The same folder now shows a minus sign, provided there's no share symbol. The minus indicates that the directory has subdirectories which are now showing, and that it is collapsible. A plus sign shows an expandable directory. You should see an entry for the Windows for DOS or Windows NT directory – you may have to use the scroll bars to find it if you have a lot of directories at this level. The Windows directory folder contains a plus sign.

3   Expand the Windows directory, by double clicking, to see the tree of its subdirectories.

4   Collapse the Windows directory, by double clicking, to hide the entries.

The files in a selected directory are displayed automatically provided View, Tree and Directory is turned on.

5   Find the file called JANE.WRI and highlight it. You have to select its directory – try USERS\DEFAULT or your home directory.

6   To complete the next step you will need to place a formatted floppy disk in drive A: (or B:).

7   With the mouse drag JANE.WRI to the icon for drive A: (or B:) and let go. As you drag you will notice a small symbol. This is a file symbol, and if you highlight and drag multiple files it shows as a multiple file symbol. You can also drag directories

---

around in a similar manner. You then have to respond to one or more confirmation messages (or possibly none at all, this depends upon any previous settings through Options, Confirmation). Answer in the affirmative and JANE.WRI is copied to drive A.

When you drag from one drive to another the file is copied. You can force Windows to move the file, that is copy it first and then delete the original, by pressing the **Alt** key as you drag. When you drag a file to a new destination on the same disk it is automatically moved. In this case, to leave the original intact, you must force Windows NT to copy rather than move. This is done by holding down the **Ctrl** key as you drag. Note that your ability to copy, delete, and move files and directories depends upon the permissions. Permissions are covered in Chapter 9 which contains more discussions on *File Manager*. Keyboard users have to choose File then Copy or Move after highlighting the file.

The previous operation is on a single file. The procedure is the same when working on a single directory. You can also work with multiple files or directories at the same time. In order to do so you must first make a multiple selection. There are various ways of doing this, it depends upon whether the files are next to each other (contiguous) or scattered throughout the directory window (non-contiguous).

To select a contiguous group of files (for example to copy multiple files in one go) click the first one and, while holding down the **Shift** key, click the last file in the group. Keyboard users need to use direction keys instead of dragging. To select a non-contiguous group of files hold down the **Ctrl** key as you click each required file. From the keyboard press and release

Shift-F8, press the **Spacebar** for each required file and press **Shift-F8** again to finish. By combining the techniques for contiguous and non-contiguous groups you can select non-contiguous groups of contiguous files, if you see what I mean. A shortcut for selecting all the files in a document window is to press **Ctrl-Forward Slash** (/) or to click File, Select Files.

For the final exercise in File Manager try and locate some of the following files in a directory window: LOGO.BMP, MEMO.TXT, CLIENTS.CRD, JANE.WRI, CUSTOMER.CRD, WEIRD.BMP.

1   Select two or more of these files. Make very sure that is all you have selected.

2   Click File then Delete.

3   Click the OK button in the subsequent dialog. Choose Cancel if you have any doubts about the wisdom of your action.

4   If a confirmation message appears click Yes or Yes to All. Choose No if doubts have just crept in, we do not want to delete files that are vital to the operation of Windows NT.

    If you did happen to delete important program files you may have to install Windows NT again.

5   Close File Manager by double clicking its application window Control menu.

Program Manager (2)

PROGRAM MANAGER (2)

■ The second of two chapters on Program Manager

■ How to create personal and common groups

■ How to set up default directories

■ Changing default icons

This part of the book assumes some previous knowledge of Windows for DOS (that is Windows 3 or Windows 3.1 on DOS-based systems). It does not assume that you're familiar with either Windows for Workgroups or Windows NT. If you're new to Windows altogether you should read (if you've not already done so) Part One: *For users new to Windows.*

If you've come to Windows NT from a Windows for DOS or Windows for Workgroups environment then Program Manager in Windows NT is reassuringly familiar. The main difference that you notice immediately is that File, Exit has been replaced by both File, Logoff and File, Shutdown. The title bar has been extended to show the computer (or workgroup) name and the current username. And minimized groups don't look quite the same – they have either a person's head or a computer attached. These attachments tell you if the minimized group is a personal or a common group – but more on this in a moment. There are other subtler changes from Windows for DOS too. For example, the Windows Tutorial option (available in Windows 3.1 for DOS) has gone from the Help menu, and there's a new choice on the Options menu: Save Settings Now. This one is quite useful and is worth investigating further.

In Windows 3.0 for DOS it was easy to lose your careful configuration of groups and icons. To keep the changes you made you had to explicitly instruct Windows to do so as you exited. The trouble with this is that next time you used Windows 3.0 for DOS you had to remember to turn off this instruction as you exited – otherwise it would keep any unwanted and accidental alterations. Windows 3.1 for DOS introduced the Save Settings on Exit item to the Options menu. As you rearranged Program Manager you turned this on if you wanted to keep your changes when you exited, or turned it off if you didn't. But it was still not foolproof. Instead most users turned it off but forced Windows to save desired settings by holding

Program Manager (2)

down the **Shift** key as they clicked File, Exit Windows. This handy technique saved Program Manager groups and icons but did not actually take you out of Windows. This still works in Windows NT, only you click File, Logoff (while holding down the **Shift** key) as there is no File, Exit. However, Options, Save Settings Now has exactly the same effect. Thus, to be sure you have Program Manager set up just as you want it, turn off Options, Save Settings on Exit and click Options, Save Settings Now when you are happy with your Program Manager arrangement. If you stay with that arrangement then, obviously, you don't need to continually click Options, Save Settings Now.

Now a word or two about those two different types of groups – personal and common groups. Personal groups look just the same as Windows for DOS groups when opened as windows. However, when minimized in the Program Manager workspace they have a person's head attached to the group icon. Common groups have a computer attached when minimized, and the word Common in parentheses on the title bar when open as a window. If you've recently installed Windows NT on a single-user machine then most (if not all) of your Program Manager groups are personal ones. Those readers on a network, or a multi-user machine, where an administrator has installed NT may be looking at one or more common groups. The distinction between personal and common groups is a straightforward one. Common groups are available to all users once they're logged on – personal groups are specific to an individual user. When you create personal groups they are only available to you. For example, if another user deletes a few icons from the Main group you can still see them when you log on. Personal groups are associated with a particular username. Thus individuals on a multi-user machine can create customized Program Managers without affecting how Program

Manager appears to the other users. Common groups, on the other hand, always appear exactly the same to all users. If a common group has a program icon added then all users see the new icon as they log on. Common groups, therefore, are ideal for a company-wide standard interface. To ensure that common groups aren't accidentally (or maliciously) tampered with, only members of the Administrators and Power Users groups can create or amend them. However, other users with fewer privileges can copy (but not move) icons from common groups into their personal groups.

If you're working on a single-user machine and you installed Windows NT yourself then your username is a member of the Administrators group by default. Here you can create common groups without explicitly logging as Administrator. On multi-user machines or if you're part of a network you may not have sufficient privileges to create common groups – if in doubt check with your system administrator.

To create an empty common group:

1   Click File, New in Program Manager.

2   In the subsequent New Program Object dialog (see FIG. 8.1) select the option button for Common Program Group and click OK.

3   In the next Common Program Group Properties dialog (see FIG. 8.2) type the descriptive name for the group and click OK.

Program Manager (2)

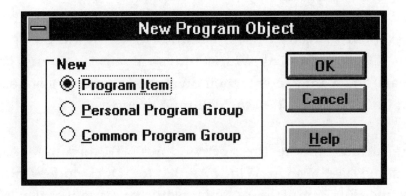

FIG. 8.1

You can then proceed to populate the group with program items. If you recall, you add icons with File, New, Program Item or drag from File Manager. To add lots of items at the same time you may find that Windows NT Setup is more convenient.

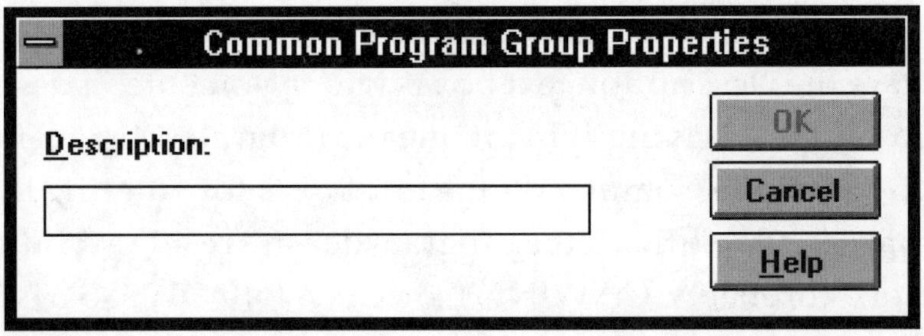

FIG. 8.2

System administrators moving from Windows for DOS networked environments will find common groups a great benefit. There is no longer any need to make GRP group files read-only, or to manually edit PROGMAN.INI to restrict users' abilities to configure groups. Under Windows NT your company-wide settings are safe in common groups. If individual users want to create their own personal groups on top of that, then that does not impact on the common groups.

There are various other features of Windows NT Program Manager that are the same as those in Windows 3.1 for DOS and Windows for Workgroups. But some of these similar features were not part of Windows 3.0 for DOS. I'm going to mention them quickly here; they're not covered in the Program Manager discussions in the part of this book: *For users new to Windows*. Hardened Windows 3.1 for DOS or Windows for Workgroups users may want to skim the rest of this chapter on *Program Manager*. If you've never used Windows at all, you should first read Chapter 6 on *Program Manager* in *Part One: For users new to Windows*.

In particular I want to mention a few of the choices in the Program Item Properties dialog (see FIG. 8.3). You see this dialog whenever you add new program icons to a group through File, New, Program Item. It's also called when you select an existing icon and click File, Properties. As you're aware the Description text box is where you enter a description of the program icon – leaving it blank means Program Manager labels the icon for you. And the Command Line text box is for entering the name of the program executable file. If the program doesn't reside in your Windows NT directory (probably C:\WINNT or C:\WINDOWS\SYSTEM32), or your path, you must preface the program executable filename with its path – for instance, C:\WORD\WINWORD.EXE for Word for Windows

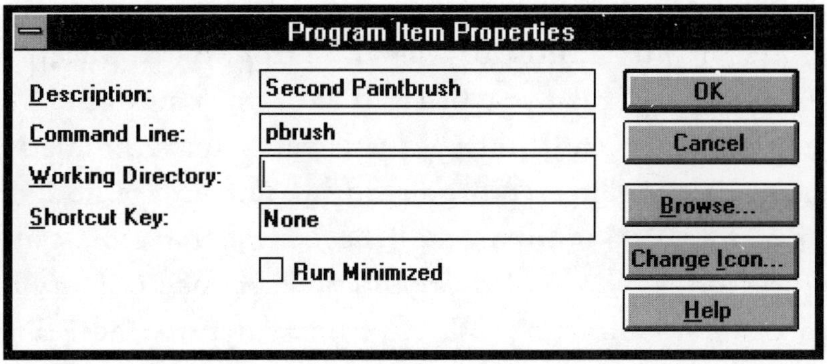

Program Item Properties

Description: Second Paintbrush

Command Line: pbrush

Working Directory:

Shortcut Key: None

☐ Run Minimized

OK

Cancel

Browse...

Change Icon...

Help

FIG. 8.3

if it's in the WORD directory on C:. If you're not sure of the path or simply want to avoid typing lengthy pathnames then you can select the program file together with its full path by going through the Browse button.

To load a data file with the application, add a space after the executable filename and type in the name of the data file. Should this be in a different directory from the executable file then once again you need to preface the data filename with its path. Suppose you want Word for Windows to open with a data file called VITAL.DOC ready-loaded, and this data file is in C:\DATA\DOCS – your entry would then read C:\WORD\WINWORD.EXE C:\DATA\DOCS\VITAL.DOC. This is all familiar territory to all previous users of Windows, but what's new for Windows 3.0 for DOS users is the Working Directory text box. Entering a directory name makes that your default directory for the application loaded by the program icon. This means that actions like File, Open and

File, Save in applications default to this working directory. In the absence of a working directory you should default to your home directory or C:\USERS\DEFAULT. A default directory is handy if you want to keep your data files in a data directory separate from the application's main directory – and this is good practice as it helps to ensure a tidy and well-ordered hard disk. A home directory helps the system administrator keep track of users' files. Again if you're already au fait with Windows for DOS or Windows for Workgroups you'll be aware that you can also set working directories for PIF files. Should you set one directory in the PIF file and a different directory for the icon that runs the PIF file from Program Manager then the Program Manager working directory takes precedence. If you're new to Windows then you may like to know that PIFs (Program Information Files) are useful for getting DOS applications to run under Windows. The method of creating a PIF file in PIF Editor is covered in due course.

The Program Item Properties dialog also has a push button labelled Change Icon. This lets you change the default icon proposed for the program icon you're adding to or editing in Program Manager. All Windows applications and some DOS applications come with a built-in icon. You may want to change the icon for an application, especially when the same program appears more than once in Program Manager groups. It's possible that you have more than one occurrence of the same icon if you have attached different data files to the same application. You'll also want to set an icon if you have more than one DOS application in your groups. The way to pick (or alter) an icon is to click the Change Icon button. This action opens the Change Icon dialog (see FIG. 8.4) which should be displaying the filename of the application. If your filename only contains one icon then you can find more by editing the filename to

Program Manager (2)

PROGMAN.EXE or, even better, MORICONS.DLL. Both of these files include quite a range of icons, one of which might be suitable for the Program Manager item. Note that changing the program name in the Change Icon dialog has no effect on the program started by the icon – that name is set in the Command Line box back in the Program Item Properties dialog.

You'll also notice a Run Minimized check box in the Program Item Properties dialog. Turning this on results in the application starting as an icon on the desktop. This minimized application is then loaded for you to work on at any time or to carry out processing in the background. A minimized program item on the desktop is not the same as the program icon in your groups. In the latter case the program has not started – generally, it's quicker to work from minimized icons but that may be at the expense of valuable memory resources. Incidentally, you can still start an application minimized even if the Run Minimized box is off – to

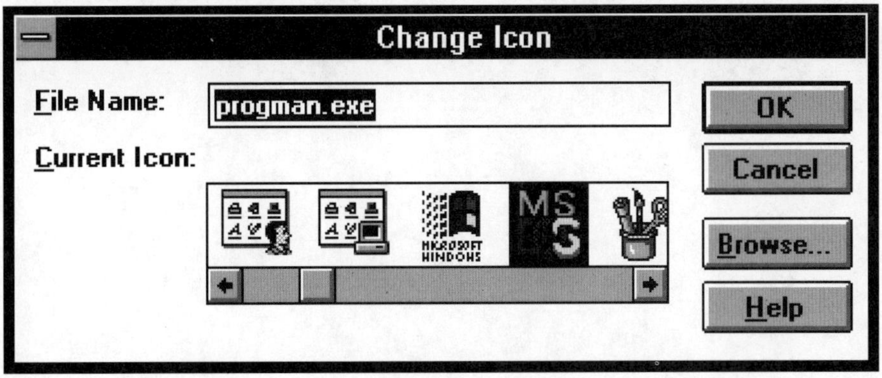

FIG. 8.4

do so simply hold down the **Shift** key as you double click the icon in Program Manager.

When you start up applications you may want to reduce Program Manager itself to an icon. You can arrange for this to happen automatically by turning on Options, Minimize on Use.

Finally, it's useful to know how to start applications automatically whenever you log on to Windows NT. You can accomplish this by adding program icons to the Startup group. These icons can be added through File, New, Program Item or by dragging from File Manager. If the icon already exists in another group you can copy or move it to the Startup group by dragging. To copy, as opposed to moving, hold down the **Ctrl** key as you drag between groups. The Startup group was a feature of both Windows 3.1 for DOS and Windows for Workgroups. It's new for Windows 3.0 for DOS users who should realise that you are no longer required to edit the load and run lines in WIN.INI to get applications to start up automatically. You can have an application in the Startup group open in a window or as an icon. To make it start as an icon turn on Run Minimized for the program icon's properties.

FILE MANAGER (2)

■   The second of two chapters on File Manager

■   How to share directories

■   How to connect to remote directories

■   Toolbar buttons

File Manager is a vital application. It enables you to carry out a number of file, disk, connectivity, and security tasks. Previous users of Windows for Workgroups will discover that File Manager in Windows NT is reasonably familiar. Previous users of Windows for DOS will find much that is new. Users with no previous exposure to Windows should first refer back to Chapter 7 on *File Manager* in *Part One: For users new to Windows*. That chapter provides an introduction to certain fundamental File Manager techniques and features. The topics covered include how to display disks, directories, and files; how to copy and move directories and files; and how to select single or multiple items displayed in the File Manager windows.

This section builds on that knowledge. It does so by looking at File Manager from three perspectives – the tasks that can be performed, the menu bar, and the toolbar.

Tasks

There's a large number of tasks that can be performed in File Manager. The tasks listed here should enable you to quickly locate the actions required for a particular task. Each task has a cross-reference to one or more items in the following section: *Menu bar*.

Disks

Displaying disks

See Disk, Select Drive; Options, Drivebar; and Options, Open New Window on Connect.

File Manager (2)

Network disks

See Disk, Connect Network Drive and Disconnect Network Drive.

Copying floppy disks

See Disk, Copy Disk.

Formatting floppy disks

See Disk, Format Disk.

Labelling disks

See Disk, Label Disk.

Searching disks

See File, Search.

Directories

Creating directories

See File, Create Directory.

Sharing directories

See Disk, Share As and Disk, Stop Sharing.

Displaying directories

See File, Open; the Tree menu items; View, Tree and Directory; View, Directory Only; and Window, New Window.

Files (viewing)

Displaying files

See View, Tree Only; View, Split; View, Name; View, All File Details; View, Partial File Details; View, By File Type; and Window, Refresh.

Sorting file display

See View, Sort by Name; View, Sort by Type; View, Sort by Size; and View, Sort by Date.

Files (manipulating)

Running applications

See File, Open; File, Run; File, Associate; and Options, Minimize on Use.

File Manager (2)

Selecting files

See File, Select Files; File, Search; and View, By File Type.

File maintenance

See File, Move; File, Copy; File, Copy to Clipboard; File, Delete; File, Rename; File, Properties; File, Print.

System administration

Security

See the Security menu.

Working with child windows

Manipulating document windows and icons

See the Window menu.

File Manager (overall)

Closing File Manager

See File, Exit and Options, Save Settings on Exit.

Customizing File Manager

See Options, Confirmation; Options, Font; Options, Customize Toolbar; Options, Toolbar; Options, Drivebar; and Options, Status Bar.

Menu bar

File menu

Open

If an executable file is selected in a File Manager window then File, Open runs the application. With a data file selected it runs the application associated with the data file type and loads the data file into the application. If a directory is selected, File, Open expands the directory provided it is expandable. Of course, if you have a mouse it's far easier to simply double click the selected file or directory.

Move

File, Move is for moving selected files and directories to a new location. Moving an object is the equivalent of first copying the object and then deleting the original. With a mouse it's easier to drag-and-drop – though in order to complete the drop operation the destination drive or directory must be displayed in File Manager. If you drag between locations on the same drive then the selected objects are moved. To force a copy operation within the same drive (that is leaving the original objects intact) hold down the **Ctrl** key as you drag.

File Manager (2)

Copy

File, Copy is for copying files or directories. Mouse users will find drag-and-drop more convenient, though the destination of the copy operation must be visible in File Manager. When you drag a selected file or directory to a destination on the same drive it is moved by default. To force a copy operation within the same drive hold down the **Ctrl** key as you drag. Dragging to another drive results in an automatic copy. To force a move operation to another drive hold down the **Alt** key as you drag.

Copy to Clipboard

This item copies the selected file contents to the Clipboard. From there it can be pasted into an application to create an embedded or linked object.

Delete

When you want to delete a file or directory use File, Delete. Alternatively you can simply press the **Delete** key. If you delete a directory you end up with a cascade deletion. In other words you also delete all files in the directory, all subdirectories, and all the files in the subdirectories. To guard against potentially dangerous cascade deletions leave the File Delete and Directory Delete warning messages turned on. These are on by default – if you want to check click Options, Confirmation.

Rename

Use File, Rename to rename a selected file or directory. Note that it's feasible to rename a directory even if it contains files and subdirectories.

Properties

File, Properties opens a Properties dialog (see FIG. 9.1) for the currently selected file. This shows information about the file and allows you to change the attributes of the file. The attributes that can be changed include read-only, archive, hidden, and system attributes. As well as the attributes of a file you can also view (but not edit) the name of the file, its size, and its creation date. If you're in a workgroup you can click the Open By button to see who's got the file open. This action opens the Network Properties dialog (see FIG. 9.2). You can use this dialog to terminate other users' connections to the file. However, to do so you must be a member of the Administrators or the Power Users groups.

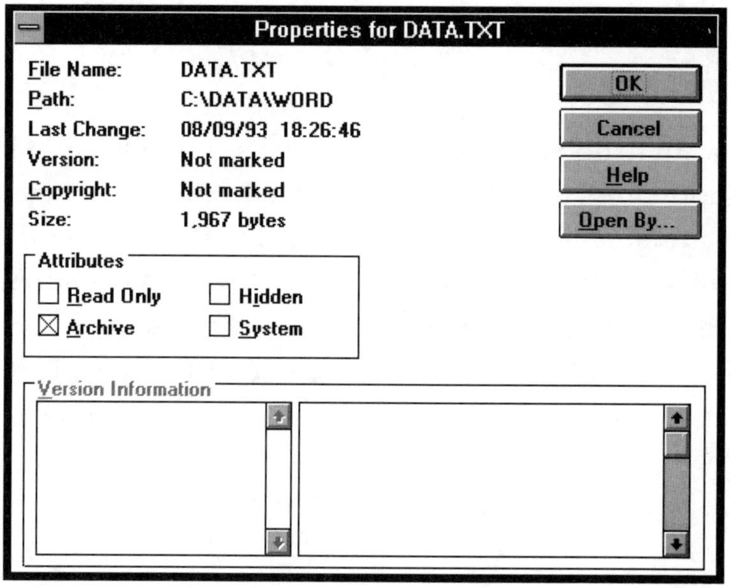

FIG. 9.1

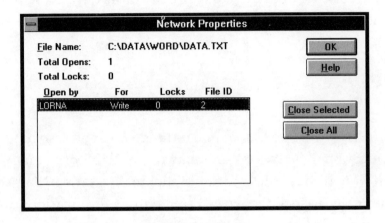

FIG. 9.2

Run

This command is the same as File, Run in Program Manager – although it does lack the handy Browse button. It enables you to run an application directly by selecting the application name, or indirectly by selecting a data file associated with an application. If the application or data file appears as an icon in Program Manager you may find it more convenient just to double click the icon. Alternatively you could double click the filename in the File Manager window.

Print

You can print straight from File Manager without opening the data file in its parent application first. To do so click File, Print. In order for this command to work the data file must already be associated with its parent application. To check on and define file associations see the next item File, Associate.

Associate

To print directly from File Manager a data file must be associated with its parent application. An association must also exist before you can start an application from its data file by double clicking the latter. Many data files are automatically associated with their parent applications when you install the applications. When you click File, Associate the Associate dialog (see FIG. 9.3) appears. The various file extensions (BMP and so on) are listed at the top of the dialog and the applications with which they are associated are listed at the bottom. To remove a file association for a particular extension select (None) from the lower list. To associate a file

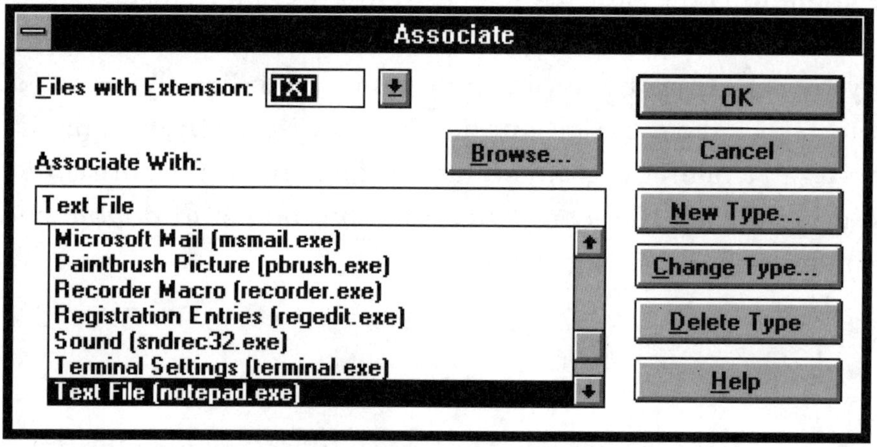

FIG. 9.3

type that does not appear automatically in the upper list, type its extension in directly or select a file with the extension before opening the Associate dialog.

If the application used for the association does not appear in the lower list you have to create an entry for that too. To do so click the New Type button to see the New File Type dialog (see FIG. 9.4). Here you click Add to place the extension in the default list and enter the program name in the Command text box. There's an Advanced button in the New File Type dialog. This should not normally be used by end users or even administrators – the information it leads to is set up when you install applications. It's probably the domain of software developers only – for

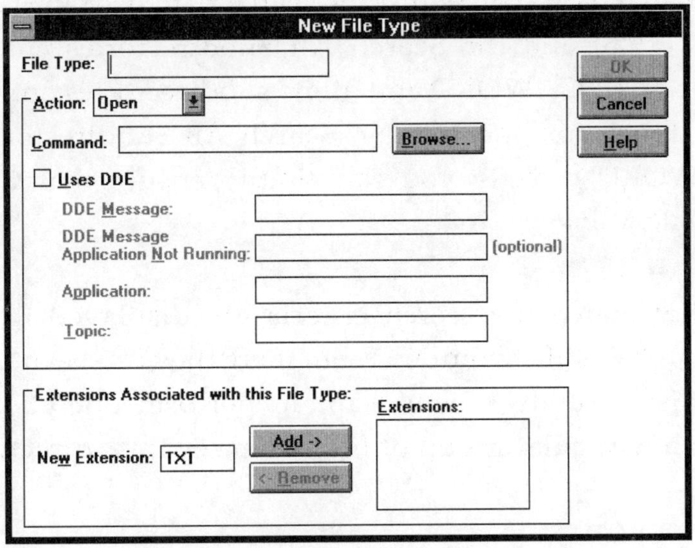

FIG. 9.4

example, it lets you specify DDE commands. Depending on your privileges you may not even be able to use the Advanced button.

Create Directory

Used for creating a directory. If the root directory is selected in File Manager then the new directory is from root level, unless you specify a different path. Similarly, you create a subdirectory if an existing directory is selected.

Search

File, Search lets you search for a specified file or a group of files. To search for a group of files use wild cards – for example, *.BMP locates all BMP files in the search path. You define the search path use the Start From text box (see FIG. 9.5) and the Search All Subdirectories check box. For example, to search C:\WORD and all its subdirectories enter **C:\WORD** in the Start From box and turn on Search All Subdirectories. To save typing C:\WORD directly you can simply ensure that C:\WORD is selected in File Manager first.

Any files that match the search criteria are displayed in a new File Manager Search Results window. From there they can be manipulated as normal – this is handy if you want to perform operations (such as copying) on a particular group of files from separate directories.

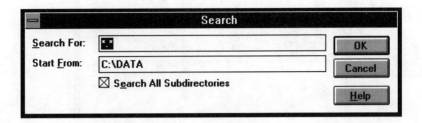

FIG. 9.5

Select Files

File, Select Files lets you select one or more files and subdirectories in the current directory window. To select all objects in a window enter the ***.*** wild card in the Select Files dialog (see FIG. 9.6). To select all files with a particular extension enter ***.extension** – for example, use ***.BMP** to select all BMP bitmaps.

Exit

This option closes down File Manager. Alternatively you might find it quicker to double click the Control menu. In either case if Options, Save Settings on Exit is turned on then all your window positions and views are saved.

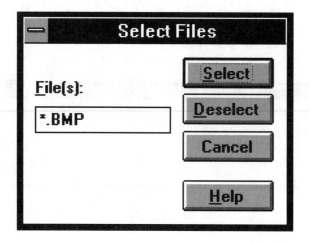

FIG. 9.6

Disk menu

Copy Disk

Disk, Copy Disk is handy for making backup copies of floppy disks. On systems with more than one floppy disk drive you can choose both the destination and the source drive for the copy operation. However, to copy from one floppy drive to another they must be capable of handling disks of the same size and format. Otherwise you must specify the same drive as the both the source and the destination.

Label Disk

Use this item to assign volume labels to hard and floppy disks. You are limited to eleven characters for FAT and HPFS disks, but with an NTFS volume the maximum is thirty-two characters.

Format Disk

Disk, Format Disk is for formatting your floppy disks. In the ensuing Format Disk dialog box (see FIG. 9.7) you can choose the drive which contains the floppy disk (assuming there is more than one such drive); specify the capacity of the newly formatted disk; create a volume label; and perform a quick format. Quick formatting can only be used on previously formatted disks – it saves time but does not mark any bad sectors. Disk, Format Disk is a fairly safe in that you can't use it to format a hard disk.

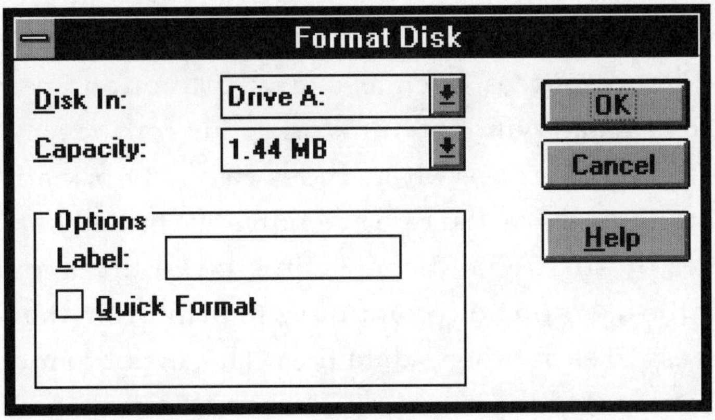

FIG. 9.7

Connect Network Drive

If you've upgraded straight from Windows for DOS then Disk, Connect Network Drive is new. Of course, Windows for Workgroups users will recognise it immediately. Its purpose is to connect your computer to a shared drive or directory on another computer within your workgroup or domain.

Once a connection is established you can view the contents of the shared directory in your own copy of File Manager. You can then copy, move, or delete files from a remote computer (subject to the necessary permissions). In addition, you can load data files into applications on your local machine and print them if you have a printer directly attached. You can also print remote files across the network if you are connected indirectly to a network printer. However, certain actions may not be possible if you don't have sufficient privileges.

Sharing and connecting are fundamental procedures for workgroup users. To illustrate the concepts let's consider a typical upgrade path for a small business with two stand-alone machines, both running Windows for DOS. To share resources, such as a laser printer and common data files, it's decided to install Windows for Workgroups on the two computers. The Windows for Workgroups kit includes two network adapter cards and a connecting cable. Now the two machines are linked in a basic peer-to-peer network. By sharing and connecting to resources appropriately it's possible for the users on both computers to print from the sole printer and to have access to each other's data files. This is not to mention other benefits like email and group scheduling. Then Windows NT is installed to derive the benefits of system integrity, security, 32-bit processing, and so on. But, to all intents and purposes, running NT is pretty much the

File Manager (2)

same as Windows for Workgroups. So it's just as easy to share resources, in fact the procedures are almost identical to those for Windows for Workgroups. The two basic procedures are connecting and sharing.

Quite simply, to use a resource you must be connected to it. But to be connected the resource must be sharable. In other words the user who 'owns' a resource must give permission for others to share it. Once a user declares a resource to be sharable other users can connect to it. Thus the single laser printer in our example can be made sharable by the user whose machine is directly attached to the printer (the print server). That done, the other user can connect to the printer and print just as if it's a local printer on the user's own machine. Printer sharing and connecting are controlled from Print Manager, but you use File Manager to share and connect to drives and directories. Suppose one user wishes to work on a data file on the other machine. The second user makes the directory containing the file sharable. The first user can then connect to that directory with Disk, Connect Network Drive in File Manager. To share the directory in the first place the second user would have used Disk, Share As in their copy of File Manager. It's not possible to connect to a resource that's not shared. When you do establish a connection, a shared directory is mapped to a drive letter on the connecting machine. Thus if the first user connects to the shared C:\DATA\WORD directory on the second machine this appears as F: (or G:, or whatever's chosen) drive in File Manager on the first machine. A file such as C:\DATA\WORD\LETTER.DOC on the second machine is then F:\LETTER.DOC on the first machine.

Clicking Disk, Connect Network Drive opens the Connect Network Drive dialog (see FIG. 9.8). The Drive box shows the drive letter that's assigned

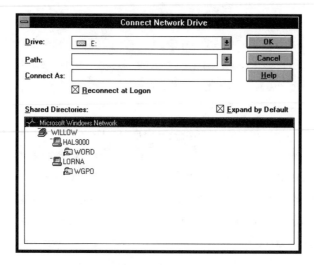

FIG. 9.8

to the shared directory on the connecting machine. The letter defaults to the first free drive, though you can select another letter (provided it doesn't already exist in File Manager) if you wish. In the Path box type a network path to the shared directory. Fortunately, File Manager remembers the last ten connections, so if you've connected to the same directory recently you can select it from the Path drop-down list. Alternatively, expand workgroups and computers by double clicking in the Shared Directories list, and click the required shared directory to copy it to the Path box. This alternative may not be available on all networks.

In the Connect As text box type a valid username, though normally you enter your own username. Turn on the Reconnect at Logon check box if you want to establish the connection automatically as you log on in the future. You may also want to turn on the Expand by Default check box to automatically display all computer names in your workgroup or domain.

File Manager (2)

To make the connection click OK. A successful connection results in the mapped drive letter appearing in File Manager's drivebar and the shared directory opening in its own window. To stop the window opening you may want to turn off Options, Open New Window on Connect.

It's important to realise that you aren't forced to log on to network drives in File Manager. For example, if you click File, Open in Notepad the Open dialog contains a Network button. You can go through this button to connect to a remote directory and open a file in that directory in Notepad.

Disconnect Network Drive

Disconnecting is rather easier than connecting. To disconnect from a shared directory click Disk, Disconnect Network Drive. In the Disconnect Network Drive dialog (see FIG. 9.9) select a mapped drive to disconnect and click OK. To assist in selecting the correct mapped drive from a list, the network path is given next to the drive letter. If you wish to disconnect from a number of network drives at the same time, select them all in the Disconnect Network Drive dialog before clicking OK.

It's important to realise that in some situations you are not totally dependent on another user to make directories sharable before you attempt a connection. Members of the Administrators group can make a remote directory sharable. To do so you first connect to the remote computer's shared root directory, usually C$. Then you can use your local File Manager to make any other directory on the remote computer sharable (see the next entry on Disk, Share As).

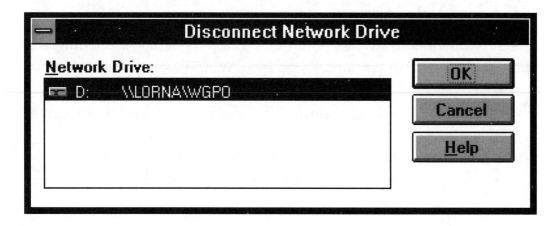

FIG. 9.9

Share As

To enable other users in a workgroup to connect to your local directories, as network drives, you must first make them sharable. That's precisely what Disk, Share As is for.

The procedure for setting up a shared directory is as follows:

1   Select the directory you wish to share in the File Manager window.

2   Click Disk, Share As. This opens the New Share dialog (see FIG. 9.10).

File Manager (2)

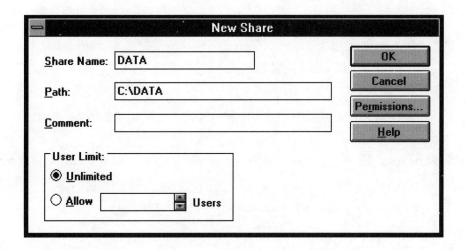

FIG. 9.10

3 In the New Share dialog the Path box indicates the directory you're sharing. If you change your mind you can edit the path to point to a different directory. The name of the directory also shows up in the Share Name box. This is the name that other users see when they set up a connection to the directory. You may want to enter a more meaningful name in this box (maximum of twelve characters). You may also want to add an explanatory comment in the Comment box. Other users can also see the comment when they attempt to make a connection.

4 By default there is no limit to the number of users who can connect to your shared directory. If you want to set a limit then make an entry in the Allow Users box in the User Limit section.

5   If you want to set permissions on the shared directory click the Permissions button. Permissions are discussed at the end of this chapter on *File Manager*.

6   Click OK in the New Share directory to complete the sharing.

You can change the properties of a shared directory at any time. To do so:

1   Select the shared directory in File Manager.

2   Click Disk, Share As to see the Shared Directory dialog (see FIG. 9.11).

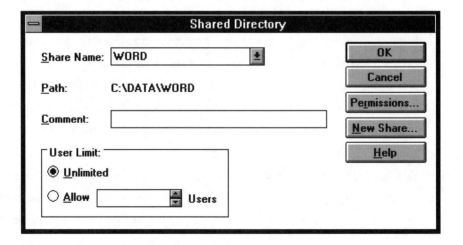

FIG. 9.11

3   Use this dialog to change the user limit, comment, or permissions for the shared directory. To share the directory under a new name click the New Share button. If you are already sharing the directory under more than one name you can select one of the existing names from the Share Name drop-down list.

4   Click OK in the Shared Directory dialog when you're finished.

Stop Sharing

As you might expect Disk, Stop Sharing removes the shared attribute from a directory. In the Stop Sharing Directory dialog (see FIG. 9.12) all of your shared directories are shown. Select one or more directories from the list and click OK to remove sharing. If users on other workstations are connected to a shared directory and you remove sharing those users may lose data. Windows NT detects that others are connected and warns you accordingly. To be on the safe side you might want to click Cancel in the

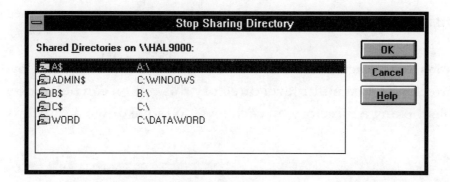

FIG. 9.12

warning dialog and back out of the stop sharing procedure – a warning dialog informs you if the other users have any files open. You may then want to tell the other users to disconnect (you could use Chat or Mail to do this) before attempting to stop sharing later.

Select Drive

Disk, Select Drive displays the selected drive in the current directory window. Mouse users will find that the drivebar or the drives drop-down list on the toolbar much more convenient.

Tree menu

Expand One Level

Expands the selected directory folder to show the next level down of subdirectories (this is assuming that the directory does contain subdirectories). Double clicking with the mouse is probably easier.

Expand Branch

Expands the selected directory to show all the subsequent levels of subdirectories. In a multi-level directory this option can be quicker than double clicking a directory on each level to move down a directory tree.

File Manager (2)

Expand All

Expands all the directories in the current directory window to show all the levels of subdirectories.

Collapse Branch

Hides all the subdirectories of the currently selected directory. If you've used Tree, Expand All then select the root directory and click Tree, Collapse Branch to show just the root again. Mouse users can simply double click a directory. Double clicking acts as a toggle. You double click an unexpanded directory to show the next level of subdirectories. But if you double click a directory that's already expanded (no matter how many levels) then it collapses.

Indicate Expandable Branches

Tree, Indicate Expandable Branches places a plus sign in directories that can be expanded (that is directories with subdirectories). Once such a directory is expanded the plus sign changes into a minus sign. This menu item acts as a toggle so you can turn it off again. Marking expandable directories can help you navigate your disk structure but it may slow File Manager down slightly.

View menu

Tree and Directory

View, Tree and Directory splits the current directory window into two panes. The left-hand pane shows the directory tree, while the right-hand pane displays files and subdirectories of the directory selected in the left-hand pane.

Tree Only

Shows only the directory tree in the current directory window.

Directory Only

Shows only the contents (files and subdirectories) of the current directory. It hides the structure of the directory tree.

Split

Splits a directory window. If the window is showing one pane only (either the tree or the directory contents) then View, Split is the equivalent of View, Tree and Directory. To move the split bar use the mouse or arrow keys. To anchor the split bar click the mouse or press **Enter**. If the window is already split then View, Split can be used to adjust the position of the split bar – although it's easier just to drag the split bar with the mouse.

File Manager (2)

Name

View, Name shows only the names of files and directories in the current window.

All File Details

Shows not only the name but also the size, modification date and time, and attributes of files and directories.

Partial File Details

You use View, Partial File Details to customize the display of files and directories in the current window. It enables you to arrive at a compromise between View, Name and View, All File Details. In addition to size, date, time, and attributes you can also choose to show DOS filenames for NTFS files.

Sort by Name

Sorts the display of directories and files alphabetically – though directories are always shown before files.

Sort by Type

Sorts the display by extension.

Sort by Size

Sorts the display by size of files.

Sort by Date

Sorts the display of files and directories by date of last modification. Again directories are shown before files.

By File Type

View, By File Type opens the By File Type dialog (see FIG. 9.13). You can further customize your display by making appropriate choices in this dialog. You can show all files by entering the wild card ***.***, or show only those matching a template (for example, ***.BMP** for BMP bitmap files). You can also decide whether or not to display directories, program files, data files, or other files. In addition, you can show or hide system and hidden files.

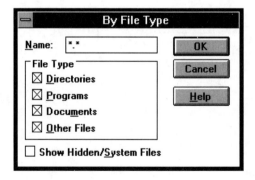

FIG. 9.13

File Manager (2)

Options menu

Confirmation

Until you are au fait with File Manager, it's best not to turn off confirmation messages. However, once you are comfortable you might want to suppress one or more of the confirmation messages. You accomplish this through Options, Confirmation and doing so can speed up certain operations. The default messages occur on file deletion, directory deletion, replacing files, mouse actions (for example, copying a file), issuing disk commands (for example, copying or formatting a floppy disk), and modifying hidden/system/read-only files. You may decide that it's advisable to keep confirmation messages for file and directory deletion – this helps to prevent possibly quite traumatic accidents.

Font

Options, Font enables you to customize the font used to display file and directory names. As well as changing font you can select a font size, font style, and whether to have lower or upper case letters. Judicious use of the Font dialog can improve the legibility of your File Manager display.

Customize Toolbar

If you want to use the toolbar (see the next item for Options, Toolbar) you might like to customize its appearance. To begin doing so click Options, Customize Toolbar or simply double click on an empty section of the toolbar. Either action opens the Customize Toolbar dialog (see FIG. 9.14). You use this dialog to add, remove, or move toolbar buttons. You can also

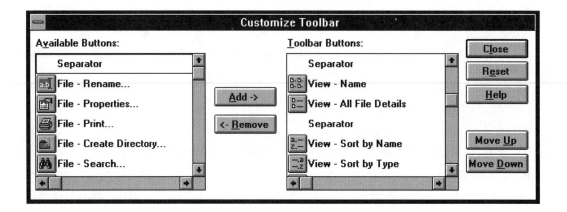

FIG. 9.14

get back to the default toolbar by clicking Reset. If you're using a mouse then there are quicker alternatives for removing or moving buttons. To remove a button from the toolbar hold down the **Shift** key as you drag a button off the toolbar. To move a button hold down **Shift** as you drag along the toolbar. However, to add a new button you must go through the Customize Toolbar dialog.

To place a new button on the toolbar select the relevant button (the menu equivalents are also listed) in the list of Available Buttons and click Add to add it to the list of Toolbar Buttons. To add a separator click Separator in the Available buttons list before clicking Add. To remove buttons or separators select the required item in the Toolbar Buttons list and click Remove. Use Move Up (which corresponds with move left) and Move Down (that is move right) to change the position of a button or separator.

File Manager (2)

Click Reset to retrieve the default toolbar. Click Close to keep any changes made.

Toolbar

Toggles the toolbar off and on.

Drivebar

Toggles the drivebar off and on.

Status Bar

Toggles the status bar off and on.

Open New Window on Connect

Options, Open New Window on Connect is a toggle which is on by default. When turned on it results in a new directory window being displayed in File Manager whenever you make a successful connection to a shared directory with Disk, Connect Network Drive.

Minimize on Use

If you select this item (it's a toggle) File Manager minimizes to a desktop icon when you run a program from within File Manager. You can launch applications by double clicking the program filename or using File, Run or File, Open. You can also start applications with the same methods but choosing a data file that is associated with a parent application. You can check and define such associations through File, Associate.

Save Settings on Exit

Options, Save Settings on Exit is handy if you want File Manager to remember the current directory windows, their arrangement, and the viewing options you've set up. Unlike Program Manager there is no Save Settings Now, however, you can achieve the same results by holding down the **Shift** key as you click File, Exit. This keeps the current layout and does not actually close File Manager. But you may want to ensure that Options, Save Settings on Exit is turned off otherwise any subsequent and unwanted changes will be saved.

Security menu

Permissions

This option is only available if you're dealing with an NTFS partition. It concerns the setting of permissions on directories and files you create. To set permissions specifically on shared directions see Disk, Share As earlier. There's a full discussion of permissions at the end of this chapter on *File Manager*. If you're working with others and/or you have an NTFS partition make sure you read the discussion.

Auditing

Security, Auditing allows you to record what happens to directories and files. For example, you can see when a directory has been deleted and by

File Manager (2)

whom. To view the audit you open Event Viewer – this is covered in some detail later in the book. And to set up auditing from File Manager in the first place you must turn on File and Object Access through Policies, Audit in User Manager – this too is covered later.

To set up file and directory auditing:

1   Select the directory or file you wish to audit.

2   Click Security, Auditing to see the Auditing dialog for the selected item.

3   If you selected a directory then the Directory Auditing dialog includes a Replace Auditing on Subdirectories check box. If you leave this check box turned off then auditing is only applied to the selected directory and the files it contains. Turn on the check box to extend auditing to subdirectories of the selected directory and the files in them.

4   Select a user or group in the Name list and turn on the auditing check boxes in the Events to Audit section.

5   If necessary, click the Add button to add users and groups to the Name list. This opens the Add Users and Groups dialog, which is discussed in detail in the section on *Permissions* at the end of this chapter on *File Manager*. You can use the Remove button to clear users and groups from the Name list.

6   Click OK in the Auditing dialog to preserve your settings.

Owner

You are the owner of a directory or file if you create it. Being the owner confers the privilege of setting permissions for the item. A member of the Administrators group can take ownership of the item and thus confer or revoke permissions. However, such a user can't transfer ownership to another user. Other users can only take ownership if the original creator/ owner grants the necessary permissions – that is Full Control is granted, or a customized set of permissions that includes the Take Ownership permission. If a user takes ownership under these conditions they can then bestow or alter permissions on the directory or file. If the creator/ owner has set up customized permissions then another user can change the permissions if the customized set includes the Change Permissions permission. Permissions are covered in the final section of this chapter. In the meantime this is how to take ownership of an item:

1   Select a file or directory in File Manager.

2   Click Security, Owner.

3   In the Owner dialog click the Take Ownership button.

Window menu

New Window

Opens a new directory window. The new window contains the same information as the current window, but you can easily navigate through directories to arrive at two different views. The best way to open a window on a different drive is to double click the drive icon on the icon bar.

Cascade

Cascades all open directory windows.

Tile Horizontally

Tiles all open directory windows horizontally. A popular way of working is to open a second directory window in File Manager and navigate so it shows a different view to the first window. Then click Window, Tile Horizontally to tidy up the display and hold down the **Shift** key as you click File, Exit. The latter action preserves the layout the next time you open File Manager.

Tile Vertically

Tiles all open directory windows vertically.

Arrange Icons

Window, Arrange Icons tidies up any directory windows you've minimized to icons in the File Manager workspace.

Refresh

This updates the display in the current directory window. This is useful if you're viewing the contents of a floppy disk and insert a new disk. Window, Refresh reads in the contents of the new floppy and obviates the need to close and reopen the directory window.

Toolbar

If you've upgraded to Windows NT from Windows 3.0 (or 3.1) for DOS the toolbar in File Manager is a new feature. Apart from one drop-down list, it contains fifteen buttons by default. The drop-down list allows you to display the contents of a particular drive and is the equivalent of Disk, Select Drive; or clicking a drive icon on the drivebar; or pressing **Ctrl-drive letter**. The fifteen buttons provide quick alternatives to some of the menu bar options. If you prefer to work without the toolbar you can turn it off by clicking Options, Toolbar. This is a toggle so choosing it again turns the toolbar back on. Nor are you stuck with the default toolbar, you can customize it to show those buttons that are most useful to you. To customize the toolbar click Options, Customize Toolbar or simply double click on a blank area of the toolbar to display the Customize Toolbar dialog. For more information about customizing the toolbar refer back to Options, Customize Toolbar in the previous *Menu bar* section.

This section details the default toolbar and indicates the menu bar equivalents of the toolbar buttons. To understand what each button is for, you may want to check back with the *Menu bar* section earlier.

File Manager (2)

Default toolbar buttons

 Connect Network Drive

Equivalent to Disk, Connect Network Drive.

 Disconnect Network Drive

Equivalent to Disk, Disconnect Network Drive.

 Share As

Equivalent to Disk, Share As.

 Stop Sharing

Equivalent to Disk, Stop Sharing.

 Name

Equivalent to View, Name.

 *All File Details*

Equivalent to View, All File Details.

 *Sort By Name*

Equivalent to View, Sort by Name.

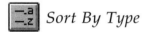 *Sort By Type*

Equivalent to View, Sort by Type.

 *Sort By Size*

Equivalent to View, Sort by Size.

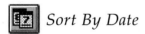 *Sort By Date*

Equivalent to View, Sort by Date.

File Manager (2)

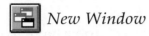 *New Window*

Equivalent to Window, New Window.

 Copy

Equivalent to File, Copy.

 Move

Equivalent to File, Move.

 Delete

Equivalent to File, Delete.

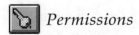 *Permissions*

Equivalent to Security, Permissions.

Permissions

If you're a single user of a stand-alone machine then you don't have to worry about permissions. If, on the other hand, you share your machine with other users or share your directories with co-workers in a workgroup then an understanding of permissions is vital. You can set, change, and revoke permissions on directories and files you create, on directories that you share, on printers, and on ClipBook pages.

The permission you set on a directory determines the type of access other users can have to that directory. For example, you can give permission for others to read the directory only or you might want to grant broader permissions including the ability to delete files from a directory.

If you're working in a FAT or HPFS partition you can set permissions on shared directories. This means you can control the actions of remote users who connect to the shared directory. If you're working in an NTFS partition you can also set permissions on all the directories and files you create. This means you can limit the actions of other local users (that is users working on the same machine) with your directories and files. On an NTFS partition you can set two separate lots of permissions on the same directory – permissions you grant as creator of the directory and permissions you grant when you share the directory with remote users. In some cases this may mean that the remote user does not have the permissions you stipulate for the shared directory. Anyone can set permissions on directories and files they create – but to set permissions on shared directories you must be logged on as a member of the Administrators or Power Users groups.

To set permissions on a shared directory you click the Permissions button in the New Share or Shared Directory dialogs. To set permissions on a directory or file you create you click Security, Permissions in File Manager. The latter is only possible if you're working from an NTFS partition.

Shared directory permissions

Let's look at what's involved in setting permissions on shared directories:

1   From a New Share or Shared Directory dialog click the Permissions button. This opens the Access Through Share Permissions dialog (see FIG. 9.15).

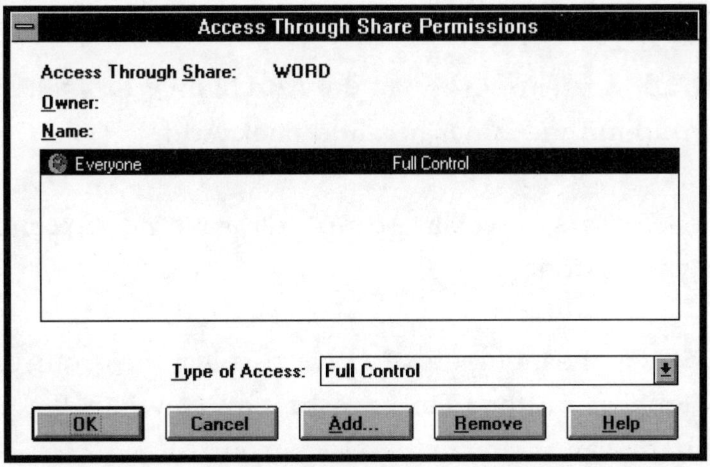

FIG. 9.15

2   To grant permissions to a user or group select the user or group and select a permission from the Type of Access drop-down list. To revoke permissions select a user or group and click the Remove button.

3   Click OK to establish the permissions set.

First, a word about the permissions. No Access prevents any access to the shared directory. Read allows remote users to display data and run programs from the directory. Change adds write and delete privileges to Read. Full Control in this instance is the same as Change. Second, an observation on the Access Through Share Permissions dialog. You can only grant permissions to the users or groups that are listed in the dialog. To grant permissions to unlisted users and groups you click the Add button. This opens the Add Users and Groups dialog (see FIG. 9.16). This dialog is met in many areas of Windows NT and is worth considering in some detail:

1   To add a user or group to the Add Names box select the user or group in the Names box and click Add.

2   To list users as well as groups in the Names box click the Show Users button.

3   To view the members of a group, select the group and click the Members button. This can be handy when you're deciding what permissions to give to a group.

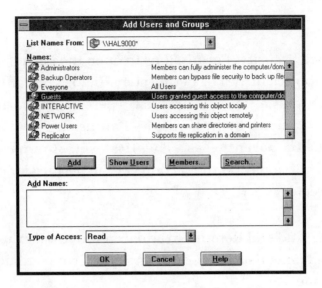

FIG. 9.16

4 If you're part of a Windows NT Advanced Server domain you can first search for a user or group by clicking on the Search button and adding them to the Names list.

5 To assign permissions to users and groups, add them to the Add Names list and select the necessary permissions from the Type of Access drop-down list. Click OK to return to the Access Through Share Permissions dialog.

Directory and file permissions

Setting permissions on directories or files you create is almost the same as setting permissions for shared directories. To do so:

1 Select the directory or file in File Manager.

2   Click Security, Permissions to open the Permissions dialog for the object. In the File Permissions dialog you can see parentheses after entries in the Name list. These contain a summary of the permissions. In the Directory Permissions dialog there are two sets of parentheses. The first set summarises directory permissions and the second set the permissions for files in the directory.

3   Use Add and Remove to add or remove users and groups from the Name list. The Add Users and Groups dialog is discussed above.

4   Turn on the Replace Permissions on Subdirectories check box if you want the permissions to extend to the subdirectories (and their files) of the selected directory. This option is only available if you selected a directory.

5   Select a user or group in the Name list and select a permission from the Type of Access drop-down list.

6   Click OK when you're finished.

Customized permissions

There may be occasions when you find that the default permission sets are not flexible enough. In such a situation you can create your own set of customized permissions for a directory or file. To establish customized permissions:

File Manager (2)

1   Select the directory or file in the File Manager window and click Security, Permissions.

2   In the Permissions dialog select the user or group to be granted a customized set of permissions.

3   Select Special Directory Access (for directories) or Special File Access (for files) from the Type of Access drop-down list. Alternatively you can simply double click the user or the group in the Name list. All of these actions open a Special Access dialog.

4   Select the relevant permissions in that dialog and click OK twice.

Print Manager

PRINT MANAGER

■ How to install and configure printers

■ Sharing printers

■ Connecting to remote printers

■ Toolbar buttons

Print Manager

Print Manager (see FIG. 10.1) allows you to install printers, configure installed printers, and control most aspects of printing. You can control printing on both local printers and those accessed remotely across a network. There are two ways of starting Print Manager: either double click the Print Manager icon in your Main group or choose the Printers icon in Control Panel.

Windows for Workgroups users will find much that is familiar. Windows for DOS users are going to notice a lot of changes from the Windows for DOS version of Print Manager. Fortunately, certain procedures in Print Manager are similar to those in File Manager – I have in mind sharing and connecting to printers. These procedures are the equivalent to sharing and connecting to network drives in File Manager.

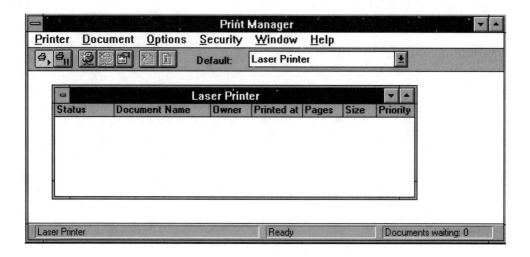

FIG. 10.1

Print Manager

Menu bar

Printer menu

Connect to Printer

Printer, Connect to Printer enables you to print remotely across a network. If you're on a Windows network you don't even need to install the remote printer for your local computer. You don't use Printer, Connect to Printer to print to a local printer directly connected to your workstation. Before you can connect to a remote printer then that printer must be sharable. To make a printer sharable you use Printer, Properties (see below). Typically, the system administrator would arrange for the remote printer to be sharable. Then other users can connect to that printer in order to print.

When you click Printer, Connect to Printer the Connect to Printer dialog (see FIG. 10.2) appears. In the Shared Printers list in this dialog double click your network to show the workgroups or domains. Next double click a workgroup or domain to see the computers in that group. Then double click the computer (print server) to which the remote printer is directly attached. Finally click the relevant printer shown for that computer to place the printer name in the Printer text box. Click OK to make a connection to that printer. The Expand by Default check box can be turned on to automatically expand the tree in the Shared Printers list the next time you make a connection.

Note that if you're trying to print to a remote printer on a non-Windows network you may be asked to install a driver for the remote printer. In that eventuality follow the instructions that appear on screen.

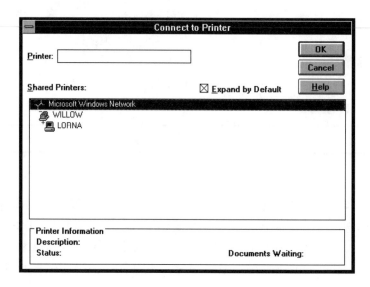

FIG. 10.2

Create Printer

You employ Printer, Create Printer when you want to install a new printer or to print to file. It's likely that you installed a printer when installing Windows NT, but you may wish to install another printer or to print to file. Note that some users may not have sufficient privileges to install a printer – members of the Administrators and Power Users groups do possess the relevant privileges. It's important to note that you can create two or more printers for each physical printer. You install them both in the same way but you must give each one a distinct name (see Printer Name shortly). Such an approach confers a number of advantages. For example, you can give each logical printer a different priority so you can send vital jobs to the one with the higher priority. This means that the urgent job will print in precedence to spooled jobs sent to the lower priority printer (remember both printers are the same physical printer).

Print Manager

Or you might assign differing print times to each logical printer. Long, and non-urgent, print jobs might be sent to the logical printer that only prints during the night (you can send the print job at any time) and shorter, more urgent, tasks directed to the logical printer that prints during the day. To set both print priorities and print times you have to go through Printer, Properties – there is a *Menu bar* section on Printer, Properties below.

The Create Printer dialog (see FIG. 10.3) contains a number of text boxes, drop-down lists, and buttons. In fact, it's identical to the Printer, Properties dialog except the Setup button is enabled in the latter. The buttons are for configuring the printer and you may find it more convenient to ignore the buttons as you install the printer. Once the printer's installed you can go through Printer, Properties and use the Printer Properties dialog buttons

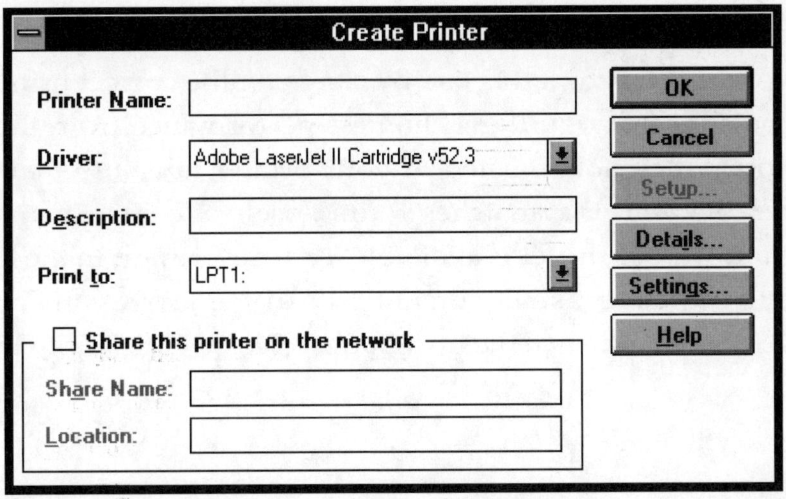

FIG. 10.3

to configure your printer. The various options are discussed under Printer, Properties shortly. However, you must complete a few of the entries in the Create Printer dialog to install the printer in the first place. Those entries are discussed here. After making relevant entries click OK and you'll be asked to provide further information (this is the equivalent of clicking the Setup button if it had been enabled – see Printer, Properties below). The entries are:

- **Printer Name**

This is the name of the printer and appears in the title bar of the printer window. It's also the name that other users will see (provided it's a shared printer) when they connect to a remote printer. The name can be up to thirty-two characters in length, thus allowing for fairly descriptive names.

- **Driver**

Choose your printer from this list. By choosing the correct printer driver you can be sure that you'll get the best performance from the printer. Some printers may not be listed. If your printer falls into that category then either select one that matches yours closely or contact your dealer to see if a Windows NT driver is available for your printer. In the latter case you have to postpone installation until the driver arrives on floppy disk. When you do recommence the installation choose Other from the Driver list.

Print Manager

■   Description

You can enter details about the printer here. Others users connecting to the printer across a network will see the description in their Connect to Printer dialog.

■   Print to

This is where you select the destination for your printout. For a local printer you might choose LPT1. To print to file select File and when you print you'll be prompted for a filename. Should the correct port not be listed then select Network Printer followed by Local Port in the subsequent Print Destinations dialog (see FIG. 10.4). Then enter the correct name of your port in the next Port Name dialog. The port is then added to the Print to list and can be selected.

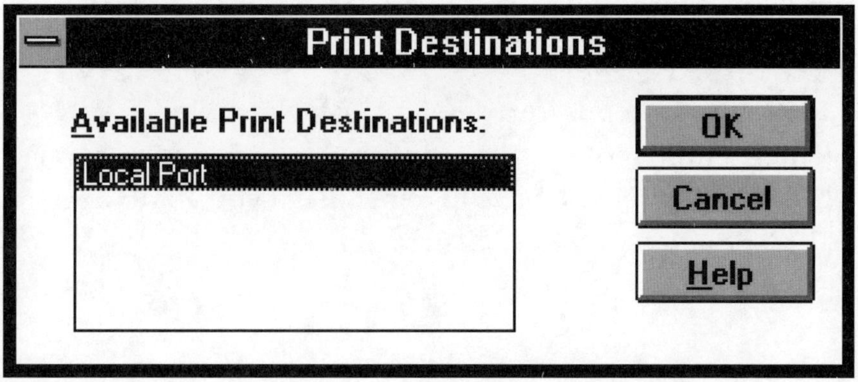

FIG. 10.4

■ Share this printer on the network

Turn on this check box if you want remote users to be able to connect to the printer. You can alter any choice you make through Printer, Properties later.

■ Share Name

If you turn on the sharing check box you need to enter a share name. This is the name other users see in their Connect to Printer dialog when establishing a connection to the printer.

■ Location

Any entry you make here can be seen by other users in their Connect to Printer dialog. You may like to record the physical location of the printer so remote users know where to pick up their printout.

Remove Printer

Printer, Remove Printer is for deleting local installed printers or for disconnecting from remote server printers to which you're connected. If you delete a local printer you have to reinstall it if you want to use it again.

Properties

Before trying Printer, Properties make sure that the desired printer window or icon is selected in the Print Manager workspace. Printer,

Print Manager

Properties is important if your printer doesn't perform well after installation. You can also use it to specify that a printer is to be sharable. The subsequent Printer Properties dialog is identical to the Create Printer dialog. You may want to refer back to Printer, Create Printer earlier to read about the text boxes and drop-down lists. Printer, Create Printer also explains how to make a printer sharable. Here I'm concentrating on the buttons in the dialog. There are three to consider in detail:

1   Setup

Clicking Setup results in a dialog that is specific to the currently selected printer in the Print Manager workspace. Typically, the printer-specific dialog lets you choose paper size, a paper tray, and how much memory your printer has. Choosing an incorrect figure for memory may result in printing problems – it's best to keep the default setting until you've checked with the system administrator. Other options may allow you to define which font cartridges to use and to configure font substitution. Font substitution is handy if some of your Windows TrueType fonts are similar in appearance to your built-in printer fonts. If a font substitution option is available you can arrange to download TrueType fonts or to stick with your matching printer fonts. If you want you can combine both approaches – for example, your printer may have Helvetica which is a good match for TrueType Arial but may not have Wingdings. In this example you may want to substitute Helvetica for Arial but to download (that is with no substitution) Wingdings.

2   Details

Many users can afford to ignore the options in the Printer Details dialog (see FIG. 10.5) which is accessed by first clicking Printer, Properties and then clicking the Details button in the Printer Properties dialog. However, you may find the Job Defaults button, which leads to another Document Properties dialog, useful. The Printer Details dialog is covered here.

The Printer Details dialog allows you to set a number of parameters. These include:

- The times when the printer is available

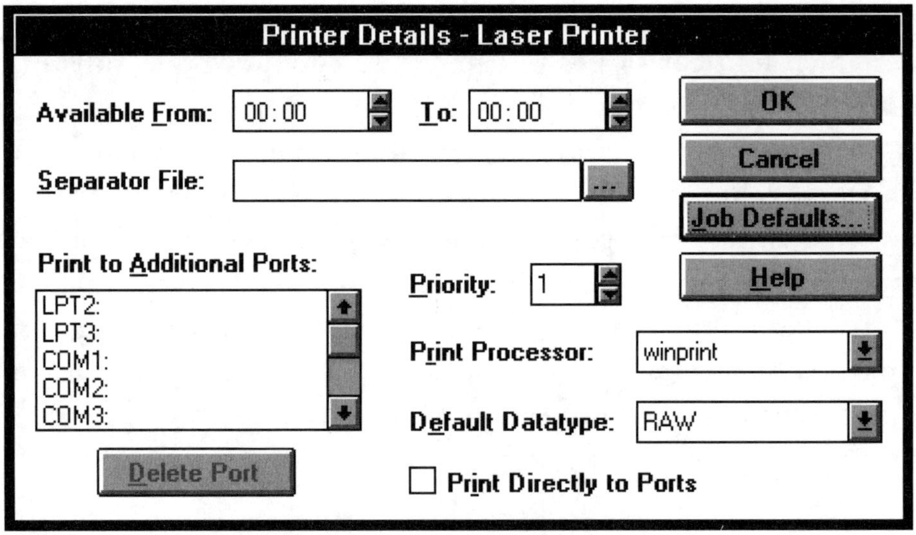

FIG. 10.5

■ Whether to print a separator page (for keeping print jobs distinct), or not

■ Whether to have a bank or pool of printers acting as one printer, or not

■ The priority of the printer to make sure urgent print jobs are printed first

■ The print processor and datatype (it's unlikely that you'll ever have to changes these two settings)

■ Whether to spool print jobs or not

Let's look at these parameters in more detail:

Printer times

By default you can print to a printer twenty-four hours a day. To restrict the availability of the printer adjust the spin buttons in the Available From: and To: sections of the dialog. Note that you can send documents at any time but they will only print within the prescribed limits.

Separator pages

You use separator pages (or separator files) to insert a page before each print job. DEFAULT.SEP is for PCL printers and PSLANMAN.SEP is for PostScript printers. To specify a separator page use the browse button to the right of the Separator File text box and select the relevant page. You can also use a separator file to switch to PCL mode (PCL.SEP) or to PostScript mode (PSCRIPT.SEP) – but you can ignore these if you always print in only one of either PostScript or PCL.

Printer pool

A printer bank or pool is a collection of printers that functions as a single printer. When a print job is sent to the print server then the first free printer in the pool will print it. To add another printer to your current printer in the pool select its port in the Print to Additional Ports list. You can remove a printer from the pool ports list by clicking it again. To remove a port from the list click the Delete Port button. It's important that all the printers in the pool are the same model to achieve consistency of printout.

Printer priority

Setting a printer priority is important if you have two or more logical printers assigned to the same physical printer. By establishing different priorities you can print non-urgent jobs to the one with the lowest priority. When an urgent job needs printing you send that to the printer with the highest priority. The urgent job prints in preference to all pending non-urgent jobs – in effect you are changing the print order of one physical printer. The priority setting can range from 1 to 99, 99 being the lowest priority.

Printer processor and datatype

In the general course of events you shouldn't have to change the default settings for print processor or datatype. If you do have to change them then select the relevant option from the Print Processor and Default Datatype lists respectively. Any application that requires you to alter these settings will include instructions about which choices to make.

Printer spooling

Unless you specify otherwise Print Manager spools all print jobs. This has the great advantage of freeing up your applications as quickly as possible. Once the job is spooled you can continue working while printing takes place in the background using the spool on disk. If you disable spooling then the application is not freed until printing is complete. This means that you must wait to continue with other work, but it may speed up printing. Should you have cause to disable spooling then turn on the Print Directly to Ports check box.

3   Settings

For printers connected via a parallel port you can establish timeouts. The default setting is 45 seconds and this is time Print Manager waits for a printer to be ready. After the timeout has elapsed, and the printer is still not ready, you'll receive an error message. You may want to give your printer more (or less) time in which to respond. You do so by clicking the Settings button in the Printer Properties dialog and changing the figure for Transmission Retry in the subsequent Configure Port dialog (see FIG. 10.6).

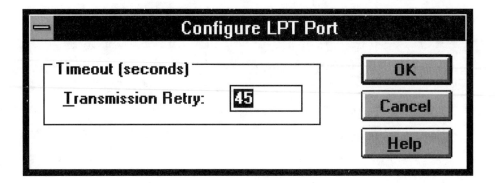

FIG. 10.6

Forms

Windows NT comes with a number of forms for use with your printers. A form specifies the paper size and margins. When installing or configuring a printer you can choose a particular form from the default list. However, there may be occasions when you are using an unusual paper size or wish to change the default margin settings for an existing paper size. You may want to do the latter to give room for logos and similar items on pre-printed stationery.

If you want to establish a new paper size and/or margins then click Printer, Forms to display the Forms dialog (see FIG. 10.7). To create a new paper size enter a name for the form in the Name text box and specify the dimensions of the form and the margins in the boxes provided. When you're finished click the Add button. To change the margins for an existing form select it in the Forms on this Computer list and edit its name

Print Manager

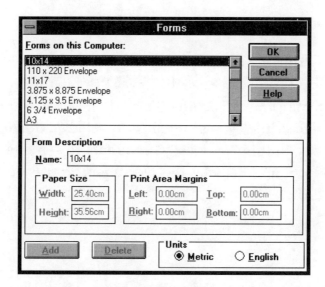

FIG. 10.7

in the Name box. Set the new margins appropriately before clicking Add. To delete a form select it from the list and click the Delete button.

Once you've established a new form and/or margins you can instruct your printer to use the new form by going through Printer, Properties, Setup. To use a new form with a particular printer you must create the form on the computer acting as the print server.

Pause

Printer, Pause causes all printing on the current printer to be suspended. It's important to be aware of the difference between Printer, Pause and Document, Pause – the former suspends all print jobs while the latter suspends only the currently selected print job. In order to pause a printer you must make sure that the window or icon for the correct printer is selected in the Print Manager workspace. If the printer has a print job listed (and selected), you can't use the Pause Printer button on the toolbar – it's replaced by the Pause Document button. In such an event either use the menu bar item Printer, Pause or click the selected document with the right-hand mouse button (or press **Spacebar**) to remove the selection from the print job, and replace the Document Pause button with the Printer Pause button.

Resume

Printer, Resume starts a paused printer again. Like Printer, Pause you have to remove the selection from a document in the printer window to see the Resume Printer button on the toolbar. And once again you must check that the window or icon for the correct printer is current.

Purge Printer

This item deletes all pending print jobs for the current printer. You should use this option with caution as you may be inadvertently removing urgent print jobs from another user connected to your shared printer.

Server Viewer

When you install, configure, or remove printers you would normally do so from the computer that acts as a print server to the printers. However, you can also carry out these tasks from a remote machine on the network. In order to do so you must be a member of the Administrators or Power Users groups, or otherwise have full control permission.

You gain access to the print server by clicking Printer, Server Viewer. This invokes the Select Computer dialog (see FIG. 10.8) where you select the required print server machine from the list presented. After selecting the print server and clicking OK a Server window opens in Print Manager and shows the printers controlled from the server. To work on a particular printer you first select it from the server printers listed. Having done that your actions are identical to working on a local printer; Printers, Remove Printer to remove a printer and Printers, Properties to configure a printer. If you want to install a new physical or logical printer go through Printers, Create Printer.

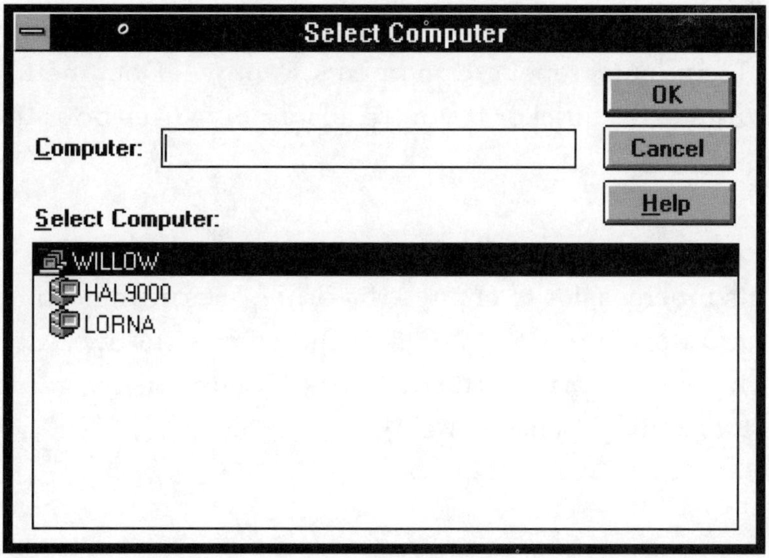

FIG. 10.8

Exit

Printer, Exit closes Print Manager. Of course, it's much easier simply to double click the Control menu. To get Print Manager to recall the positions and sizes of printer windows or icons in its workspace make sure that Options, Save Settings on Exit is turned on. Unfortunately, unlike Program Manager or File Manager, you can't hold down the **Shift** key and click Printer, Exit to save the layout and remain in Print Manager.

Document menu

Remove Document

Document, Remove Document deletes a pending print job from the list in the current printer window. First, you must select the document otherwise you might inadvertently remove an urgent print job. To remove all the pending documents repeat Document, Remove Document – though Printer, Purge is far quicker if you're absolutely sure about the result of your actions.

Don't be tempted to remove a document so one later in the list prints earlier – it's much easier to change the order of printing. You do that by selecting and dragging documents in the print window. Alternatively, you can change the print priority of the document by going through Document, Details (discussed next).

Print Manager

Details

You can view details about a print job in the printer window, such as the number of pages and the priority. To see rather more information and to have the opportunity to change the priority and a couple of other settings you click Document, Details. The ensuing Document Details dialog (see FIG. 10.9) is where you can change the priority of the print job, or who to notify on completion, or the start and stop times.

Normally the owner of a document is notified when the job completes. You can arrange for Print Manager to notify another user instead by entering the username in the Notify text box. The Start Time and Until Time spin buttons enable you to limit the time when the current document can print. For example, you might want to delay a long print job so it prints after you leave the office for the evening. The time range you

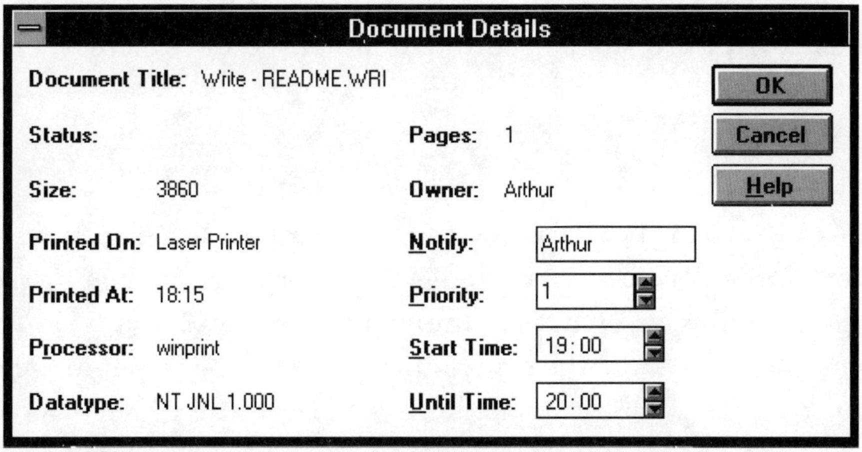

Document Details			
Document Title: Write - README.WRI			OK
Status:		Pages: 1	Cancel
Size: 3860		Owner: Arthur	Help
Printed On: Laser Printer		Notify: Arthur	
Printed At: 18:15		Priority: 1	
Processor: winprint		Start Time: 19:00	
Datatype: NT JNL 1.000		Until Time: 20:00	

FIG. 10.9

specify must fall within the time range for the printer (see Printer, Properties, Details earlier).

You get a print job to jump the queue (or go further back) by changing the document's priority. However, you can only move it up relative to other documents pending on the same printer. If there is another printer with a higher priority and with pending jobs then they print first. A document's priority are ultimately governed by the printer priority. To set the printer priority you use Printer, Properties, Details (see earlier).

Pause

Document, Pause is not to be confused with Printer, Pause. Document, Pause suspends printing of the selected print job only.

Resume

Document, Resume resumes printing of a paused document.

Restart

Document, Restart is not the same as Document, Resume. You resume a document after it's been paused – you restart a document to begin printing again from scratch. Beginning again is useful if you experience problems like you started the print job with the wrong paper in the paper tray. To restart a print job make sure you have the correct document selected in the printer window. It's only possible to restart printing if you're spooling print jobs (the default).

Print Manager

Options menu

Toolbar

Toggles the Print Manager toolbar off and on.

Status Bar

Toggles the status bar off and on.

Save Settings on Exit

Options, Save Settings on Exit is a toggle. When turned on it causes Print Manager to remember the layout of your printer icons and windows the next time it's opened.

Security menu

The Security menu includes options for setting permissions, auditing policy, and taking ownership of printers. For some background on these topics you are referred to the section on the *File Manager Security menu* in Chapter 9 on *File Manager*. This section on the Print Manager Security menu shows how to apply security to printing operations.

Permissions

To set or alter the permissions on a printer you must be the owner of the printer or have been given the necessary permission to do so. When granting or changing permissions take care not to remove the CREATOR OWNER user. This user is anyone who creates a document – the creator of a document has certain permissions over the document even if they have No Access permissions for the printer. To establish or amend permissions:

1   Select the window or icon for the printer in the Print Manager window.

2   Click Security, Permissions to see the Printer Permissions dialog (see FIG. 10.10). The two sets of parentheses after some of the entries in the Name list show the permissions over the printer and over documents respectively.

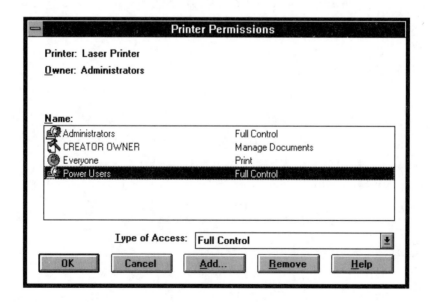

FIG. 10.10

Print Manager

3   Grant, change, or revoke permissions as appropriate.

4   Click OK when you're finished.

Auditing

To fully audit a printer involves a few steps. First, set up your overall audit policy in User Manager. Second, set your printer audit policy through Security, Audit in Print Manager. Third, view the audit results in Event Viewer. Both User Manager and Event Viewer are considered later in the book. This section looks at the Print Manager aspects:

1   Select the window or icon of the printer you wish to audit (or remove auditing from).

2   Click Security, Audit.

3   In the Printer Auditing dialog (see FIG. 10.11) select users or groups and events to audit as appropriate.

4   Click OK to register your changes.

Owner

To take the ownership of a printer:

1   Select the printer in the Print Manager window.

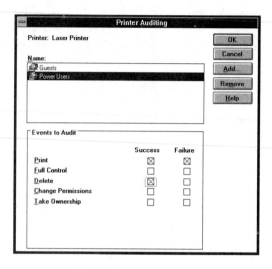

FIG. 10.11

2 Click Security, Owner.

3 In the Owner dialog (see FIG. 10.12) click the Take Ownership button.

Window menu

Cascade

Cascades any open printer windows.

Tile Horizontally

Tiles printer windows horizontally.

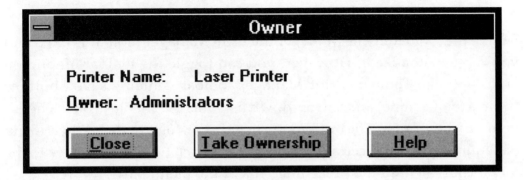

FIG. 10.12

Tile Vertically

Tiles printer windows vertically.

Arrange Icons

Arranges printer icons neatly along the bottom of the Print Manager workspace.

Refresh

Window, Refresh updates the list of documents in the current printer window.

Toolbar

Unlike the toolbar in File Manager the Print Manager toolbar is fixed and you can't customize it. However, you can toggle the toolbar off and on with Options, Toolbar. Print Manager toolbar contains seven buttons (from a total of nine) and a drop-down list. This list enables you to choose your default printer. The buttons are listed next, together with their menu bar equivalents. To ascertain the purpose of each button refer back to the menu equivalent in the preceding look at the menu bar.

Toolbar buttons

 *Pause Printer*

Equivalent to the menu item Printer, Pause.

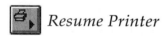 *Resume Printer*

Equivalent to the menu item Printer, Resume.

 *Pause Document*

Equivalent to the menu item Document, Pause.

Resume Document

Equivalent to the menu item Document, Resume.

 Connect to Printer

Equivalent to the menu item Printer, Connect to Printer.

 Disconnect Printer

Equivalent to the menu item Printer, Remove Printer.

 Printer Properties

Equivalent to the menu item Printer, Properties.

 Remove Document

Equivalent to the menu item Document, Remove Document.

 *Document Details*

Equivalent to the menu item Document, Details.

Control Panel

CONTROL PANEL

- A detailed guide to each icon

- How to configure your computer, network, and desktop

- Working with fonts, services, and UPS

- And lots more...

Control Panel is one of the application icons in the Main group window. Starting Control Panel displays the Control Panel window. This window itself contains a large number of icons. The icons that are visible may differ slightly from system to system, and the exact order in which the icons appear may not always be the same. But no matter which icons you have they are all accessible by double clicking or through the Settings menu in Control Panel. However, you might be denied access to some of the icons if you are not a member of the Administrators group. Double clicking an icon opens a corresponding dialog box. Any changes you make and keep are going to affect the way you work and how Windows NT looks. Most of the changes you make only affect Windows NT for your username – other users logging on won't see or experience the changes you've made. One important exception to this rule concerns any fonts you install or remove through the Fonts icon. Before moving on to a detailed discussion of each Control Panel icon here's a list which gives an overview of each of the icons you're most likely to see. The list (and the following more detailed discussion) is in alphabetical order by icon title.

Control Panel overview

 **Color**

For changing the colour scheme of your Windows NT desktop. You alter other aspects of the desktop through the Desktop icon.

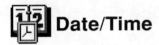 **Cursors**

Lets you customize the appearance of the mouse pointer and cursor. You can choose from a number of pre-defined effects.

 **Date/Time**

For changing the system date and time. You can also specify your time zone and ask that NT adjusts automatically for daylight saving.

 **Desktop**

This icon leads to quite a complex dialog. It enables you to define a desktop pattern and wallpaper, Program Manager icon spacing and icon titles, the invisible desktop grid, a screen saver and screen saver password, the cursor blink rate, and how **Alt-Tab** works for switching applications.

 **Devices**

Devices allows you to stop and start various device drivers. You can't stop all of them (for example, your floppy disk driver) – these are started automatically by NT. Others you can stop and start at will. In addition, you can customize the startup parameters for some drivers, for example, whether they are started at boot time. Most of the drivers are fairly low-level and it's unlikely you'll have to bother much with Devices.

 **Drivers**

For installing and configuring various device drivers, for example, sound and video cards, and CD-ROMs.

 **Fonts**

Typically used for adding, showing, and removing TrueType fonts. It is not used for installing printer fonts.

Control Panel

 **International**

Allows you to specify the nationality of your keyboard layout, currency symbol, date/time formats, and measurement system.

 **Keyboard**

The Keyboard icon is used to adjust the delay and repeat rate for your keyboard. To adjust the nationality of your keyboard go through International.

 **MIDI Mapper**

For configuring settings that determine how a MIDI device (for instance, a synthesizer) works with your computer.

 **Mouse**

This icon is handy if you have to alter the double-click speed of your mouse. It's also invaluable for left-handed users who wish to click with the right-hand mouse button.

 **Network**

This is handy for changing the name of your computer or workgroup. It also enables you to install and configure network cards.

 **Ports**

Ports is for serial ports only (that is, not parallel). Use it to fine-tune the communications settings of your serial ports.

 **Printers**

This one has changed for Windows for DOS users. In Windows for DOS the Printers icon was for installing and configuring printers. In Windows

Control Panel

NT it simply starts Print Manager. You can then use Print Manager to install and configure printers. It's probably easier to start up Print Manager directly from Program Manager rather than going through Control Panel first.

 **Server**

Server controls various aspects of a computer in a workgroup or domain. It's useful for seeing which resources are shared and connected users on remote machines.

 **Services**

Services lets you control the services available on your computer. You can stop, start, pause, and configure these services.

Sound

For associating sounds with specific system events. You can also suppress the warning beep through Sounds.

 **System**

System lets you choose the default operating system and the timeout on dual-boot systems. It's also used to define the size of your paging file (virtual memory).

 UPS

For configuring an uninterruptible power supply attached to your computer or network.

Control Panel in-depth

Color

Color gives access to a range of colour schemes for Windows, should you get bored with the default colours. When you are tired of the alternative colour schemes on offer you can always create your own. Double clicking the Color icon summons the Color dialog box (see FIG. 11.1). This is where you choose the colour scheme, through the Color Schemes drop-down list box. If you want to alter the existing schemes (or create one of your own) then click the Color Palette button. This button has a double chevron which means it extends the present dialog. The expanded dialog reveals another button labelled Define Custom Colors. Use this button to alter the range of colours available for the colour schemes. To keep a new (or

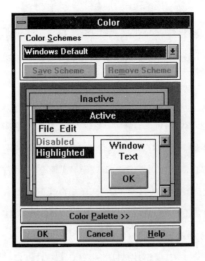

FIG. 11.1

altered scheme under a different name) scheme click the Save Scheme button. To assign a new colour to part of your desktop click on the relevant section of the sample desktop in the Color dialog, or select the section by opening the Screen Element drop-down list. You don't have to save a scheme as Windows NT implements it all the same. However, as soon as you change a colour or choose a new scheme an unsaved scheme is lost.

Cursors

Windows NT uses a lot of different mouse pointers and cursors. These include various move pointers and the I-beam as well as the normal mouse pointer and hourglass wait indicator. In addition, NT has an application starting indicator which will be new if you've upgraded from Windows for DOS. The application waiting indicator combines the usual mouse pointer with the busy hourglass. It means that Windows is busy (usually loading a file) but unlike the plain hourglass you can continue working.

The Cursors icon in Control Panel allows you to alter the appearance of any pointer, indicator, or cursor. In the Cursors dialog (see FIG. 11.2) select the pointer (or indicator or cursor) you want to change from the System Cursors list. Then click Browse and select a suitable ANI cursor file from the list presented. Your choice is shown in the preview window. To get back to the original Windows NT cursors click the Set Default button. Some of the ANI cursor files are quite difficult to work with. If

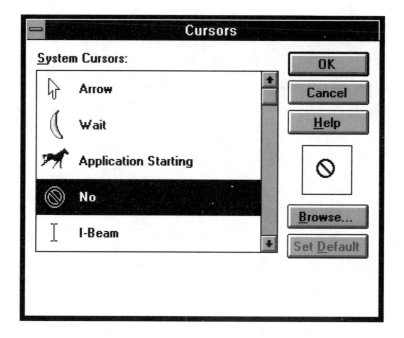

FIG. 11.2

Control Panel

they're available on your system then Wagtail makes a good arrow pointer, and perhaps something like Banana for the wait indicator and Horse for the application starting indicator. Banana is best avoided for the arrow mouse pointer – as the banana gets eaten it's not easy to work out exactly where to click.

Date/Time

This is for resetting system date and time (see FIG. 11.3). First, you select the element of time or date that you wish to modify, for example, day or minute and type in the correct number. Or you can select the element and use the spin buttons to wind backwards or forwards. You should also set the correct time zone for your place of work. To do so select the required option from the Time Zone drop-down list. You can have your system automatically adjust for daylight saving time – simply turn on the check box for that purpose. If you do want this daylight saving adjustment then be sure to choose carefully from the Time Zone drop-down list. Some areas of the world normally have the same difference from GMT but implement and remove daylight saving on different days.

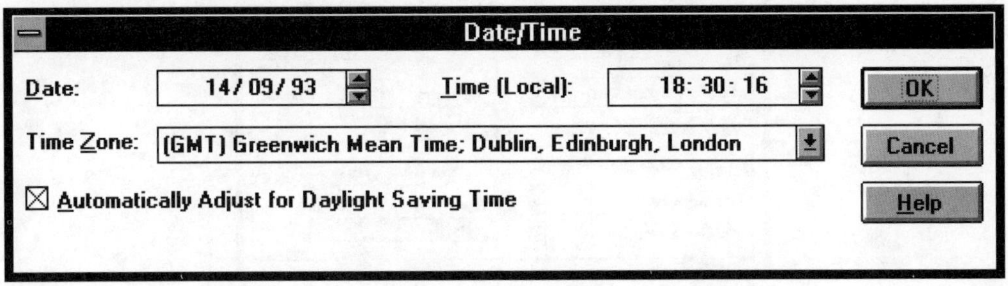

Date/Time			
D<u>a</u>te: 14 / 09 / 93	<u>T</u>ime (Local): 18 : 30 : 16		OK
Time <u>Z</u>one: (GMT) Greenwich Mean Time; Dublin, Edinburgh, London			Cancel
☒ <u>A</u>utomatically Adjust for Daylight Saving Time			<u>H</u>elp

FIG. 11.3

Desktop

The Desktop dialog (see FIG. 11.4) is fairly complex. From the dialog you can control various aspects of your desktop. Let's work through these in sequence.

Pattern

A pattern provides a backcloth to your desktop. This backcloth is best seen by minimizing all open applications and Program Manager. By default Windows NT has no pattern but does use a wallpaper bitmap.

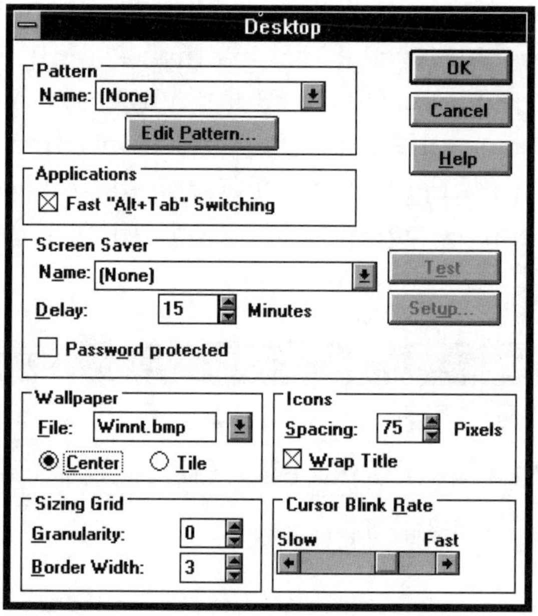

FIG. 11.4

You can have both by selecting a pattern. You can have just a pattern by selecting a pattern and turning off your wallpaper.

To select a pattern click an item in the Name drop-down list. In addition, you can edit, create, and delete patterns. To do this click the Edit Pattern button to see the Desktop - Edit Pattern dialog. To edit an existing pattern select it from the Name drop-down list and click in the painting grid. To create a new pattern enter its name in the Name box and click in the painting grid before clicking the Add button. To remove an existing pattern make sure it's current in the Desktop - Edit Pattern dialog and click the Remove button.

Applications

By default **Alt-Tab** cycles application windows by displaying a banner in the centre of the screen. This is known as fast **Alt-Tab** switching. You can suppress fast **Alt-Tab** switching by turning off its check box in the Applications section of the Desktop dialog. If you do so then **Alt-Tab** cycles applications by highlighting their title bars.

Screen saver

You can add a screen saver to Windows NT. This reduces phosphor burn-in and can provide security while you're away from the computer. You choose the screen saver you want from the Name drop-down list in the Screen Saver section of the Desktop dialog. To specify the timeout before the screen saver comes into operation you adjust the figure in the Delay box. For example, a setting of 1 means the screen saver starts one minute after you last use the mouse or keyboard. If you turn on the Password protected check box then you must supply your logon password to remove the screen saver and continue working – this helps to prevent unauthorised access while you're not at the machine. You can configure the screen saver display by going through the Setup button. To see how the screen saver looks before quitting the Desktop dialog click the Test button. Note that you do not need to enter your password for a password protected screenshot while in test mode.

Wallpaper

Wallpaper allows you to display a bitmap (BMP) graphic on the background. Some may cover all the background, others are too small for this. The latter type can be made to cover the whole screen by turning on the Tile option button. In general, wallpaper produces a more pleasing effect than a pattern – you can combine both if you wish. If you like you can create your own wallpaper in Paintbrush (save it as BMP not PCX) and type its name in the Wallpaper File text box. If the bitmap file is not stored in the Windows directory you have to specify its full pathname. To remove a wallpaper from the list presented delete the BMP file from your Windows NT directory.

Sizing grid

The Sizing Grid section of the dialog contains defaults for two parameters. Granularity determines layout of the invisible grid that lies behind Program Manager. A setting of 0 indicates that the grid is not in effect. Any positive number creates a grid, and windows and icons snap to this grid. An entry of 1 sets an eight pixel grid, 2 a sixteen pixel grid, and so on. Grids keep icons and windows neatly aligned. Border Width alters the width of borders around windows – this is only true for windows that can be resized.

Icons

The Icons section enables you to alter the space between icons in group windows. This is especially handy if icon descriptions tend to overlap. You could of course always shorten descriptions, though descriptions can word wrap. To adjust the space between icons adjust the figure in the Spacing box. To toggle icon title word wrap turn the Wrap Title check box on and off.

Cursor blink rate

The Cursor Blink Rate section does exactly as it says, complete with a little demonstration to the side. To alter the blink rate drag the slider.

Devices

The Devices dialog (see FIG. 11.5) lets you start, stop, and configure device drivers. If a device has started then it has a Status of Started. The Startup column shows how the driver is started. Some of the started device drivers can be stopped by clicking the Stop button. However, if the device driver is essential for running your system the Stop button is disabled. If a particular device driver has not been started then you can do so by clicking the Start button.

You can determine how a particular device driver is started by going through the Startup button. To configure startup you must be a member

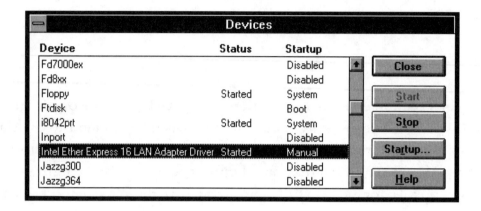

FIG. 11.5

of the Administrators group. Each device that can be configured has its own dialog box. The choices given are Boot, System, Automatic, Manual, and Disabled. Boot, System, and Automatic mean the device driver is started for you. Boot drivers are loaded first followed by System and then Automatic drivers. Boot and System device drivers are essential to the proper functioning of your computer and their startup option should not be changed. If you do so you may be locked out of your system, or at best make it unworkable. The Manual setting means you can start the driver yourself or have it started under application control. Disabled means that the driver can't be started manually, though it can still be started automatically.

Control Panel

Drivers

Use this icon to add drivers for hardware. Drivers are simply programs that control the hardware. For example, if you have a sound card then this is where you install the driver for that card. To install (or remove) a driver you must be a member of the Administrators group. You do not use this option to add drivers for printers or network cards. To add printer drivers use Print Manager – this can be started from Program Manager or by double clicking the Printers icon in Control Panel. To add network card drivers go through the Network icon in Control Panel.

When you double click the Drivers icon you see a list of installed drivers in the Drivers dialog (see FIG. 11.6). To remove a driver select it from the list and click the Remove button. To add a new driver click the Add button to see the Add dialog. Select a device from the list or for a device not

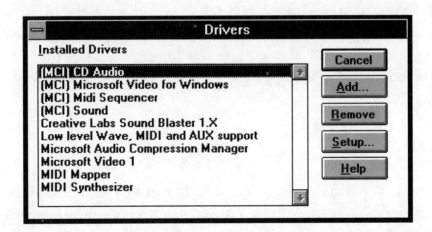

FIG. 11.6

shown in the list select Unlisted or Updated Driver. Click OK to continue. If the driver already exists you are given a choice between sticking with the existing one or installing a new one. When you go for a new driver you'll be asked to insert a floppy disk containing the driver. You may be presented with further dialogs (the nature of which depends upon the driver) allowing you to set up the driver. Once the driver's installed you should restart Windows NT for it to take effect, NT asks if you want to restart or continue with the current session.

If you merely wish to configure an existing driver click the Setup button in the Drivers dialog. You are presented with one or more dialogs – these are specific to the currently selected driver. For changes to take effect you have to restart NT.

When you install drivers be careful that they do not conflict with existing drivers. If NT detects such a conflict it displays a warning message. In that event reconfigure one or more drivers to remove conflicts. If you do not do so then one or more drivers may not function correctly. In some cases, for example, a conflict of interrupt levels, Windows NT may be able to handle the conflict. NT also detects the conflicts at boot time. You can view the conflicts by using Event Viewer in the Administrative Tools group.

Fonts

This option is normally accessed only if you buy extra fonts for your printer or for the screen. Adding TrueType fonts is straightforward. Click the Add button in the Fonts dialog (see FIG. 11.7), select the name in the Add Fonts dialog for the font and click OK. You may have to switch drives

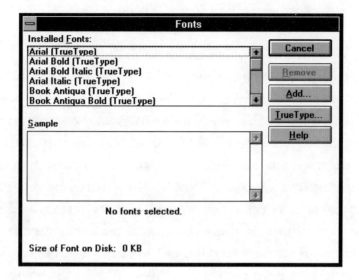

FIG. 11.7

and directories to view the fonts you want to install. The Network button lets you view fonts held on network drives. To remove unwanted fonts click the Remove button with the font highlighted back in the Fonts dialog (but do not ever remove MS Sans Serif which is used by NT itself). Going into Fonts is a handy way of viewing your fonts. Click the font name in the Installed Fonts list box and you see a sample of the font in the Sample box.

The button labelled TrueType leads to the TrueType dialog where you can specify that only TrueType fonts are available in your applications. This is not the place to enter into a technical discussion of the different styles of fonts. Suffice it to say that the font actually printed by your printer is often different from the font shown on screen. This is particularly noticeable when word processing. Windows word processors use a graphics screen. This allows you to see a fair representation of the typeface, size and style of your text on screen. When the screen display matches the printout it is called a WYSIWYG display. WYSIWYG is an acronym for *what you see is what you get*. Many Windows applications give you a more-or-less WYSIWYG display. However if the font used by Windows to put the text on screen does not exactly correspond to the font used by your printer, it is not full WYSIWYG. For example, in Word for Windows, you may see a line of text extending beyond the right-hand margin of the page in Page View. Windows has attempted to find a screen font that matches, as closely as possible, size, typeface, and style of the font selected for printing. In this example the nearest screen font available is wider than the printer font and hence the same line of text takes up more room on screen, and goes past the right-hand margin. When you print, however, the same line of text stops at the margin.

It is more important to see line breaks, the word on which the line ends, than to have a neat display with all the text wrapping at or before the margin. If you are lucky, on the other hand, your printer might have the same fonts as the Windows screen fonts, in which case you have the best of both worlds – you see the correct point of the line break while the screen wraps the text at or before the right margin. Try varying the font in a trial document and see if you can achieve a true WYSIWYG display for one or more fonts. If you use TrueType fonts then the screen and printer fonts match exactly. If you want this full WYSIWYG display, without TrueType, you will have to install extra screen fonts that are replicas of your chosen printer fonts. There are a couple of packages around that allow you to do just this, whether for a dot matrix, HP Laserjet-compatible or PostScript-compatible laser printer. In addition they improve the sometimes bitty appearance of characters on the screen.

International

This icon is for changing those parameters that are likely to differ from country to country. These parameters include formats for dates, times, currency and numbers, and units of measurement (Measurement drop-down list). The first three settings in the International dialog box (see FIG. 11.8) are labelled Country, Language and Keyboard Layout. Although they might sound as if they do pretty much the same thing, they are in fact different. Changing Country changes many options to reflect conventions in the particular country, for example the Date Format might change, the Currency Format almost certainly will. Language governs the way in which applications carry out sorting and case conversion. Keyboard Layout varies special characters and symbols normally available on the

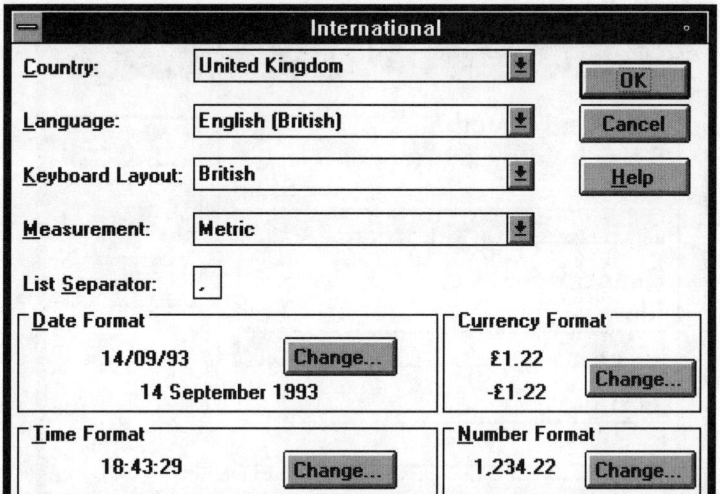

FIG. 11.8

keyboard. There is also a small box (List Separator) which is for defining the character used to separate items in a list.

Having selected a particular option under Country you are not tied to its defaults for date, time, currency, and number. The four relevant sections all have a Change button which allows further customization. Each leads to a particular dialog (Date Format, Time Format, Currency Format, and Number Format) where you specify the settings. Hopefully, all of the options are self-explanatory so I won't go through them here.

Keyboard

This icon has one purpose only, to adjust the rate at which a keystroke is repeated if you hold the key down. The Keyboard dialog (see FIG. 11.9)

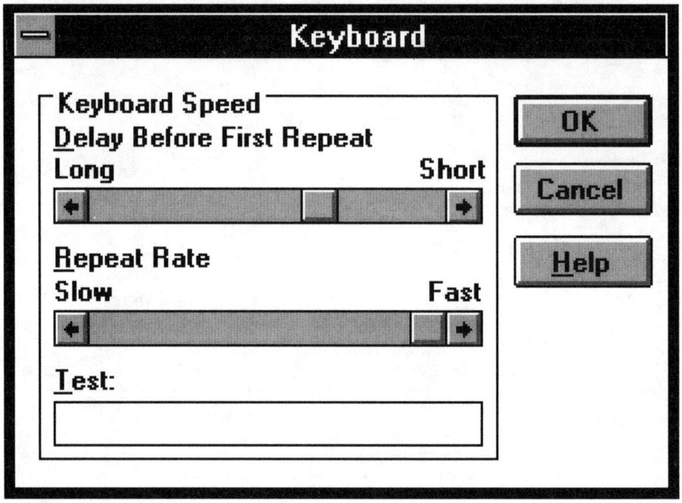

FIG. 11.9

Control Panel

has two scroll bars where you drag the scroll box anywhere from Long to Short (or Slow to Fast). The top slider determines the delay before the first repeat when a key is held down. The lower slider sets the speed at which the key subsequently repeats (that is after the first repeat). To try out any changes click in the Test box and press and hold down a character key.

MIDI mapper

The MIDI Mapper icon is for configuring how NT works with MIDI-compliant devices such as certain synthesizers. You should only use this icon if you have a thorough understanding of MIDI devices. The options in the MIDI Mapper dialog (see FIG. 11.10) are not relevant to most users (and outside the experience of the author) and are not discussed further here. If you are connecting a MIDI device that is compatible with Windows NT then the documentation that accompanies the device should give you guidance on how to use MIDI Mapper. In the meantime, interested

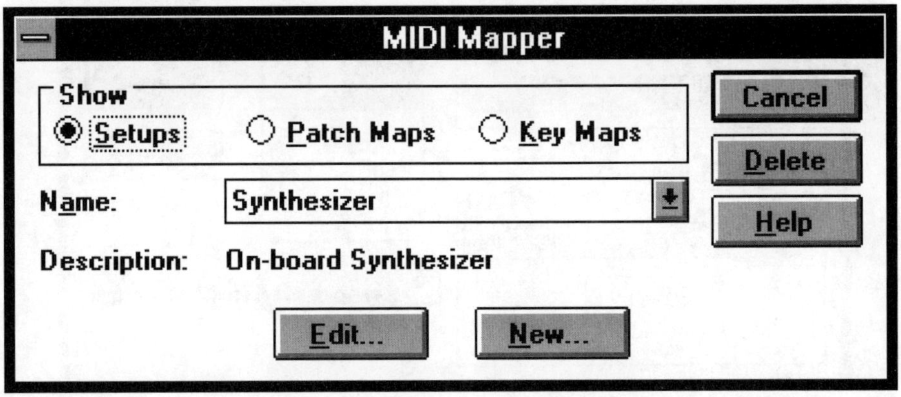

FIG. 11.10

readers can click the Help button in the MIDI Mapper dialog for more information. I hope it means more to you than it does to me!

Mouse

This icon is essential if you are left-handed and invaluable if you are having trouble double clicking. The Mouse dialog (see FIG. 11.11) includes a check box (Swap Left/Right Buttons) which, if turned on, reverses the left and right mouse buttons. When selected, the index finger of the left hand resting on the right button can be used for normal clicking and double clicking. The Double Click Speed scroll bar is to adjust the speed at which you must double click. If you experience any problems in double clicking quickly enough, drag the scroll box towards the Slow end of the scroll bar. You can try out the new speed by double clicking the Test

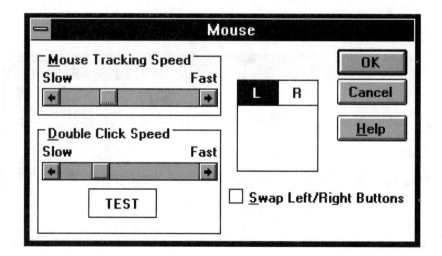

FIG. 11.11

button. This is highlighted (and the highlight removed in turn) if your double click is successful. The scroll bar for Mouse Tracking Speed dictates responsiveness of mouse pointer to mouse movements. A Slow mouse tracking speed makes for a very lazy pointer. A Fast speed gives the pointer the appearance of being hyperactive.

There may be differing icons with their own setup dialogs for different pointing devices. The standard mouse option is the one discussed above as it is the one relevant to most users.

Network

Clicking the Network icon in Control Panel opens the Network Settings dialog (see FIG. 11.12), though you must be a member of the Administrators

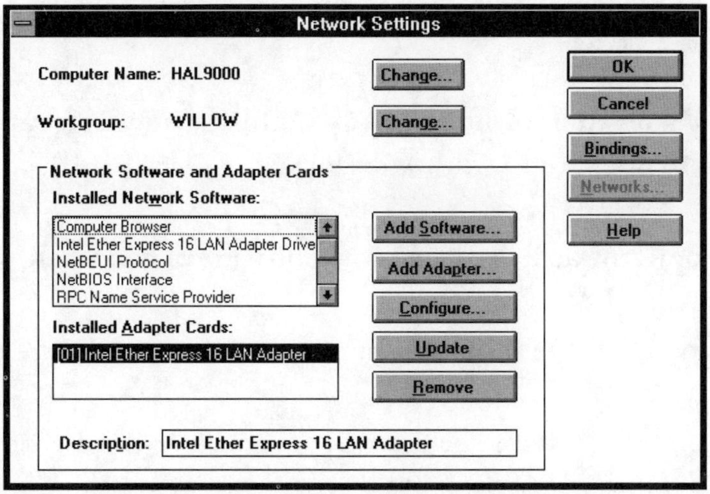

FIG. 11.12

group to see the dialog. The Network Settings dialog is the starting point for exercising control over various aspects of your network or workgroup. Some of the options are fairly advanced. Fortunately, many users will never need to use the Network icon, and if they do so it's probably only to alter their computer or workgroup name. Here's some of the things that are possible from the Network Settings dialog. The entry in parentheses corresponds to a dialog button and further details can be found after this next list:

- Change the name of your computer (Change – Computer Name).

- Change the name of your workgroup or domain. This is the equivalent of joining a new workgroup or domain (Change – Workgroup).

- Add an item of software to your network setup (Add Software).

- Add an item of hardware – that is, a network card – to your network setup (Add Adapter).

- Configure an item of network software or hardware (Configure).

- Update an item of network software or hardware (Update).

- Remove an item of network software or hardware (Remove).

- Add and remove network bindings (Bindings).

■ Specify a network search order if you're on more than one network (Networks).

Change – Computer Name

Changing the name of your workstation is fairly straightforward. Simply click the Change (Computer Name) button and enter the new name in the ensuing Computer Name dialog (see FIG. 11.13). However, if you're part of a Windows NT Advanced Server domain you should check that the new name is valid – if it's not you may not be able to log on.

Change – Workgroup

This button is only enabled if you haven't changed the computer name in your current work session. It's used to change the name of your current workgroup or domain. But by changing the name you are effectively joining a new group. In order to join a new domain you must have an

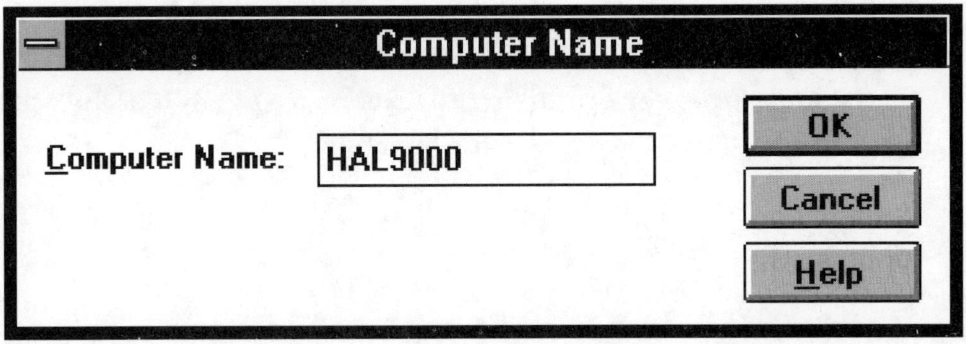

FIG. 11.13

account for your computer in that domain. If you're logged as a domain administrator you can create the computer account at the same time as joining the computer to the domain. The restrictions on joining domains do not apply to workgroups. A workgroup is a loose collection of computers, typically in a peer-to-peer network – if you've experience of Windows for Workgroups you'll know what a workgroup is. A domain, on the other hand, is a tighter grouping of machines. A domain is normally administered centrally in a client-server network. Typically, you would be part of a Windows NT Advanced Server network.

Joining a workgroup

Joining a workgroup should be reasonably straightforward, although you must be careful to ensure that your computer name is not the same as the workgroup name. If that's the case then change your computer name first. To join a workgroup:

- Click the Change (Workgroup) button.

- In the resulting Domain/Workgroup Settings dialog (see FIG. 11.14) turn on the option button for Workgroup and enter the name of the workgroup in the text box to the right of the option button. Click OK to register the change.

Joining a domain

To join a domain you follow exactly the same procedure as joining a workgroup except you turn on the Domain option button in the Domain Settings dialog and enter the name to the right of that button.

Control Panel

```
┌──────────────────────────────────────────────────────────────┐
│ ─           Domain/Workgroup Settings                          │
│                                                                │
│  Computer Name:   HAL9000                      ┌─────────┐     │
│  ┌─ Member of: ──────────────────────┐         │   OK    │     │
│  │                                    │         └─────────┘     │
│  │  ◉ Workgroup:  [WILLOW        ]    │         ┌─────────┐     │
│  │                                    │         │ Cancel  │     │
│  │  ○ Domain:     [              ]    │         └─────────┘     │
│  │                                    │         ┌─────────┐     │
│  └────────────────────────────────────┘         │  Help   │     │
│                                                └─────────┘     │
│  ┌─ □ Create Computer Account in Domain ─────────────────┐     │
│  │                                                        │     │
│  │  Domain Administrator User Name:  [             ]      │     │
│  │                                                        │     │
│  │  Domain Administrator Password:   [             ]      │     │
│  │                                                        │     │
│  │  This option will create a computer account on the     │     │
│  │  domain for this computer. It is for use by domain      │     │
│  │  administrators only.                                  │     │
│  └────────────────────────────────────────────────────────┘     │
└──────────────────────────────────────────────────────────────┘
```

FIG. 11.14

Creating a domain account

To create a domain account you must be logged on as the domain administrator. The steps involved are:

- Join a new domain (see previous section).

- Turn on the check box for Create Computer Account in Domain.

- Enter your domain administrator username and password in the appropriate text boxes. Click OK to accept the changes.

Add Software

You use the Add Software button to install additional network support software. In the subsequent Add Network Software dialog (see FIG. 11.15) select the software from the list and click Continue. If the software is not in the list select Other. You may be asked to insert a floppy disk or to specify a local or network path for the software. You may also be asked to insert your original Windows NT disks. When you've completed all the steps you have to restart NT for the changes to take effect.

Add Adapter

Adding a new network adapter is the same as adding software (see previous section), but you click Add Adapter rather than Add Software, and use the Add Network Adapter dialog (see FIG. 11.16) rather than the Add Network Software one.

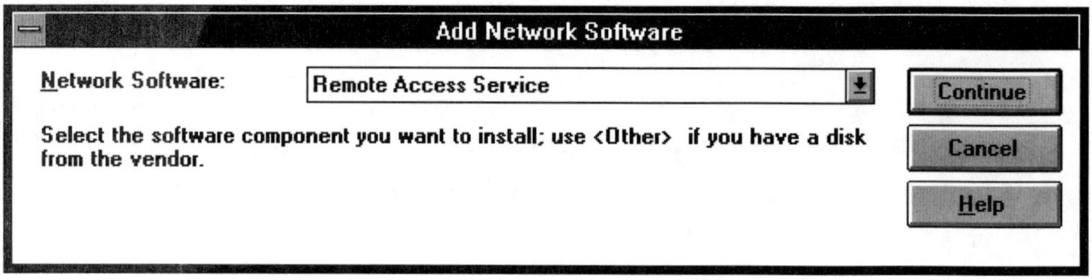

FIG. 11.15

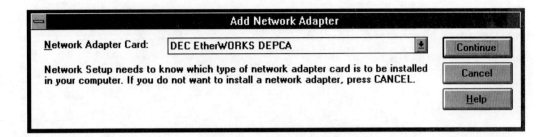

FIG. 11.16

Configure

The Configure button is for configuring your network software or adapter. First, select the software from the Installed Network Software list or the adapter from the Installed Adapter Cards list in the Network Settings dialog. Click Configure and you are presented with a dialog box that is specific to the software or card. For example, you may be able to reset interrupt levels or I/O addresses for a network adapter. Click OK in the specific dialog to keep any changes.

Update

From time-to-time suppliers provide updated drivers for your network components. To update a driver select the software or card in the Network Settings dialog and click Update. Then follow the instructions that appear on screen.

Remove

To remove an existing network component select the software or card in the Network Settings dialog and click Remove. Follow the instructions that appear on screen.

Bindings

Bindings dictate how the network software layers interact. You can use the Bindings button to look at your network bindings. You can also enable and disable bindings, and change the binding order. Under no circumstances should you attempt to disable a binding or change the order unless you're absolutely sure of the wisdom of doing so.

To view the bindings click the Bindings button to see the Network Bindings dialog (see FIG. 11.17). Enabled bindings have a lit light bulb

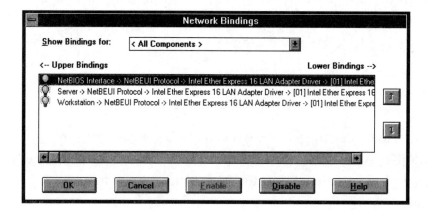

FIG. 11.17

Control Panel

next to them. To disable a binding select it and click the Disable button – the light bulb goes out. To enable a binding again click the Enable button. To change the order first select All Components from the Show Bindings for drop-down list. Then select a binding and use the up and down buttons to reposition it. If you're tempted to experiment, don't be – I advise that you merely view the bindings.

Networks

The Networks button is normally disabled. However, if you're on more than one kind of network it's enabled. Clicking the enabled button shows the Network Provider Search Order dialog. To change the order in which NT tries to establish network connections select the network and use the up and down buttons.

Ports

Ports applies to your serial ports only and has no effect at all on the parallel port. The parallel port (LPT1 for instance) is the one to which most of us connect our printer on stand-alone machines. Serial ports (COM1 for instance) are frequently the connections for modems, mice, and occasionally printers. If you wish to use a modem, for example, possibly with Terminal, then you can also set the parameters through Terminal. However, some applications and devices do not provide options for customizing the serial port to which they are attached. In that case use the Ports icon in Control Panel. A typical parameter that needs specifying is the speed at which data is transmitted through the port, called the baud rate. You can set this in the Ports dialog (see FIG. 11.18). To do so, select the COM port from the list presented and click the Settings button to see

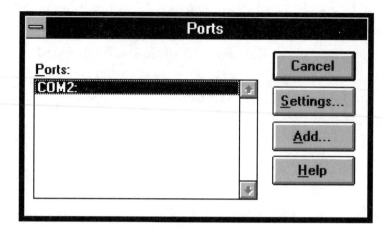

FIG. 11.18

the Settings dialog. For some COM ports you may need to specify more settings than are shown in the Settings dialog. To accomplish this click the Advanced button. Follow the instructions that came with your serial device and software when making choices.

Printers

This icon starts Print Manager from where you can install, configure, remove, and control printers. It's probably easier to start Print Manager directly from the Main group in Program Manager. However, the Printers icon in Control Panel is handy if you're already working in Control Panel or you've removed the Print Manager icon from Program Manager.

Server

If your machine is part of a network then it's valuable to be able to see which users are connected to your computer and what shared resources they are using. The Server icon in Control Panel allows you to do precisely that. It also lets you disconnect users and turn off sharing – but if you recall you turn on sharing (and off if you like) in File Manager and Print Manager. You can also control directory replication and alert messages through Server. Let's look at some of the Server functions in more detail.

When you double click the Server icon the Server dialog box (see FIG. 11.19) opens. This dialog contains five main buttons for opening further dialogs. The Description text box is for entering and changing the description (not the name) of your computer. At the top is the Usage

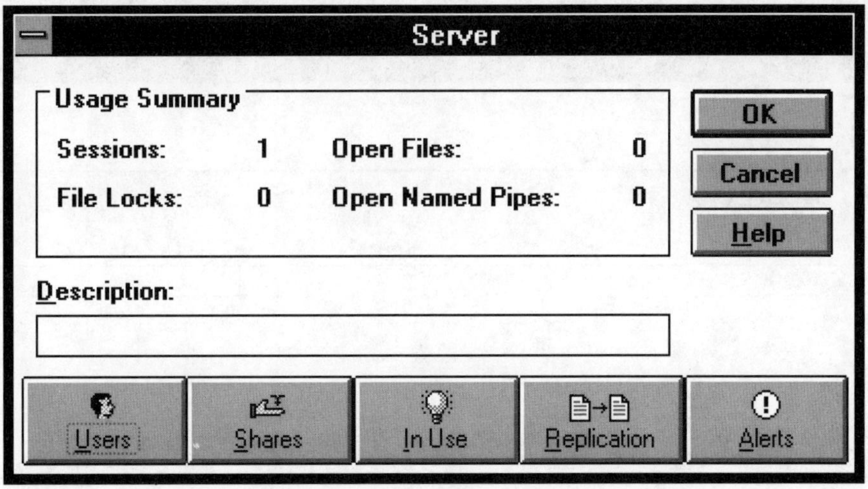

FIG. 11.19

Summary section. Sessions shows the number of remote users connected to the computer. File Locks shows the number of file locks. Open Files indicates the number of shared resources on the computer, and Open Named Pipes is for the number of pipes open. The five main buttons are labelled Users, Shares, In Use, Replication, and Alerts.

Users

Clicking the Users button leads to the User Sessions dialog (see FIG. 11.20). This dialog shows which users are connected and the shared resources they are using. To see the resources that a particular user is connected to select the user in the upper list. You can disconnect the selected user by clicking the Disconnect button, or disconnect every

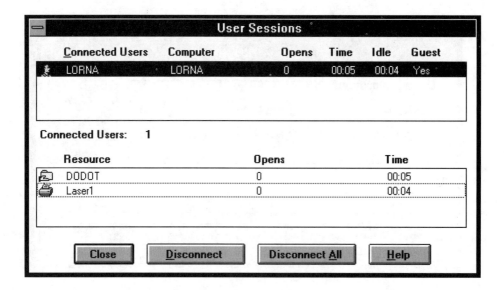

FIG. 11.20

remote user by clicking Disconnect All (you should always warn users, if possible, that they are about to be disconnected. Chat or Mail enable you to send a message).

Shares

The User Sessions dialog discussed in the preceding section lets you view shared resources by user. You use that dialog to disconnect users but not to stop the sharing of resources. Conversely, you can view users by shared resource. You do this in the Shared Resources dialog (see FIG. 11.21) which you access by clicking the Shares button. You can also disconnect individual or all users in the Shared Resources dialog. However,

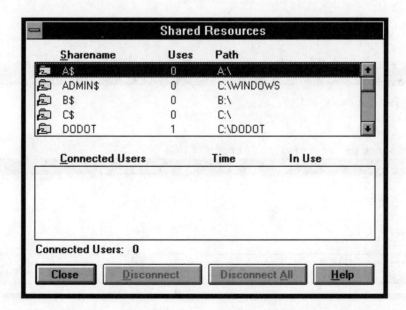

FIG. 11.21

to remove sharing from a resource you must go through the In Use button, which is discussed next.

In Use

Clicking the In Use button opens the Open Resources dialog (see FIG. 11.22). Here you can see the resources opened by remote users. For example, if a remote user has opened a file in one of your shared directories you can see the username, the path of the open resource, and the privileges the remote user has over the resource. By clicking the Close Resource or Close All Resources button you can stop sharing on individual or all resources. You use the Refresh button to update the display.

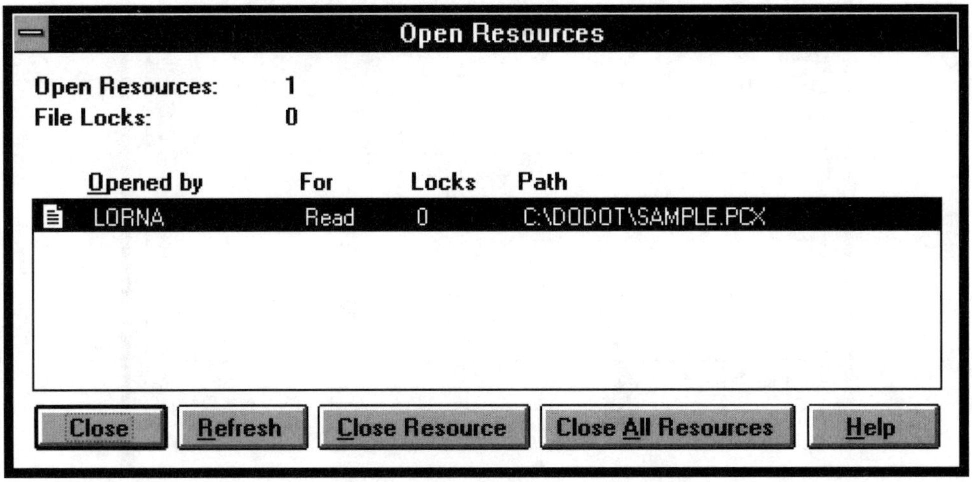

FIG. 11.22

Control Panel

Replication

Directory replication involves copying master sets of directories from a domain server to other computers on the network. Your Windows NT workstation can only act as the destination (importer) and not as the source (exporter) of these directories. The export server must be running Windows NT Advanced Server. The Replication button allows you to configure the importing of the replicate directories. But before you can do this the exporter must be set up to work with your importer. For further details about configuring both the export and import of replicated directories see your Windows NT Advanced Server documentation.

Alerts

Alerts occur whenever Windows NT thinks there's a problem (or potential problem) on the computer or network. To generate alerts the Alerter and Messenger services must be running on the computer where the problem is encountered. To generate the alert on another computer then that computer must be running the Messenger service. You may find that your computer is set up to start the Alerter and/or the Messenger services automatically. You can check the status of these services (and start them if necessary) by going through the Services icon (see the next section).

The Alerts button is used to direct the alerts to specific users and machines. It opens the Alerts dialog (see FIG. 11.23). Here you enter the username or computer name and click Add to place the user (or computer) on the alerts list. To delete users (or computers) from the list select the entry from the list and click remove.

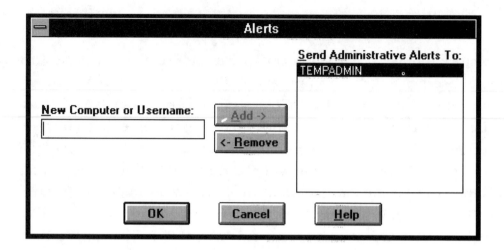

FIG. 11.23

Services

The Services icon opens the Services dialog (see FIG. 11.24). This dialog lets you start, stop, pause, and continue some of the services available on your computer. For example, you may be able to start the Alerter service mentioned in the previous section. In addition, you can configure the startup mode for services if logged on as a member of the Administrators group. To start, stop, pause, or continue a paused service first select the service from the list and click the relevant button. Note that stopping the Server service disconnects all connected remote users.

To configure the startup of a service select the service and click the Startup button to see a dialog for the selected service. Here you can specify that the service is started automatically or that it has to be started manually. To start a service manually you must use the Services icon. If

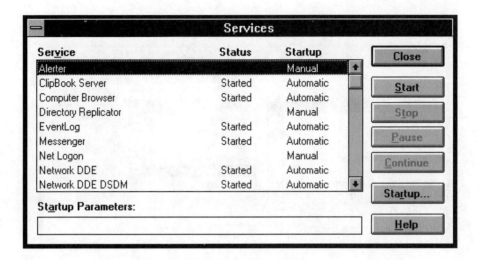

FIG. 11.24

you disable a service then it can't be started until you remove the disabled setting. You can also specify whether the service logs on to the system account or to another account.

Sound

The sound icon allows you to attach sounds to system events. For example, you can get Windows NT to sound a fanfare whenever you log on. However, in order to hear sounds you must have an NT-compatible sound card. You must also install the driver for the sound card first – use the Drivers icon to install a sound card driver.

Once you see the Sound dialog (see FIG. 11.25) you can begin attaching sounds to system events. The sounds you attach are in WAV format and some are included with NT. But there's no reason why you can't use other

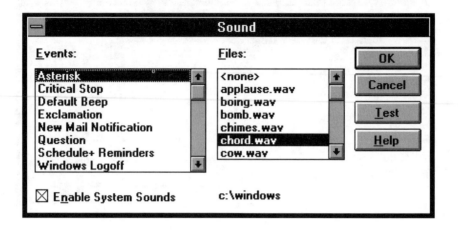

FIG. 11.25

WAV files that you may have. To assign a particular sound to an event select the event in the Events list and a WAV file in the Files list. If you don't want a sound for an individual event select <none> from the Files list. To hear a sound click the Test button. You can also assign sounds but turn them off until you're ready by deselecting the Enable System Sounds check box. This action suppresses all the assigned sounds except the Windows Logon and Windows Logoff events. You have to select <none> if you want to suppress sounds for those two events.

System

The System icon is valuable for a couple of reasons. One, it lets you alter the size of your paging file (virtual memory). Two, it enables you to choose the default operating system and timeout on a dual-boot computer.

Control Panel

In addition, you use the System icon to change environment variables and specify the foreground application priority.

First, let's look at the operating system startup options. You select the default operating system in the Startup drop-down list (see FIG. 11.26). For example, on an Intel-based PC you may have a choice of either Windows NT or DOS – the choices available depend upon how you installed NT, you may be restricted to NT only. Under the Startup drop-down list is a box labelled Show list for. This governs how long you have

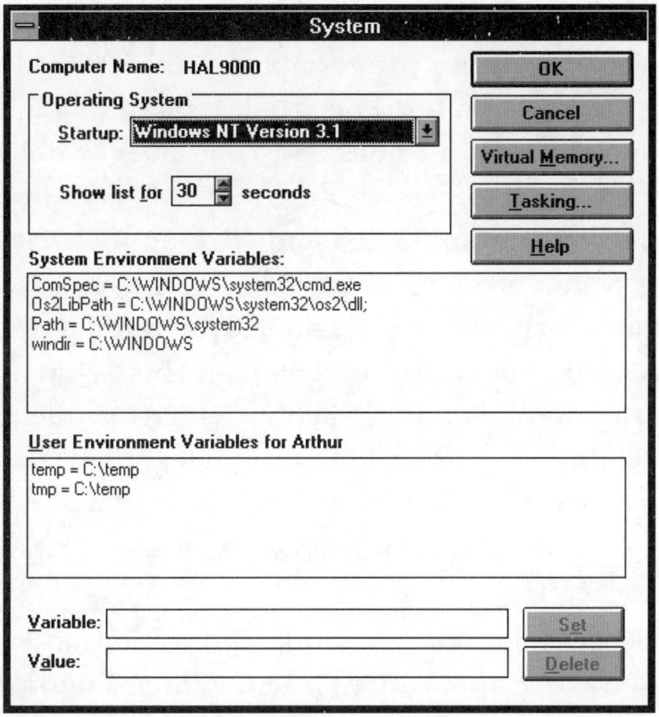

FIG. 11.26

to switch from the default operating system to another one at boot time. Select the operating system you are most likely to work in as the default and reduce the timeout to a couple of seconds. By reducing the timeout you give yourself just enough time to switch the operating system for the current session. Even if you have a long timeout (say, thirty seconds) you don't have to wait that long – simply press **Enter** when you've highlighted the right operating system at boot.

The lower portion of the System dialog box shows the User Environment Variables for the current user. Normally, you won't need to change any of the variables shown, but you can if you wish. For example, you may want to alter the TEMP directory. You do so by first selecting the variable in the list of user environment variables. This copies the name of the variable into the Variable text box. Then type in a new setting for the variable in the Value box and click Set. You can even delete the variable (which is not advisable unless you're absolutely certain of what you're doing) by selecting it from the list and clicking the Delete button. You can't alter any of the entries in the System Environment Variables list, but you can amend them by typing the name of the variable and its new value in the Variable and Value boxes respectively. This overwrites the existing value for a system variable and again this is not recommended unless you have an overriding reason to do so. However, the Path variable is cumulative so any value you enter is appended to the existing value. You may have to restart Windows NT in order to see the effects of any changes.

When you are running more than one application under NT then one application (the active application) is in the foreground while the others remain in the background even if they're processing. By default the foreground application is given most processor time. You can reduce the

Control Panel

amount of processor time dedicated to the foreground application through the Tasking button in the System dialog. Clicking this button opens the Tasking dialog (see FIG. 11.27). In this dialog you have three options for foreground and background application responsiveness. These three options give the foreground application the best possible response time (which is the default), make it more responsive than the background applications (which speeds up background applications), and make the foreground application equally responsive as the background applications. To get the best from your foreground application leave the default tasking as it is. To improve the performance of applications in the background consider one of the other two settings.

Windows for DOS users will be familiar with the concepts of virtual memory or swap files which artificially increase the amount of RAM on a computer by simulating memory in a free area of the hard disk. This has the effect of allowing more applications and data files to be open simultaneously but at the expense of performance. Memory on disk is much slower than 'real' memory. Windows NT continues this tradition, only the swap file is now called a paging file. This paging file is set up for

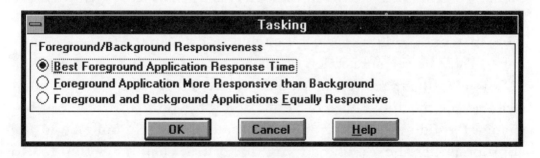

FIG. 11.27

you when you install NT, and unlike Windows for DOS there is no choice between using a permanent or a temporary paging file – it's permanent under NT. To be of any use this paging file has to be quite large (generally well over twenty megabytes if you've got sixteen megabytes of RAM) and that helps to explain why NT requires so much disk space for installation. The paging file is called PAGEFILE.SYS and can be found in your system partition. You can't delete this file while in NT but you can from another operating system such as DOS or Windows for DOS. If it does get deleted then NT recreates it automatically when you next run NT.

You might want to consider reducing the size of the paging file if you are short of disk space. Alternatively, you may wish to increase its size if NT is strapped for memory. In the latter case you'll see system dialogs appearing as you run NT – to eliminate these dialogs either close a few open applications or increase the paging file. If you have more than one hard disk you can also create additional paging files on those disks. To adjust the paging file size you must be logged on as a member of the Administrators group.

To check on, or to alter, the size of your paging file click the Virtual Memory button in the System dialog. This opens the Virtual Memory dialog which contains a number of entries. If necessary (that is if you've more than one hard disk) select the relevant drive in the Drive [Volume Label] list. The second section of the Virtual Memory dialog (see FIG. 11.28) shows the space available on the selected drive and both the initial size and the maximum size of your paging file on that drive. You can change the figures for both the initial and the maximum size in the appropriate text boxes. Should you do so then click the Set button to register your altered figures. The final section of the Virtual Memory

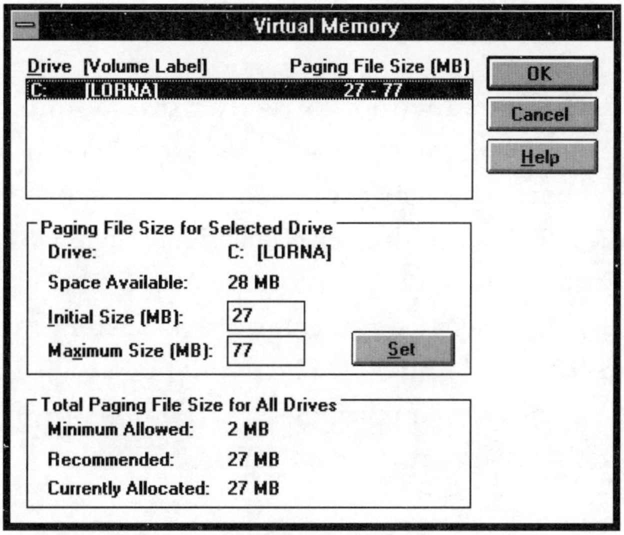

FIG. 11.28

dialog shows the cumulative total for all the paging files on all the available drives. The Currently Allocated figure should be more than the Minimum Allowed and as close as possible to the Recommended figure. When you've made changes you want to keep, remember to click OK and not Cancel.

UPS

The UPS (uninterruptible power supply) icon is for controlling your battery backup power supply, if you have one. An UPS keeps NT running in the event of a mains power cut and lets you shutdown NT correctly, thus avoiding any potential data loss. NT warns you when the mains power fails and can automatically shutdown safely before the UPS itself runs down its batteries. The latter is an extra security measure which means that data is safe even on an unattended system.

For the UPS service to function correctly you should check that the Alerter, Messenger, and Event Log services are started automatically by your system. To check whether these services are started automatically go through the Services icon (discussed earlier). Once you've configured your UPS its services are started automatically by NT. You'll need the Alerter and Messenger services to ensure that system messages (in the event of a power cut) are displayed. The Event Log service, if it's running, means that you can view power outages and their results in Event Viewer. Event Viewer is discussed later in the book.

You can test your UPS service by disconnecting the power supply. Try and have as many users as possible logged on with the maximum number of applications and data files open (though only use dummy data or data which has already been saved). Make sure that Windows NT notifies the right users at the right intervals after you've turned off the power. You should also check that NT is closed down successfully as the UPS batteries begin to run low. Use Event Viewer to double check that no errors were encountered.

Let's work through the large number of settings in the UPS dialog (see FIG. 11.29):

Uninterruptible Power Supply is installed on

Turn this check box on to set up your UPS. The drop-down list to the right allows you to specify the serial port (for example, COM2) to which your UPS is connected.

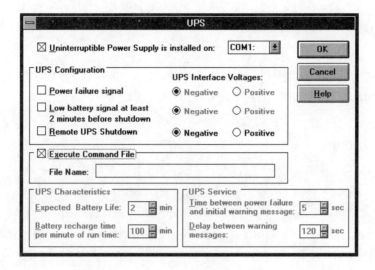

FIG. 11.29

Power failure signal

Turn on this check box for NT to warn in the event of a power cut.

Low battery signal at least 2 minutes before shutdown

Use this check box for NT to warn as the UPS batteries run low.

Remote UPS Shutdown

Enable this check box for the UPS device to close down automatically.

UPS Interface Voltages

To determine which option buttons to turn on in this section refer to the documentation that accompanies your UPS system.

Execute Command File

Turn on this check box if you want a file to execute before shutdown. Such a file might disconnect you from other linked services. The file to be executed is entered into the File Name text box. The file should reside in your main NT directory and be an EXE, COM, BAT, or CMD file.

Expected Battery Life

Use this box to enter the amount of time the UPS can keep NT running.

Battery recharge time per minute of run time

This box contains the setting for battery recharge times.

Time between power failure and initial warning message

This box is for the amount of time between a power cut and the first warning message.

Delay between warning messages

This box specifies the gaps between successive warning messages.

Command prompt

COMMAND PROMPT

■ Customizing the command prompt

■ How to run applications from a prompt

■ How to enter commands

An introduction to the command prompt

DOS users will find the command prompt (see FIG. 12.1) a familiar sight after all the graphical niceties of Windows NT. It looks pretty much like any character-based operating system. Windows for DOS users will note its close similarity to the DOS window (DOS in a box) in enhanced mode. However, the Windows NT command prompt is rather more than simply running DOS in a character screen. For example, you can run any NT-compatible application or command from the command prompt. This includes NT, Windows for DOS, DOS, OS/2 1.x, and POSIX applications and commands, provided they are feasible under NT. You can enter NT commands, most DOS commands, and even some LAN Manager ones as well. Windows NT commands are similar to many DOS commands and

```
┌─────────────────────── Command Prompt ───────────────── ▼ ▲ ┐
│ Volume Serial Number is 2F5F-1EF1                            │
│                                                              │
│  Directory of C:\                                            │
│                                                              │
│ COMMAND   COM            47845 09/04/91  05:00               │
│ DOS           <DIR>            05/04/92  23:42               │
│ WINDOWS       <DIR>            05/04/92  23:47               │
│ ALDUS         <DIR>            05/09/93  19:28               │
│ DATA          <DIR>            06/04/92  17:17               │
│ SBPRO         <DIR>            23/12/92  19:33               │
│ WORD          <DIR>            07/04/92  19:01               │
│ PM5           <DIR>            05/09/93  19:33               │
│ DODOT         <DIR>            12/09/93  13:59               │
│ SBASE         <DIR>            07/01/93  14:49               │
│ SPC           <DIR>            07/01/93  14:49               │
│ CONFIG    SYS             564 17/06/93  15:37               │
│ AUTOEXEC  BAT             816 07/08/93  14:48               │
│ TEMP          <DIR>            29/08/93  14:26               │
│ USERS         <DIR>            29/08/93  14:26               │
│ WIN32APP      <DIR>            29/08/93  14:26               │
│ PAGEFILE  SYS         26214400 18/09/93  11:43               │
│            17 File(s)   26263625 bytes                       │
│                         3909632 bytes free                   │
│                                                              │
│ C:\>                                                         │
└──────────────────────────────────────────────────────────┘
```

FIG. 12.1

Command prompt

include quite a few new additions. In addition, you can transfer data between applications via the Clipboard and even pipe data from one subsystem to another. A subsystem is a self-contained operating environment for each operating system run from Windows NT. For example, your 32-bit NT applications run in the NT subsystem and your 16-bit Windows for DOS and DOS applications in the DOS subsystem.

To start the command prompt (CMD.EXE) you double click the Command Prompt icon in the Main group. You can then enter commands at the prompt, which to all intents and purposes functions just like the DOS prompt under Windows for DOS. You then have a choice of what to do next:

- Type **start** to open a second command prompt window. This allows you to work in two windows independently.

- Type a program name to start up an application. There are two ways of doing this. One, simply type the name of the executable file (for example, **notepad**) and press **Enter**. This particular example opens Notepad in a separate window – however, you can't work back at the prompt until you close Notepad. Two, type **start** followed by the program name (for example, **start notepad**) and press **Enter**. This too opens Notepad in a separate window but enables you to work back at the prompt without closing Notepad. You can also run a batch file by keying in its name. Both batch files and normal application executables can take command line parameters if appropriate. Batch files under Windows NT can have either a BAT or a CMD extension.

■ Type an NT native command. Many of these commands are similar to the DOS versions but are full 32-bit implementations. For example, you could try **dir** to see a listing for the current directory. Some will be familiar to LAN Manager users, for example, **net print**. To see a list of most of the commands type **help**. To see a list of the net commands type **net help**. To get help on a specific command type the name of the command with **help** – for example, **help dir** or **net print /help**. Alternatively, double click the Windows NT Help icon in your Main group and click the Access the Command Reference Help hot spot in the first help window. From there you can select and browse all the command prompt commands.

■ Type a DOS subsystem command. These differ from the native commands being only 16-bit implementations. As such they are exactly the same as they were in DOS or Windows for DOS. For example, you could type **edlin** to see the famous (if that's the right word!) old DOS text editor. To get help on any of the DOS subsystem commands type **/?** after the command, for example, **edlin /?**. However, you get more comprehensive help (in this case information on how to use Edlin) go through the Windows NT Help icon, as described above. Some DOS subsystem commands are redundant under NT – for example, you don't need share any more as its functions are built into NT. Some of the DOS configuration commands are supported, such as device and install. These should go into your CONFIG.NT file in your NT directory if possible. CONFIG.NT is the equivalent of CONFIG.SYS in DOS machines – the AUTOEXEC.BAT equivalent is AUTOEXEC.NT.

■ Type a command from another category such as the TCP/IP utilities. You can view the TCP/IP commands through the Windows NT Help icon in your Main group. These commands are only meaningful if you're connected via the TCP/IP protocol to a host that supports TCP/IP. Many NT users can safely ignore this category.

■ Copy from and paste into the command prompt window. This is discussed more fully shortly.

■ Configure the appearance of the command prompt. This, too, is covered in more detail below.

■ Recall previous commands to save typing and reduce the possibility of errors. DOS users may like to know that Doskey is supported automatically by NT. For example, press **F7** to see a history (see FIG. 12.2) of the previous commands entered (and select a command from the history list if you wish) or use **F3** to show the last command.

■ Exit the command prompt. You exit the command prompt by entering **exit** or double clicking its Control menu. You exit any applications started from the command prompt by using the application's normal exit procedure. If a badly-behaved application prevents you from closing the command prompt in the usual manner you may have to resort to terminating the prompt. You do this by clicking the Control menu in the command prompt window, clicking Settings in the menu, and then clicking the Terminate button in the subsequent dialog.

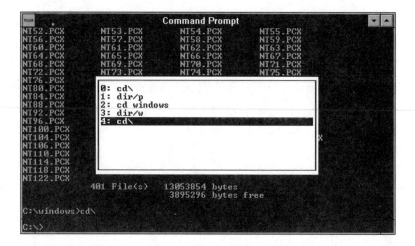

FIG. 12.2

Just because Windows NT provides the command prompt doesn't mean it's obligatory. Most of the functions you can access from the command prompt are directly available from the graphical user interface of NT. For example, most people would prefer to start Notepad by double clicking the Notepad icon in the Accessories group rather than starting command prompt and typing **notepad**. Nor can I imagine many readers wishing to edit a text file in Edlin when Notepad is available. For copying files and other housekeeping tasks you'll probably find File Manager more convenient than typing in the commands (for instance, copy and del) at the command prompt. Even if you want to run old DOS programs then it's easier to start them from Program Manager icons rather than in the command prompt window. There's a section on running DOS applications and PIF files later in the book. PIF files, incidentally, control the way your 16-bit DOS applications run in the DOS subsystem.

Command prompt

Configuring the command prompt

There's quite a bit you can do to change the appearance of the default command prompt window, including getting rid of the window altogether. This section looks at the various configuration options available.

Turning off the window

You can run the command prompt full-screen if you prefer. To toggle between a windowed and a full-screen display press **Alt-Enter**.

You can also change the default mode so the command prompt always starts full-screen. To do so click the Control menu and click Settings in the menu. In the ensuing Command Prompt dialog (see FIG. 12.3) turn on the option button for Full Screen (or Window if you want to get back to the

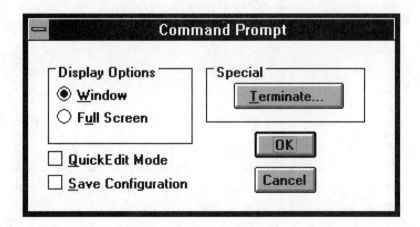

FIG. 12.3

original default). If you want NT to remember your setting for subsequent logons, turn on the check box for Save Configuration.

Window size and position

The window size and position only applies to the command prompt in a window and not when it's running full-screen. You change the window position by dragging the command prompt title bar, and you can have NT recall the window position when you reopen the command prompt. You change the window size by dragging the window borders. However, you can't resize the window so it's larger than the current screen buffer size. You can, though, increase the screen buffer size and then enlarge the window by dragging borders. If the current window is smaller than the current buffer size the command prompt window shows scroll bars. To get the window size to match the screen buffer size exactly simply maximize the window. Note that you can't resize the window by dragging borders after maximizing the window, you must restore it first. If you wish, after changing the screen buffer size, you can ask NT to remember the new size.

To alter the screen buffer size:

1   Open the Control menu and click Screen Size And Position.

2   In the ensuing Screen Size And Position dialog (see FIG. 12.4) make changes to the figures for Width and Height in the Screen Buffer Size section. Click OK to preserve the changes for the current command prompt. The figure for the width is in characters and the figure for the height is in lines. Thus the

Command prompt

```
┌─────────────────────────────────────────────┐
│ ▬        Screen Size And Position            │
├─────────────────────────────────────────────┤
│  ┌─Screen Buffer Size─────────┐              │
│  │                            │  ┌─────────┐ │
│  │ Width:      │70│   │▲│     │  │   OK    │ │
│  │             └──┘   │▼│     │  └─────────┘ │
│  │                            │  ┌─────────┐ │
│  │ Height:     │25│   │▲│     │  │ Cancel  │ │
│  │             └──┘   │▼│     │  └─────────┘ │
│  └────────────────────────────┘              │
│   □  Save Screen Buffer Size                 │
│   □  Save Window Size and Position           │
└─────────────────────────────────────────────┘
```

FIG. 12.4

screen buffer size is dependent upon the current font. A smaller font makes for a smaller screen buffer size and maximum window size.

To get NT to recall the new setting the next time you open the command prompt, turn on the Save Screen Buffer Size check box. To ask NT to remember the current window size (which may be smaller than the screen buffer size) and the window position turn on the check box for Save Window Size and Position.

Colour scheme

The command prompt uses two colour schemes. The screen colours (text and background) refer to the normal command prompt window. The popup colours (text and background) refer to the history list (and others) that you can see by pressing **F7** – though you must have entered at least one command for **F7** to work. To view or alter the current colour schemes:

1   Open the Control menu and click Screen Colors.

2   In the subsequent Screen Colors dialog (see FIG. 12.5) select one of the four option buttons and click a colour for the item in the palette. You can see a preview of your colour schemes at the foot of the dialog.

3   To keep your changes for this and all future command prompt sessions turn on the Save Configuration check box and click OK. To keep changes for the current command prompt only

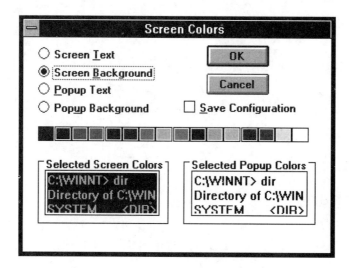

FIG. 12.5

Command prompt

click OK with the Save Configuration check box turned off. To discard any changes made click Cancel.

Fonts

Changing the command prompt font can increase (or decrease) the legibility of commands you type and the output you see in the command prompt window. The size of the font also affects the actual size of the current screen buffer (and hence a maximized window) on screen. To change the current command prompt font:

1   Open the Control menu and click Fonts.

2   In the subsequent Font Selection dialog (see FIG. 12.6) select a font size from the Font list. The font sizes are in pixels and you can see a preview of the font in the Selected Font section. In

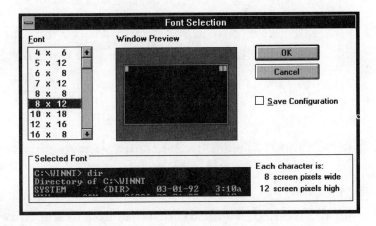

FIG. 12.6

addition, you can see how a new font is going to affect the current window in the Window Preview section. This section shows the window size and position in relation to the whole desktop. Click OK to keep any desired changes.

You can ask Windows NT to use the new font in all future command prompt sessions by turning on the Save Configuration check box in the Font Selection dialog.

Copying and pasting with the command prompt

The command prompt provides limited Clipboard support when compared with Windows for DOS or Windows NT applications. For example, you can't cut information from the command prompt (or a DOS application you run from the command prompt). You are limited to copying and pasting. To copy text from the command prompt to the Clipboard:

1   Make sure the command prompt (or character-based application) is running in a window and not full-screen.

2   Open the Control menu and click Edit, Mark.

3   With the mouse select the text you want to copy.

4   Either click the right-hand mouse button or click Edit, Copy from the Control menu to copy the text to the Clipboard.

Command prompt

Once on the Clipboard you can use the data in the normal (Windows) way. For example, you can paste it into a Windows application or another command prompt. To share the data (or save it for later) you may want to place it into your ClipBook – although you can also save directly from Clipboard in CLP format.

You can also copy the entire command prompt window to the Clipboard by pressing **Alt-Print Screen**, though here it's copied as a bitmap and not as text. To copy the entire desktop as a bitmap press **Print Screen** by itself.

To paste Clipboard text data into the command prompt (or character-based application) whether running in a window or full-screen:

1   Position the cursor insertion point where you want to paste.

2   Open the Control menu and click Edit, Paste. As a reminder, you can open the Control menu when running full-screen by pressing **Alt-Spacebar**.

You'll probably discover that the Edit, Mark - Edit, Copy sequence is rather cumbersome. Of course, in Windows applications it's a simple Edit, Copy but you can make copying to the Clipboard easier from character-based applications too. Windows NT enables you to do this by supporting QuickEdit – this is a feature that was not available in Windows for DOS.

Before you can avail yourself of QuickEdit you must turn it on. However, once it's on you can still use Edit, Mark - Edit, Copy if you prefer. To turn QuickEdit on, open the Control menu in the command prompt and click

Settings. In the ensuing Command Prompt dialog enable the QuickEdit Mode check box. You can now use the QuickEdit shortcut:

1   Drag the mouse over the text you wish to copy to the Clipboard.

2   Click the right-hand mouse button to effect the copy operation.

3   Place the cursor where you want to paste and click the right-hand mouse button once again.

QuickEdit is so much easier than Edit, Mark - Edit, Copy you might be wondering why it's not on by default. The answer's quite straightforward – it stops you from using the mouse normally in those DOS applications that support the use of a mouse. As an experiment change to your Windows NT directory in the command prompt and type **edit**. This starts the MSDOS 5/6 text editor (which you might find more congenial than Edlin!). Try starting Edit with QuickEdit on and then with QuickEdit off – you'll find it makes quite a difference when trying to open the pull-down menus in Edit with your mouse.

DOS applications

DOS APPLICATIONS

■ How to run DOS applications

■ Using PIF files

■ How to create your own PIF files

DOS applications

Windows NT allows you to run applications from a variety of operating systems. In addition to 32-bit applications written specifically for Windows NT you can also run many 16-bit Windows for DOS and DOS applications as well as some OS/2 and POSIX-compliant character ones. Most readers are most likely to have Windows for DOS and DOS applications so it's these that I want to concentrate on.

Many Windows for DOS applications run unmodified under Windows NT, thus preserving your investment in existing Windows software. Indeed running such applications is no different from running full-blown Windows NT ones – simply add an icon for the application to a Program Manager group and away you go. Not all Windows for DOS applications are fully-compatible, however. You may find that applications that drive hardware directly have to be updated. Either contact your dealer for further information or experiment – only don't use real data until you're happy with the results.

Traditional DOS applications on the other hand may present additional problems. In particular you might need to juggle with a few settings to achieve optimum performance. You do this by creating a special PIF (Program Information File) for each application. You can ask Windows NT to build the PIF for you or do it manually. But before looking at PIF settings let's investigate just some of the different ways of running a DOS application from NT.

Add the application to Program Manager and run it from there. You can specify the executable filename (EXE or COM) in the Command Line of the Program Item Properties dialog. If you do this, then NT looks for an existing PIF file with the same filename and runs that first. Typically, such

DOS applications

a PIF file sets up the environment for the DOS application (for example, the minimum amount of RAM required) and then chains to the executable. Should the relevant PIF file not exist then NT falls back on a generic PIF file called _DEFAULT.PIF. The latter contains settings that are adequate for many (but not all) DOS applications. In the event of _DEFAULT.PIF not providing an environment in which the DOS application can run you must design your own PIF, specifically for the recalcitrant application. Designing PIFs is discussed shortly, but you should be aware that you can ask NT to create a PIF in some circumstances. NT will be able to create a PIF if it has information about the DOS application built in. Thus it can create PIFs if the application is relatively well-known. If it can't, it bases the PIF on _DEFAULT.PIF. You ask NT to create a PIF by going through Windows NT Setup (covered later). Alternatively, you might want to have a go at designing your own PIF. Here you can start from scratch or use _DEFAULT.PIF as a template. In the latter case you ought to be careful to save the PIF under a new name, usually with the same name as your application's executable file. Some applications require to be started from batch files. Often a batch file loads a separate TSR (terminate and stay resident) program that is required before the main executable is loaded. If you have the batch file in the Command Line of the Program Item Properties dialog then the batch file, the TSR it loads, and the main executable it loads all use the parameters in _DEFAULT.PIF. Once again, you might consider creating a dedicated PIF to start the batch file.

As an alternative to Program Manager you can start programs from File Manager by double clicking the filename. Like Program Manager you can try this by double clicking a dedicated PIF for the main program, the main program executable itself, a batch file that calls the main executable, or a PIF created for the batch file. If you experience any problems then using a dedicated PIF may be a solution. Both File Manager and Program Manager also allow you to run programs through File, Run.

If all the alternatives in Program Manager and File Manager weren't enough then there's always the command prompt. Here you type in the name of the name of the application's executable, or its PIF, or a batch file that loads the executable. But here you must be careful. When you start a DOS application from the command prompt its PIF (or _DEFAULT.PIF if there's no dedicated PIF) sets up the environment for any other DOS applications started from the same command prompt. This is true even when a subsequent application has its own PIF with different settings from the PIF (or _DEFAULT.PIF) of the first application started. If a subsequent application requires different settings then it may not run correctly. In that case start each individual application from a fresh command prompt. You do this by closing and reopening the current command prompt, or reopening another command prompt window, or prefacing the application name with **start** (for example, **start dosprog**). When you start a TSR by itself from the command prompt (that is outside of a batch file), NT informs you when it's loaded. On seeing the message you should press **Ctrl-Z** to return to the command prompt.

PIF Editor

PIF Editor may be familiar if you've tried to run DOS applications from Windows for DOS. In Windows NT too, a PIF created in PIF Editor may be necessary for those awkward DOS programs. As a reminder you may already have a PIF for your application – it may have been created automatically by NT during installation or added later through Windows NT Setup. If a dedicated PIF does not exist then the application uses

DOS applications

_DEFAULT.PIF. When there is no dedicated PIF and _DEFAULT.PIF is clearly not appropriate you have a number of choices. One, you can check to see if the supplier of your DOS application provided a PIF. If so then copy the PIF to your NT directory. Two, you can see if NT can create a PIF for you by going through Windows NT Setup – this option is covered in the chapter on *Windows NT Setup*. Three, you can design your own PIF using PIF Editor. And here you have the option of starting from scratch or using _DEFAULT.PIF as a template. Should you use _DEFAULT.PIF as a template be careful to save out with another PIF name otherwise you will lose the generic settings in _DEFAULT.PIF.

PIF Editor in Windows NT is almost identical to PIF Editor in Windows for DOS. The main differences lie in the fact that NT lets you specify a couple of startup files as well as the PIF and that NT PIFs do not use all the Windows for DOS PIF parameters. However, all the parameters are compatible – NT simply ignores the ones it doesn't use. This means you can use your old Windows for DOS PIFs as the basis for your Windows NT PIFs. Incidentally the startup files used by PIFs in NT are, by default, AUTOEXEC.NT and CONFIG.NT. As you might expect these are broadly equivalent to AUTOEXEC.BAT and CONFIG.SYS respectively in DOS. Under NT, though, you can substitute other files and fine tune your system for particular DOS applications.

It's worth pointing out that you can create two (or more) icons for the same DOS application in Program Manager and assign a different PIF to each icon. This enables you to use the application with differing environment settings. For example, you might run an application called Dosprog from either LOW.PIF or HIGH.PIF – these could provide the application with minimum and maximum amounts of memory respectively. You might want to have the low memory situation when you're working with smaller data files, and thus leaving more memory free for other applications. Conversely, the high memory allocation would be suitable for larger data files.

Let's now work quickly through the settings available when you first open PIF Editor (see FIG. 13.1). Only a few of the available settings have any effect on Windows NT – those not mentioned are applicable only to Windows for DOS:

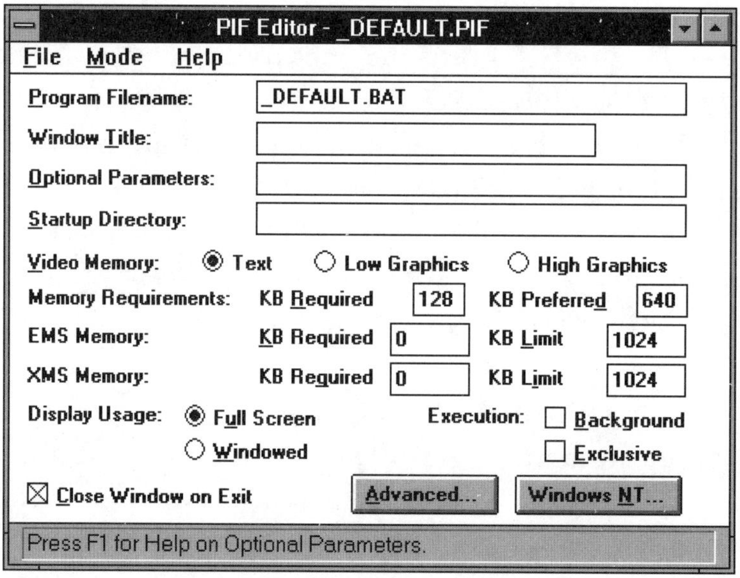

FIG. 13.1

DOS applications

Program Filename

This where you enter the filename of the application's executable file (typically with an EXE or COM extension). Should you want to use a batch file to load the main program then enter the name of the batch file instead. If the program is not on your path then enter the full path for the program.

Window Title

The name you enter here is the title that's shown in the title bar of the application's window (when it's running in a window) and the title of the icon when you minimize the application. If you don't make an entry then NT uses the name of the PIF file you save. In Program Manager there's also a Description text box in the Program Item Properties dialog for Program Manager icons. Any entry you make there overrides the one you make under Window Title in PIF Editor.

Optional Parameters

If you normally start the application under DOS with a command line parameter you can enter that parameter here for it to take effect. The exact parameter you enter depends upon the application in question. For example, many DOS applications allow you to enter a data file as a parameter and start up with that file ready-loaded into the application. When you don't know in advance what the parameter will be, you can enter a question mark (**?**) in the Optional Parameters box. This means that NT will prompt you to enter a parameter when you start the application.

Startup Directory

When you start an application it's often handy to have the application defaulting to your data directory for the application. You can specify a data directory by entering its name in the Startup directory box. The Program Item Properties dialog in Program Manager also has a text box called Working Directory. Should you have an entry there too then the Program Manager setting takes precedence.

EMS Memory

Some DOS programs require the existence of expanded memory (EMS). Windows NT can emulate expanded memory if you ask it to in a PIF. You specify the details in the KB Required and KB Limit boxes of the EMS Memory section of PIF Editor. The KB Required and KB Limit settings work together. NT tries to provide the amount required – if more expanded memory is available (actually, normal memory used to emulate expanded memory) then it's provided up to the maximum asked for in the limit box. If NT can't meet the demands of the required box it does not start the application and displays a message accordingly. If your application does not need any expanded memory then make both the KB Required and KB Limit boxes 0 (zero). If an application does not need expanded memory but performs better if there's up to a megabyte, then have settings of 0 and 1024. To give as much expanded memory as possible to an application then enter -1 in the KB Limit – this means NT tries to emulate as much expanded memory as it can, though this will prejudice the operation of other applications.

DOS applications

XMS Memory

Very few DOS applications can work with extended (XMS) memory. For those that do, you can have NT emulate extended memory. The settings are identical to those for expanded memory, thus a KB Required of 0 and a KB Limit of 0 gives no extended memory to the application. To give an application up to one megabyte then enter 0 and 1024. An entry of -1 for KB Limit tells NT to emulate as much extended memory as possible for the application.

Display Usage

You can have a DOS application run in a window or full-screen, and toggle between the two by pressing **Alt-Enter**. To have the application start every time in a window (the default) or full-screen then you can turn on the relevant option button in the Display Usage section of PIF Editor.

Advanced options

There are a couple of further settings that are accessed when you click the Advanced button in PIF Editor.

Reserve Shortcut Keys

Some DOS applications may respond to keys that you normally use with Windows NT. You might wish to reserve those keys for the application so when it's running in the foreground NT ignores the keys. For example, **Alt-Tab** cycles all open applications in NT. If your DOS application uses **Alt-Tab** you may want to suppress application cycling. You can do this by reserving that key combination for the application. To reserve **Alt-Tab** (and other standard NT keys) click the Advanced button in PIF Editor and turn on the relevant check box in the Reserve Shortcut Keys section of the resulting Advanced Options dialog (see FIG. 13.2).

Application Shortcut Key

You can cycle open applications with **Alt-Tab** or use **Ctrl-Esc** to show Task List. However, to go immediately to the application of your choice you may want to define a shortcut key combination for the application.

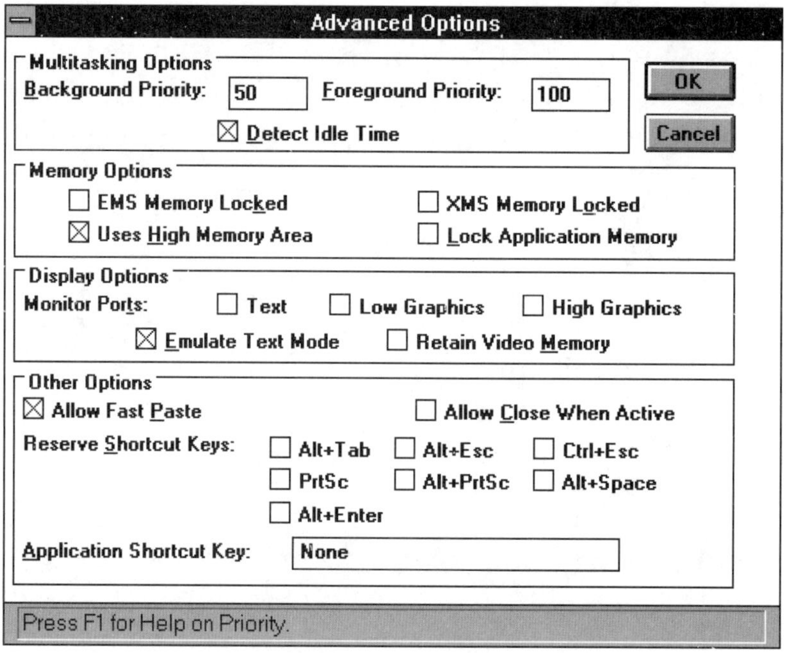

FIG. 13.2

DOS applications

Pressing the defined keys brings the associated application to the foreground. You specify the key combination in the Application Shortcut Key section of the Advanced Options dialog. To do so click in the text box and press the desired keys. The combination must include the **Alt** or **Ctrl** key – for instance, **Alt-F7**, **Alt-Shift-F10**, **Ctrl-F2**, or **Alt-Ctrl-F3**. Be careful to choose a key combination not used in other applications – the shortcut key always takes precedence. Should you want to turn off the application shortcut key then press **Shift-Backspace** in the Application Shortcut Key box.

You can also define a shortcut key for an application in the Shortcut Key box of the Program Item Properties dialog in Program Manager. Any Program Manager settings override those made in PIF Editor.

Startup files

You also set the startup files for a DOS session by going through the Windows NT button in PIF Editor. The default initialization files are called AUTOEXEC.NT and CONFIG.NT. Together they can determine various aspects of the DOS subsystem that are responsible for running DOS applications under NT. If a particular application requires a fine-tuned environment that can't be created by the previous settings in PIF Editor or a batch file that you run, then you might need to create alternatives to AUTOEXEC.NT and CONFIG.NT.

Custom DOS initialization files

As already mentioned, Windows NT uses a couple of startup files to configure the environment for DOS applications. By default these are

AUTOEXEC.NT and CONFIG.NT. These are broadly equivalent to
AUTOEXEC.BAT and CONFIG.SYS in a DOS operating system. Unless
you indicate otherwise NT automatically employs these two files.
However, there may be occasions when these files aren't adequate. For
example, you may have a DOS application that requires specific changes
to the environment in the DOS subsystem. If you can't use any of the PIF
Editor settings or a batch file to implement these changes you might have
to tweak AUTOEXEC.NT and/or CONFIG.NT. But rather than edit those
two files, they are used by every DOS session, you could create two new
files to replace them for a particular application. The new files would be
based on AUTOEXEC.NT and CONFIG.NT and you have to instruct NT
to substitute them.

To substitute another file for AUTOEXEC.NT and/or CONFIG.NT click
the Windows NT button in PIF Editor. This opens the Windows NT
Options dialog (see FIG. 13.3). In this dialog enter the name of any
substitute for AUTOEXEC.NT in the Autoexec Filename text box, and
similarly for CONFIG.NT in the Config Filename box.

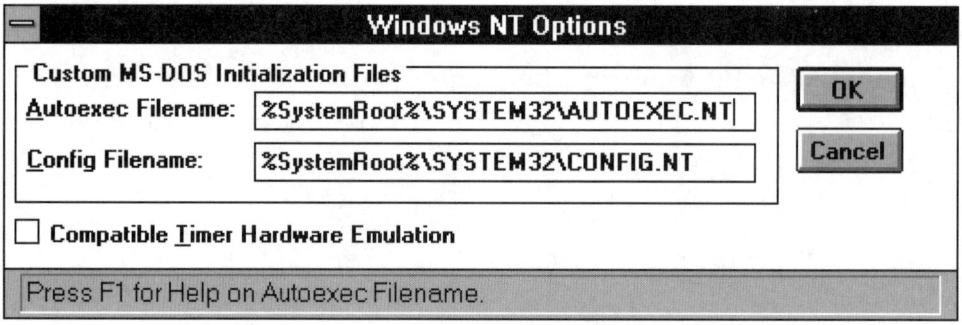

FIG. 13.3

Windows NT Setup

WINDOWS NT SETUP

- Changing your display

- How to create PIFs automatically

- How to reclaim disk space

When you install new hardware you normally have to tell Windows NT about it. Exactly how you do this depends upon the hardware. Basically, it boils down to three choices: Print Manager, Control Panel, and Windows NT Setup (see FIG. 14.1). To install a new printer, for instance, go through Print Manager. You use the Network icon in Control Panel to install a new network card. For sound cards (and other multimedia devices) go through the Drivers icon in Control Panel. Other hardware devices are often installed in Windows NT Setup. The list includes graphics drivers, mice, keyboards, SCSI adapters, and tape drives. You can also use Windows NT Setup to alter the driver for your current graphics card – you might want to switch from VGA to SVGA mode (or vice versa), providing your graphics card and monitor can support both modes.

As well as allowing you to install and configure hardware Windows NT Setup has a number of other purposes. It enables you to delete user profiles and add or remove Windows NT files. In addition, you can build PIFs for DOS applications in Windows NT Setup. Removing files can be

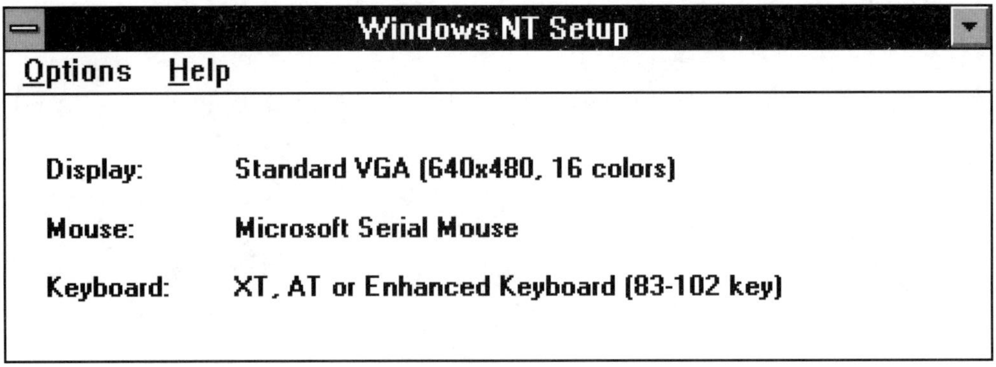

▬	Windows NT Setup	▼
Options Help		
Display:	Standard VGA (640x480, 16 colors)	
Mouse:	Microsoft Serial Mouse	
Keyboard:	XT, AT or Enhanced Keyboard (83-102 key)	

FIG. 14.1

Windows NT Setup

handy when you're running short of free disk space. This section looks at all aspects of Windows NT Setup. Let's begin by looking at graphics cards, mice, and keyboards.

System settings

When you first start Windows NT Setup its dialog shows the currently installed display (graphics card), mouse, and keyboard driver. You can change any of these settings. However, if you have a keyboard problem check out the International icon in Control Panel first. That's where you determine the nationality of your keyboard – in other words it dictates which characters are produced by the keys. The keyboard option in Windows NT Setup is for defining the *physical* characteristics of your keyboard, like exactly how many keys it has. You should never have to change the keyboard setting in Windows NT Setup as the default option covers most 83 to 102 key keyboards. You are more likely to want to alter the display and mouse setting. You change the mouse driver if your existing or new mouse doesn't respond to the existing driver. The display setting allows you to set up the right driver for your graphics card and monitor. In addition, with some drivers you can experiment with differing screen resolutions and numbers of colours. For instance, you may want to switch from 16 colours in 640 by 480 pixel resolution to 256 colours in 1024 by 768 pixels. Note that not all graphics cards and monitors give you a choice.

To alter any of these hardware settings click Options, Change System Settings to see the Change System Settings dialog (see FIG. 14.2). Open the required drop-down list and make the selection that matches your display, mouse, or keyboard. If you can't find a match, select Other from the list.

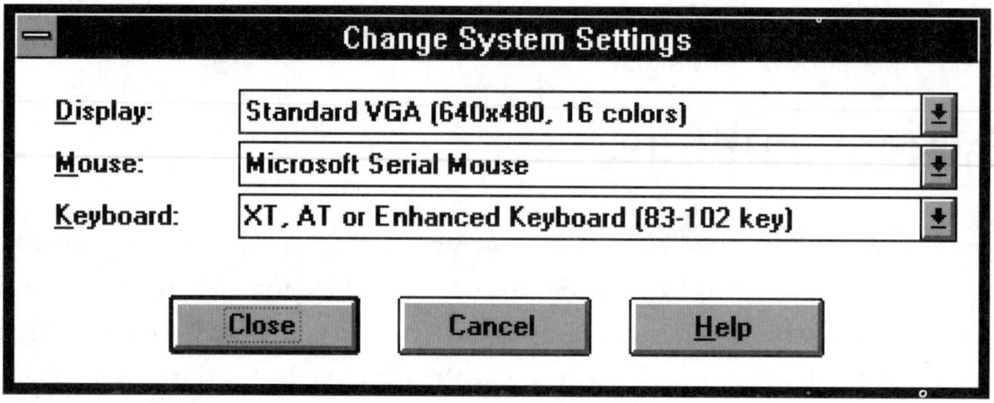

Change System Settings

Display:	Standard VGA (640x480, 16 colors)
Mouse:	Microsoft Serial Mouse
Keyboard:	XT, AT or Enhanced Keyboard (83-102 key)

[Close] [Cancel] [Help]

FIG. 14.2

In that case you need a floppy disk containing the driver, or the driver must be on a disk accessible from your computer. Whether you choose a listed option or Other you may be asked to insert one or more of your original NT disks. After the installation (or modification) is complete you must restart Windows NT for the changes to take effect.

SCSI adapters and tape drives

The procedure for adding (or removing) a SCSI adapter or tape drive is slightly different from the method discussed in the previous section. To install a SCSI adapter:

1   Click Options, Add/Remove SCSI Adapters.

2   In the subsequent SCSI Adapter Setup dialog (see FIG. 14.3) click the Add button.

3   In the next Select SCSI Adapter Option dialog select a driver and click the Install button.

4   Follow any instructions given and click the Continue button to close the SCSI Adapter Setup dialog.

5   For the installation to take effect you must shutdown and restart NT.

To remove an existing SCSI adapter click Remove rather than Add in the SCSI Adapter Setup dialog. Adding or removing a tape device is exactly the same as for a SCSI device. The only difference is in the dialog names: Tape Device Setup and Select Tape Device Option.

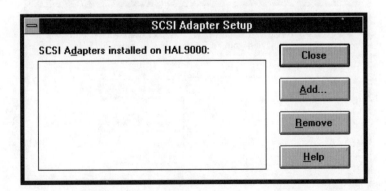

FIG. 14.3

Setting up applications

To set up individual applications it's probably easier to use Program Manager and create the icons from within Program Manager (with File, New, Program Item). However, Windows NT Setup is preferable when you want to add multiple application icons to Program Manager. Windows NT Setup can add more than one application in one operation. In addition, using Windows NT Setup can automatically create PIFs for DOS applications. When you add programs with Windows NT they go into your Applications group in Program Manager. If you want them in different groups then it's a simple matter to drag them from the Applications group. To add application icons to Program Manager from Windows NT Setup:

1   Click Options, Set Up Applications in the Windows NT Setup dialog. This opens the first (see FIG. 14.4) of two Set Up Applications dialogs.

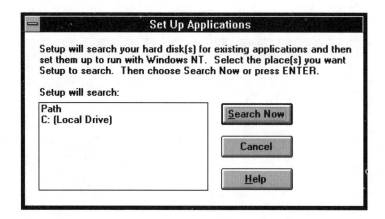

FIG. 14.4

2   In the first of these dialogs select your path or drives to search
          for applications and click Search Now.

3   The results of the search are displayed in the second (see FIG.
          14.5) Set Up Applications dialog. Select the programs found
          that you wish to install and click Add followed by Continue. If
          you want to install all the found programs click Add All rather
          than Add. Should you decide not to install one you've added to
          the right-hand list, select it from the list and click Remove
          before you click Continue.

If NT can, it creates a PIF file for any DOS applications that you've chosen.

Adding and removing Windows NT files

When disk space is at a premium you may be tempted to delete some of
your NT files from your hard disk. It's not recommended that you use File
Manager for this purpose as you may accidentally delete files that are

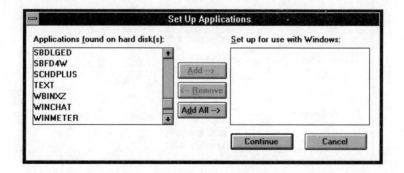

FIG. 14.5

essential to the NT system. Rather you should use Windows NT Setup as it only removes files that aren't vital to the functioning of NT. Such files include screen savers, wallpaper bitmaps, games, and those programs that appear in the Accessories group. Conversely, you might consider reinstalling any deleted files as your disk situation improves – or you may simply wish to add files you left out when Windows NT was initially installed. To add files you must have your original NT floppy disks to hand, or have access to a network directory where the files are stored.

To add or remove NT files safely:

1   Click Options, Add/Remove Windows Components to see the Optional Windows Components dialog (see FIG. 14.6).

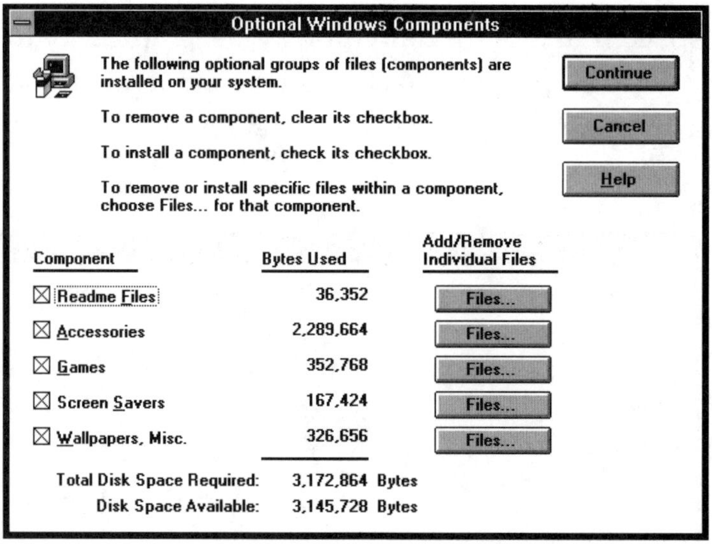

Optional Windows Components		
The following optional groups of files (components) are installed on your system.		**Continue**
To remove a component, clear its checkbox.		**Cancel**
To install a component, check its checkbox.		
To remove or install specific files within a component, choose Files... for that component.		**Help**

Component	Bytes Used	Add/Remove Individual Files
☒ Readme Files	36,352	Files...
☒ Accessories	2,289,664	Files...
☒ Games	352,768	Files...
☒ Screen Savers	167,424	Files...
☒ Wallpapers, Misc.	326,656	Files...

Total Disk Space Required: 3,172,864 Bytes
Disk Space Available: 3,145,728 Bytes

FIG. 14.6

2   In this dialog you turn off the Component check boxes to remove groups of files. To install groups of files turn on the relevant check boxes. The foot of the dialog shows how much disk space is required and how much is free. These two figures change to reflect whether you're removing and/or adding files.

3   Click Continue when you are happy with the proposed deletion/addition of groups of files.

Should you not want to add or delete whole groups of files you can choose files on an individual basis. You do so by clicking the Files button for a particular group in the Optional Windows Components dialog. For example, as part of a productivity drive you decide to remove the Games group but can't bear to live without Freecell. To get rid of Solitaire and Minesweeper only, click the Files button next to the Games entry. This opens the Customize Games dialog. In this dialog select the files to remove and click the Remove button followed by OK.

Removing user profiles

To set up and configure user accounts on a multi-user machine you use User Manager in the Administrative Tools group. Once an account has been created for a particular user then that user can configure Windows NT to look and work as required. For example, users can create personal groups in Program Manager and add applications to those groups. In addition, desktop and colour schemes can be customized. Or users might establish directory and printer connections across a network. All of these personalized details are held in a profile for each user. As a system administrator you may have cause to delete user profiles from time-to-time. This gives users the opportunity to build their working environments from scratch again – though they must still work with any common Program Manager groups that have been established. Not all users have the necessary permissions to delete user profiles and you can't delete the profile of the currently logged on user. To delete user profiles:

1   In the Windows NT Setup dialog click Options, Delete User Profiles.

2   In the subsequent Delete User Profiles dialog (see FIG. 14.7) select the user from the list and click Delete.

3   Repeat the previous step for any other profiles that you wish to remove and click OK to exit the dialog.

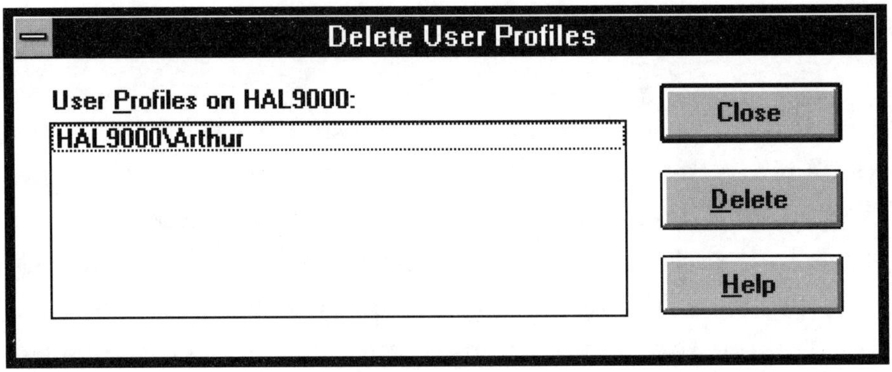

FIG. 14.7

Clipboard and ClipBook

CLIPBOARD AND CLIPBOOK

- How to save Clipboard data

- Sharing your ClipBook

- Connecting to remote ClipBooks

Clipboard and ClipBook

Windows for DOS users will be familiar with the Clipboard but not with ClipBook, although Windows for Workgroups users may have already come across the ClipBook Viewer. To start Clipboard and ClipBook, double click the ClipBook Viewer icon in the Main group. The ClipBook Viewer window (see FIG. 15.1) contains two child windows or icons. One of these will be the normal Clipboard. The second window or icon will be your local ClipBook. In addition, your ClipBook Viewer window can contain further windows or icons, each one representing a connection you've made across the network to a remote ClipBook belonging to another user. Perhaps a word or two of explanation is required concerning the Clipboard and local and remote ClipBooks.

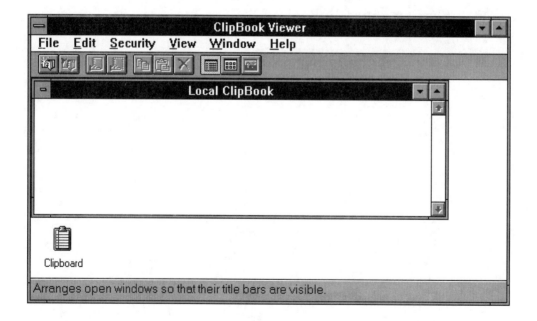

FIG. 15.1

Clipboard and ClipBook

When you select text or graphics in an application and click Edit, Copy (or Edit, Cut) you copy (or move) the selected object to the Windows Clipboard. The Clipboard is a temporary storage area – normally the data you placed on the Clipboard is lost when you place more data on the Clipboard or log off. Before the data is lost you can use Edit, Paste to place it back into any application that supports the Clipboard. Or you might want to save the data from the Clipboard before it is lost. You can save the Clipboard data in one of two ways. First, you can use File, Save As from Clipboard. This saves the contents of Clipboard to a CLP format file which can be reopened (File, Open) to retrieve the contents to the Clipboard at any time. Second, you can copy data from your Clipboard to your local ClipBook. The ClipBook is like a scrapbook where you store one or more items of text and graphics from the Clipboard. It differs from the Clipboard in that the data is held permanently until you explicitly delete it. It also differs as you can store multiple items of text or graphics in ClipBook – generally, Clipboard can only contain one item at a time. To create items (called pages) in ClipBook you paste from Clipboard. To retrieve ClipBook pages into Clipboard you copy the page back. You can also share your ClipBook pages with other users in a workgroup or network domain. And if other users have set up their ClipBook pages for sharing, you can connect to them and copy the data into your local Clipboard. From there you can paste directly into your own applications.

If you do connect to another user's ClipBook you end up with three windows or icons within ClipBook Viewer. You move around these windows or icons by going through the Window menu or pressing **Ctrl-F6**. If a window is visible you simply click on it to bring it to the foreground. Indeed, if you're already versed in File Manager or Print

Manager (or any other MDI application) you'll be right at home in ClipBook Viewer.

The following sections present a few of the tasks you can carry out in ClipBook Viewer. After that there's a brief look at the ClipBook Viewer toolbar which provides quick alternatives to commonly-used menu bar options.

Creating a page in a local ClipBook

Before you create a ClipBook page you must first have some data on the Clipboard. This normally done by using Edit, Copy or Edit, Cut in an application. However, some applications present a variety of methods – you may be able to transfer data to the Clipboard under DDE (dynamic data exchange) control or with the macro or programming language of the application.

Once the required data is on the Clipboard you click Edit, Paste (that's Edit, Paste in ClipBook Viewer and not in your application). This opens the Paste dialog (see FIG. 15.2) where you enter a name for the page and enable immediate sharing if you wish.

Sharing a local ClipBook page

You can either share a page as it's created (see the previous discussion on creating pages) or do so later. To share a page in retrospect first select the page in the ClipBook and click File, Share. This opens the Share ClipBook Page dialog (see FIG. 15.3). Click OK in this dialog to begin sharing. To set permissions on the shared page click the Permissions button. If you think

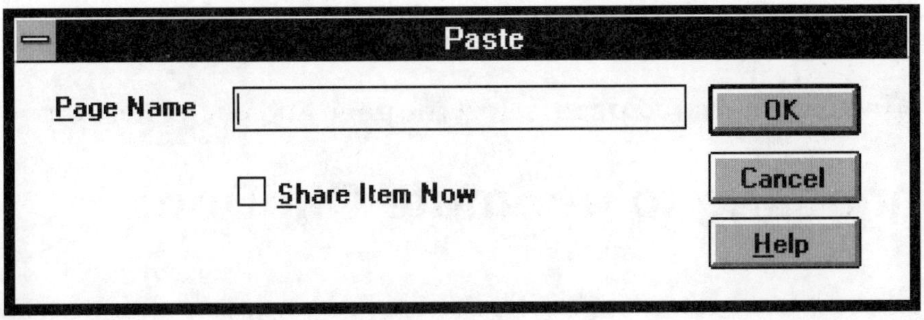

Clipboard and ClipBook

FIG. 15.2

the page is going to be used for object linking (as opposed to object embedding or a basic 'cold' paste) turn on the check box for Start Application on Connect. This means the server starts up when a remote user connects to your shared page – if it doesn't they won't be able to set

FIG. 15.3

up a link. You can also use the Run Minimized check box in conjunction with the Start Application on Connect one.

To stop sharing a shared page, select the page and click File, Stop Sharing.

Connecting to a remote ClipBook

You can use a remote user's ClipBook pages to copy data to your own local Clipboard. From there you can save it to your own local ClipBook, save it as a CLP file, or paste into one of your Windows applications. Depending upon the nature of the data this results in either a 'cold' paste or an embedded or linked object. To see a remote ClipBook in your ClipBook viewer you must first connect to the remote computer – and the remote user must have at least one shared ClipBook page.

To establish a remote connection click File, Connect. In the subsequent Select Computer dialog (see FIG. 15.4) select a remote computer and click OK. This opens the remote ClipBook in your local ClipBook Viewer. From there you can manipulate it just as you would your own ClipBook.

To end a remote connection select the remote ClipBook and click File, Disconnect.

Copying a page to the Clipboard

Select a page in the ClipBook window and click Edit, Copy.

Clipboard and ClipBook

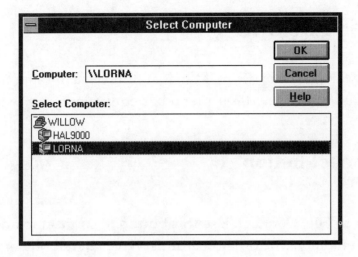

FIG. 15.4

Viewing a ClipBook page

You can view the pages in your ClipBook (or a remote one to which you're connected) in one of three ways. To see a list of all the pages click View, Table of Contents. To see a miniature representation of the data on each page click View, Thumbnails. Finally, to view an individual page in full (as it would appear on the Clipboard), select the page and click View, Full Page.

Setting security for a ClipBook page

You use the Security menu to determine security for your ClipBook pages. Through this menu you can set permissions, specify your auditing policy, and take ownership of another's page. There's a full discussion of permissions, auditing, and ownership in Chapter 9 on *File Manager*.

Toolbar buttons

Like File Manager and Print Manager there's a toolbar in ClipBook Viewer. The buttons and their menu bar equivalents are listed next.

 ### Connect button

Equivalent to File, Connect. Use this button to connect to another user's ClipBook remotely. The other user must have shared one or more pages before you can establish a connection.

 ### Disconnect button

Equivalent to File, Disconnect. You can disconnect from a remote ClipBook with this button.

 ### Share button

Equivalent to File, Share. You must share a ClipBook page before remote user's can make a connection. Select a page in ClipBook and click this button to make the page sharable.

Clipboard and ClipBook

 Stop Sharing button

Equivalent to File, Stop Sharing. Use this button to remove all sharing from a selected page. Any remote users connected to the page will lose their connection.

 Copy button

Equivalent to Edit, Copy. This button copies the contents of the currently selected ClipBook page to the Clipboard. From there it can be pasted into an application.

 Paste button

Equivalent to Edit, Paste. This button pastes the current contents of the Clipboard into a ClipBook page. You are prompted for a page name and are given the option of making the new page sharable immediately. If you decline to do so you can make the page sharable at any time in the future.

 Delete button

Equivalent to Edit, Delete. This button serves two functions. If you make the Clipboard window active it clears the contents of the Clipboard – this can be handy if there's a lot of data on the Clipboard and memory is extremely tight. If the local ClipBook window is active then it removes the currently selected page. Unless the data is also on the Clipboard or saved as a CLP file you lose the data for good – although you might be able to copy it from an application or from a remote ClipBook page.

Table of Contents button

Equivalent to View, Table of Contents. This shows a list of all the pages in the current ClipBook window (whether local or remote). The alternatives to table of contents view are thumbnails or full-page view.

Thumbnails button

Equivalent to View, Thumbnails. This shows the contents of ClipBook pages as a collection of small pages (thumbnails).

Full Page button

Equivalent to View, Full Page. This shows the full contents of the currently selected page or thumbnail in the ClipBook window.

CHAPTER 16

OLE

OLE (OBJECT LINKING AND EMBEDDING)

■ How to embed objects

■ How to link objects

■ Maintaining links

Many Windows NT and Windows for DOS applications support OLE. In addition, some of the NT accessories can function as OLE servers or clients. For example, Paintbrush is a server and Write is a client. But first a little background for those readers to whom OLE is a new concept.

The traditional way of transferring data between Windows applications is to use a 'cold' Clipboard. Let's take the example of copying a graphic from Paintbrush and inserting it into Write under Windows for DOS version 3.0. The initial step is to select part (or all) of the graphic in Paintbrush and click Edit, Copy (or Cut if you're moving rather than copying). This action places the selected graphic onto the Clipboard. You then switch to Write and click Edit, Paste – the graphic appears in your Write document. Once you've done that there is no longer any relationship between the pasted graphic and the original graphic (or indeed any relationship between the pasted graphic and its parent application, Paintbrush). You can demonstrate that no relationship exists by editing the original graphic in Paintbrush – doing so has absolutely no effect on the copy in Write. Nor can you select the copy in Write and edit it from there. In such a situation you are forced to Edit, Copy and Edit, Paste the graphic all over again. This is a real chore when the pasted data is complex and/or the pasted data appears in more than one destination.

Windows for DOS 3.1 introduced OLE and for the first time Windows kept the relationships intact. Embedding an object kept the relationship to the parent application (the server) – thus you could edit the object starting from Write even if the original had long since been deleted. Linking an object went even further as the relationship with the original data was preserved. This meant that changes to either the copy or the original were reflected in the other. If you had copies in multiple destinations these were updated too – and ensured data integrity. To return to the Paintbrush and Write example, when you embed the graphic in Write it remembers its relationship to Paintbrush, but not to the original data which may not have even been saved. If the original were saved and you edited it, this would have no effect on the Write copy. Indeed the original may no longer exist – it might not have been saved in the first place or it may have been deleted in the meantime. However, you can still edit the copy in Write. With OLE version 1, editing the copy automatically starts Paintbrush. You make your changes there and exit – the copy back in Write is updated to reflect your editing. Instead of embedding you may choose to link the graphic. In this case the graphic must be saved as a separate Paintbrush file. And this time the copied graphic remembers not just its parent application but the original file from which it came. Thus, like an embedded object you can edit the object starting from Write. But unlike an embedded object changes to the copy are reflected in automatic changes to the original data. This works in the opposite direction too – changes to the original graphic in Paintbrush result in corresponding changes to the Write copy. If there are other copies in other documents and applications then these too are updated. Linking an object is therefore extremely valuable when it's vital that all occurrences of the data remain identical. Windows for Workgroups extended, and Windows NT consolidates, the OLE concept by allowing you to embed and link objects across a workgroup or network. You use shared ClipBook pages to do this and it means a team of people can work on the same data, safe in the knowledge (assuming the objects are linked) that they are all using the latest version of the data.

You can embed or link an object directly if the source application is an OLE server and the destination application an OLE client. In some circumstances you can use File Manager to drag and drop embedded or linked objects. Or you can wrap objects up in bundles first with Object Packager (PACKAGER.EXE). All I want to do here is to show in general terms (the exact procedures may vary from application to application) how to embed and link directly on a stand-alone machine and across a workgroup or network.

To embed an object from within the client:

1   Click Edit, Insert Object. This opens the Insert Object dialog (see FIG. 16.1).

2   Select an object from the list presented and click OK.

3   The previous step starts up the server application associated with the object chosen. Create the object in the server.

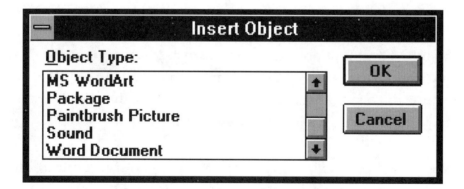

FIG. 16.1

4   Click File, Exit & Return (or a similar command) in the server. The server closes and an embedded object appears in Write.

Instead of starting from the client you may prefer to embed an object by starting from the server application, especially if it's already running:

1   Create the data in the server and select it.

2   Click Edit, Copy.

3   Switch to the client application and click Edit, Paste. This action, of course, is identical to normal clipboarding except that if used between an OLE server and client it creates an embedded object instead of a 'cold' copy.

You can also embed an object created on another computer:

1   Ask another user to create some data in a server application.

2   They must then use Edit, Copy to place the data on their Clipboard.

3   From their ClipBook Viewer ask them to click Edit, Paste to create a page in ClipBook.

4   They must then click File, Share in ClipBook Viewer to share the page.

5   From your computer open ClipBook Viewer and click File, Connect to connect to the remote page containing the data.

6   Click Edit, Copy to copy the data from the remote ClipBook page to the Clipboard.

7   In your client application click Edit, Paste.

To edit most embedded objects simply double click them. However, double clicking some objects such as sound or video clips causes them to play. With those types of objects you should select them then click Edit, Edit Object.

Now to consider object linking. This differs slightly from embedding in that the server data must be saved in a file and you start from the server:

1   In the server application create and save your data.

2   Copy selected data to the Clipboard with Edit, Copy.

3   In the client application click Edit, Paste Link (not simply Edit, Paste as that would create an embedded object). Some applications may not have Edit, Paste Link and you must use Edit, Paste Special followed by a Paste Link button.

You can also link data across a workgroup or network. The procedure for linking workgroup data is the same as for embedding, except you use Edit, Paste Link rather than Edit, Paste in the client application. The nice thing about linking to data on another computer is that any changes to the original object are reflected in your local object. When you edit a linked document you must save the changes to the source data – for embedded objects this is not necessary.

Once you have a linked object you can leave it in automatic update mode (the default) or you can set the update mode to manual. If you do the latter you must remember to update the object for yourself periodically. To switch between automatic and manual update mode, or to force a manual update, you go through the Edit, Links in the client application. The Links dialog (see FIG. 16.2) also allows you to change the link information – this is essential if the file containing the original data gets renamed or moved to a new location.

Readers with experience of DDE (dynamic data exchange) will be interested to learn that Windows NT supports this too. You can even establish DDE links across a workgroup or network. As DDE can often involve some knowledge of programming and macros in Windows

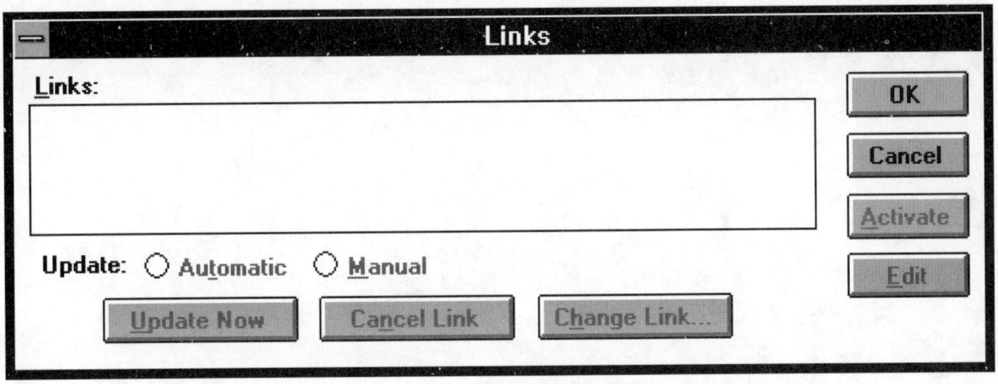

FIG. 16.2

applications it's outside the scope of this book. You are referred to the documentation that accompanies your Windows applications – but by no means all Windows applications support DDE.

Workgroup applications

WORKGROUP APPLICATIONS

- How to use Chat

- Creating a postoffice

- Working with Mail

- Working with Schedule+

Workgroup applications

In the course of this book we've seen various ways of linking computers together in a workgroup or network domain. These include using File Manager to share and connect to directories, Print Manager to share and connect to printers, and ClipBook Viewer to share and connect to ClipBook pages and OLE objects. However, there are yet more ways of linking to other machines and these involve a direct communication with other users. The applications that provide these capabilities are Chat, Mail, and Schedule+. Each of these three applications serves a different purpose and Schedule+ is very useful even on a stand-alone machine. If you've used Windows for Workgroups then all three applications are immediately recognisable, indeed the NT versions are almost identical to the Windows for Workgroups ones. Let's see what each one does.

Chat is best compared to a telephone conversation without any answer phone features for recording messages. In other words, Chat is totally interactive. Mail, on the other hand, is not interactive. Messages can be stored and read and replied to at a convenient time. You can even use it offline on, say, a portable computer. Mail is an email system and is similar to a postal service or a fax service. Schedule+ lets you plan and arrange your time. When used across a workgroup it enables users to coordinate meetings when everyone's free. Schedule+ is a bit like a personal organizer only some of the features are automated. For example, you can have it enter recurring meetings for you or to automatically arrange a meeting with other users – it can work out when everyone's free by comparing each user's Schedule+ planner.

Workgroup applications

Chat

Chat is the simplest of the three applications to use. There are three basic actions involved; dialling another user, answering a call, and hanging up. When you dial another user there's no need for them to have Chat running – it opens itself so they can answer your call. Nor is there a requirement to have shared and connected directories. As long as both users are on a workgroup or network domain all you have to do is start Chat and dial. To initiate a conversation:

1   Start Chat (see FIG. 17.1) from your Accessories group in Program Manager.

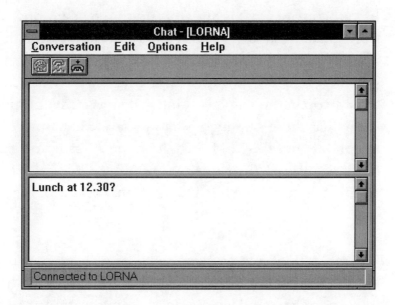

FIG. 17.1

2 Click Conversation, Dial or use the Dial button on the Chat toolbar.

3 The previous step opens the Select Computer dialog. In this dialog select the computer name of the colleague you wish to dial and click OK.

4 As soon as the other person answers you can begin typing a message. Any response is shown immediately in one half of your Chat window. You can now continue to converse at any time until either party hangs up.

To answer an incoming call:

- If your copy of Chat is already running in a window then click Conversation, Answer or use the Answer button on the toolbar. If you've a sound card you can hear that someone's dialling. If not look for the flashing Chat title bar. When Chat is not already open then an incoming call starts Chat minimized. To show that there's an incoming message the handset on Chat's telephone vibrates, and the telephone rings if you've a sound card. To answer the call simply double click the Chat icon to restore it – there's no need to use Conversation, Answer in this case.

To initiate or reply to a conversation on-screen just type in the Chat window. Your colleague's replies are shown in a separate half of the window. You can hang up and terminate the conversation at any time. To hang up:

Workgroup applications

- Click Conversation, Hang Up or click the Hang Up button on the toolbar.

And that's about all there is to Chat, although you can use the Options menu bar item to customize the Chat window. Hopefully the Option menu is self-explanatory. Chat is a handy tool but does not offer the functionality of a full email system. For this you have to turn to Mail.

Mail

Mail (see FIG. 17.2) has the advantage over Chat in that you can send messages even when the recipient is not at a computer. You can store and

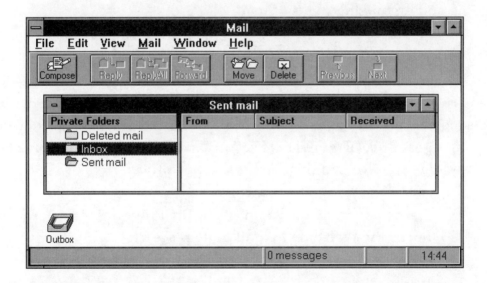

FIG. 17.2

search for messages, forward messages, share messages, and attach files to messages. In addition, you can embed packages in Mail.

But before anyone can even begin to send and read messages you must set up a postoffice. The first step is to appoint someone in the workgroup as a postoffice manager. The second step is to build the postoffice, typically in a directory on the postoffice manager's machine. The third step is for the postoffice manager to create accounts for each user in the postoffice, although users can also create their accounts instead. The postoffice must reside in a shared directory and the computer must be running before other users can use the email system, unless they specifically decide to work offline. However, working offline means the user can only compose but not send mail. Nor can the user receive or read mail until they are online. The postoffice holds all Mail user accounts and any shared folders. Private folders are stored on users' own machines. Folders are for holding and organizing items of mail.

Building a postoffice

If you're an end user who merely wishes to send and receive mail and someone else already runs the postoffice you can skip this section on creating a postoffice. If you plan to set up a mail system (or are interested anyway) you should read this. To build a postoffice:

1   Start Mail from the Main group in Program Manager. This opens the Welcome to Mail dialog (see FIG. 17.3).

2   In the dialog turn on the option button for Create a new Workgroup Postoffice and click OK. In the next dialog click Yes

Workgroup applications

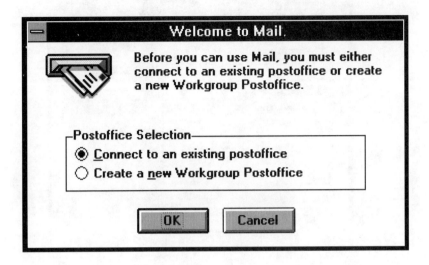

FIG. 17.3

to continue setting up the postoffice. The subsequent dialog is entitled Create Workgroup Postoffice (see FIG. 17.4).

3   In the Create Workgroup Postoffice dialog select a local hard disk and directory in which to create a WGPO subdirectory. The WGPO (Workgroup Postoffice) directory will hold the postoffice. If you want to place the postoffice on a remote network drive click the Network button instead. Click OK when you've specified a location for the postoffice.

4   You are then asked to create the first account in the postoffice, for yourself as postoffice manager. You do all of this in the Administrator Account Details dialog (see FIG. 17.5). The Name, Mailbox, and Password boxes are obligatory. The other boxes are self-explanatory and you can leave them blank if you

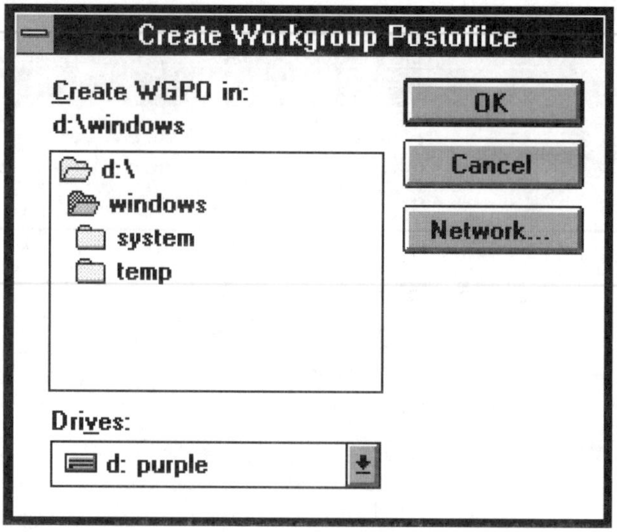

FIG. 17.4

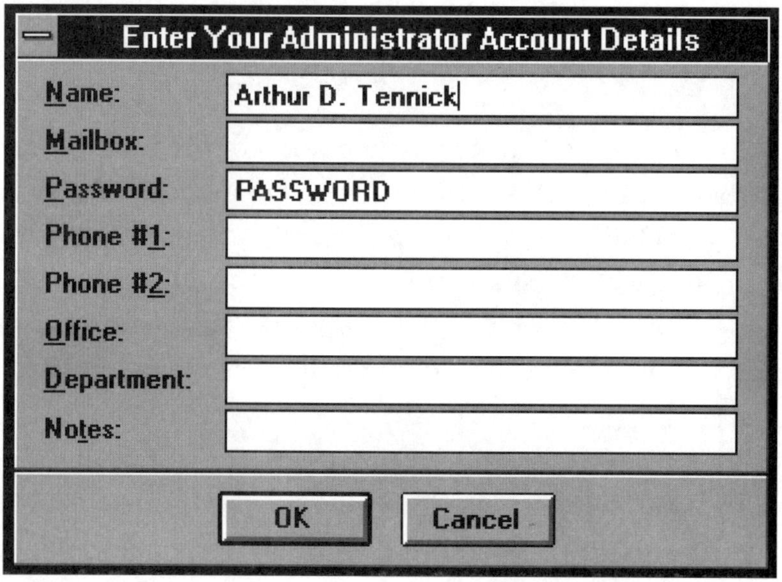

FIG. 17.5

Workgroup applications

wish. The Name box takes a maximum of thirty characters – you can leave it as your username if you want. The Mailbox text box is where you enter the name of your mailbox. This is the name used when signing in to Mail. This must be a unique name in your postoffice and can be no more than ten characters. Typically, you might use a shortened version of your username. In the Password box enter a password of no more than eight characters. Click OK when you've completed the dialog.

5   A final dialog reminds you that the postoffice directory must be shared. If it's not, other users won't be able to connect to the postoffice – they'll be forced to work offline.

After creating the postoffice and your own manager's account you must ensure that the postoffice directory is shared. You should also give full access permissions to other users. As a reminder, you share directories in File Manager through Disk, Share As.

You can easily tell if you're logged on as the postoffice manager. If you open the Mail menu in Mail the final item is Postoffice Manager. This menu option is not available to ordinary users of the postoffice.

The final step in setting up a postoffice is to notify other users that they can start Mail and create their own user accounts with the postoffice. If you prefer, you can set up accounts for other users so they can begin to send and receive email straight away. Setting up user accounts is one of your potential roles as manager. Some of the other functions you might carry out include editing existing user accounts, deleting user accounts, changing users' passwords, and checking on the disk space occupied by shared folders. Let's look at some of these management tasks in a little more detail. Incidentally, you don't have to be at the postoffice machine – you can manage the postoffice from any computer that's connected to the shared postoffice directory provided you make certain changes to the MSMAIL32.INI file. Full instructions on how to do this are in your Windows NT documentation.

Managing a postoffice

You need only read this section if you have (or plan to have) responsibility for managing a postoffice. Of course, even if you're not an actual or potential postoffice manager this section may be of interest.

Managing users

Managing users includes creating, modifying, and deleting user accounts. To carry out any of these actions click Mail, Postoffice Manager. This opens the Postoffice Manager dialog (see FIG. 17.6). This dialog lists all the current users of the postoffice. To add a new user click the Add User button. This action opens the Add User dialog (see FIG. 17.7). This dialog is identical to the Administrator Account Details dialog mentioned earlier. You fill in the relevant details for each new user – or you can let users create their own accounts when they first sign in to Mail. The Details button opens the same dialog but this time it contains the details already filled in for the selected user. One use of this is to alter user passwords – this is handy if users forget their passwords. Note that if you forget the postoffice manager password you must recreate the postoffice – keep your password in a secure place. The Remove User button is for deleting the account of the currently selected user.

Workgroup applications

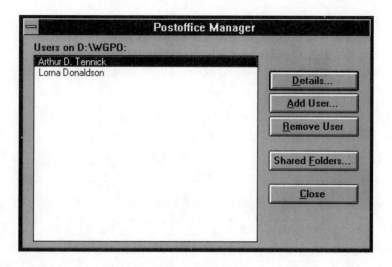

FIG. 17.6

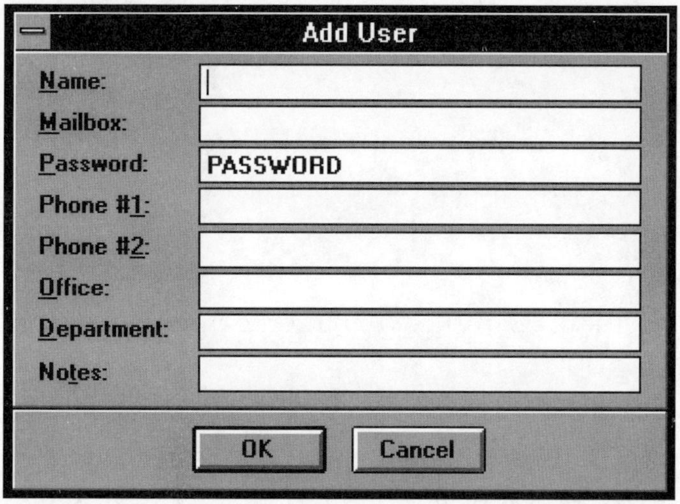

FIG. 17.7

Managing shared folders

When postoffice users choose to save their sent and received mail they can do so in private or shared folders. Private folders are held on the user's workstation whereas shared folders are stored in the postoffice directory, typically on the postoffice manager's hard disk (or possibly a network drive). The user who sets up a shared folder can then allow users to browse the mail in the folder. However, a large number of shared folders containing many items of mail can quickly take up a lot of disk space. In the first place you can check on the amount of disk space occupied by shared folders. When you do this you can find out how much disk space can be reclaimed by compressing the folders. If this is not sufficient you may have to arrange to delete some of the folders. As a last resort you could move the postoffice to another disk with more disk space. Full instructions on moving a postoffice are given in your Windows NT documentation.

Compressing shared folders

Before you attempt to compress shared folders and to reclaim disk space you must ensure that no other users are using them. To begin the compression process:

1   Click Mail, Postoffice Manager to open the Postoffice Manager dialog.

2   In this dialog click the Shared Folders button to see the Shared Folders dialog (see FIG. 17.8).

Workgroup applications

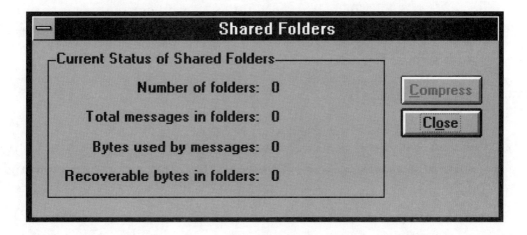

FIG. 17.8

3 This second dialog shows the total number of shared folders on your disk and the total number of messages they contain. It also shows how much disk space is currently being occupied and how much can be reclaimed. Click the Compress button to carry out the reclamation. Click the Close button when the compression is finished.

Deleting shared folders

You can only remove shared folders if the creator has given delete permissions. If not, the creator will have to delete them. Anyone with the necessary permissions can also delete messages from within folders. The permissions are set up when the folder is first created. To delete a folder you first select it in the Mail window and press **Delete**. To see the folders in the first place click View, Shared Folders. To revert back to viewing private folders click View, Private Folders. To delete messages within shared or private folders you select the message rather than the folder before pressing **Delete**.

Working with Mail

This section assumes that a postoffice already exists within your workgroup or network domain. It concentrates upon signing in, creating an account, and sending and reading mail.

Signing in for the first time

When users start Mail for the very first time they see the Welcome to Mail dialog. Assuming someone has already created a postoffice in your workgroup then you select the option button for connecting to an existing postoffice. This opens another dialog where you select the computer and shared directory on that computer which contains the postoffice. You are asked if you already have an account at the postoffice. It's possible that the postoffice manager has already created an account for you. In that case answer yes and you'll be asked for your postoffice password and you're admitted to Mail. If there is no existing account you must reply in the negative and the Enter Your Account Details dialog appears. Here you must specify your name, mailbox name, and password. You can add other details if you wish. Clicking OK in this dialog admits you to Mail.

Workgroup applications

Signing in on subsequent occasions

Once you've made the initial connection to a postoffice, and have a valid account, you need only enter your mailbox name and password (see FIG. 17.9).

Signing in automatically

If you're not too worried about security you can sign in to Mail automatically when you double click the Mail icon. To do so append your mailbox name and password to the Command Line (MSMAIL32.EXE) in the Program Item Properties dialog in Program Manager.

Signing out

There are two ways of quitting Mail. If you click File, Exit you close Mail but do not actually sign out. This is handy if you're also running Schedule+

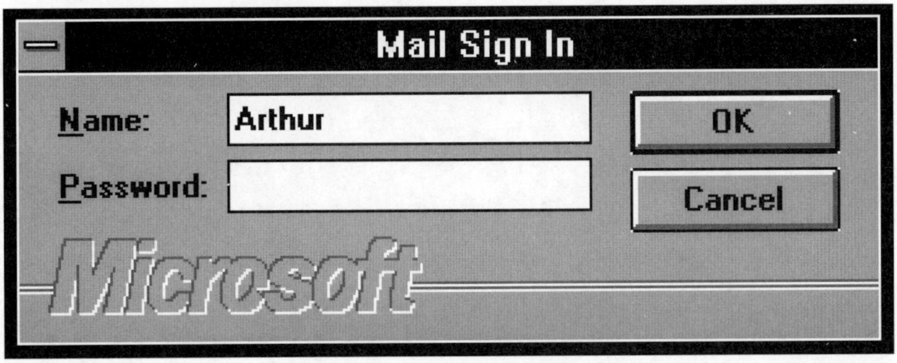

FIG. 17.9

which needs to access the postoffice as well. To sign out of Mail you click File, Exit and Sign Out. This has the effect of also closing Schedule+ if it's running.

Sending a message

Before you send a message you address it and type in the text of the message. In addition, you may want to attach a file (for example, a spreadsheet) to the message. This section takes you through the steps involved in addressing a message, entering the text of the message, and actually sending it. To prepare and send a message:

1   Click Mail, Compose Note. This opens the Send Note window (see FIG. 17.10). Notice there is a toolbar alternative to this and other menu items.

2   In the Send Note window you must enter an addressee in the To box. You can type this manually and have Mail check it's a bona fide addressee (that is someone with an account at the postoffice) by clicking the Check Names button. But a much quicker way is to click the Address button and select an addressee from the list presented (see FIG. 17.11). Click the To button followed by OK to insert the addressee in the To box back in the Send Note window. An underlined entry means it's for a valid addressee.

3   Repeat the previous step if you wish to insert an entry in the Cc box.

Workgroup applications

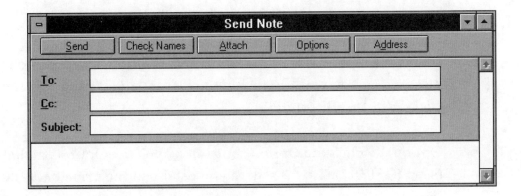

FIG. 17.10

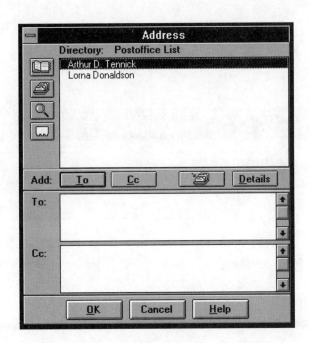

FIG. 17.11

4   Type a subject in the Subject box.

5   Click in the main area of the Send Note window and type your message. If you want to include text from an existing text file click Edit, Insert from File.

6   Optionally click the Options button to open the Options dialog (see FIG. 17.12). This is where you establish the priority of the message and ask for a receipt. Click OK to save your choices or Cancel to back out.

7   Click the Send button to actually send the message.

The message is listed in your Outbox until the message is processed by the Mail system. If the Save sent messages check box in the Options dialog

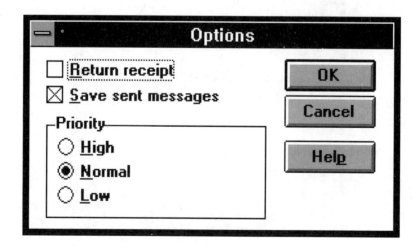

FIG. 17.12

Workgroup applications

was turned on, the message is then transferred to the Sent mail folder. Later you might want to move it from the Sent mail folder to your Deleted one.

Reading a received message

When another user sends you a message it appears in your Inbox folder. To read a message simply double click it to open the Read Note window (see FIG. 17.13). This window has a header section that provides full details of the sender, date, recipients, and subject. The main area of the window shows the message in full. Any attached files are represented by icons.

Replying to a message

After reading a message you may want to reply to it. There are two ways of responding to a received message. One, you can compose a brand new

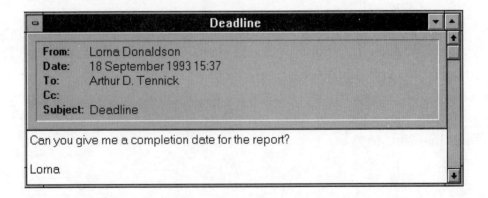

FIG. 17.13

message and send it. Two, you can reply using the received message as a basis. The second method has the advantage of automatically addressing the message to the original sender. It also reproduces the original message in the message area. You can add your reply above or below the original message or both. The original subject is also inserted in the subject box with an RE: prefix. To reply to a received message in this way:

1   Select the received message in your Inbox folder.

2   Click Mail, Reply to reply to the sender. Alternatively, you can click Mail, Reply to All to reply to the sender and also send a copy to all original recipients of the message.

3   In the Send Note window add your comments above and/or below the original message.

4   Click the Send button to reply.

Forwarding a message

There may be occasions when you wish to send a received message to a third party. You do this by selecting the message in your Inbox folder and clicking Mail, Forward. This opens a Send Note window where you address the message normally. You'll notice how the message text is already inserted for you.

Workgroup applications

Attaching a file to a message

From time-to-time you might consider sending a file to another user. One way of accomplishing this is to attach the file to a Mail message. You could also use File Manager but then you'd need to connect to a shared directory and you wouldn't be able to include an explanatory message.

To send a file from within Mail you click the Attach button in the Send Note window. This opens the Attach dialog (see FIG. 17.14) which is where you choose a file to attach. The recipient can see the attached file as an icon in the received message. They can also see which messages have files attached in their folders – an attachment is indicated by a paper clip icon. To save the attachment as a separate file the recipient clicks File, Save Attachment. Instead of using the Attach button to attach a file you can simply drag the file from File Manager into the message.

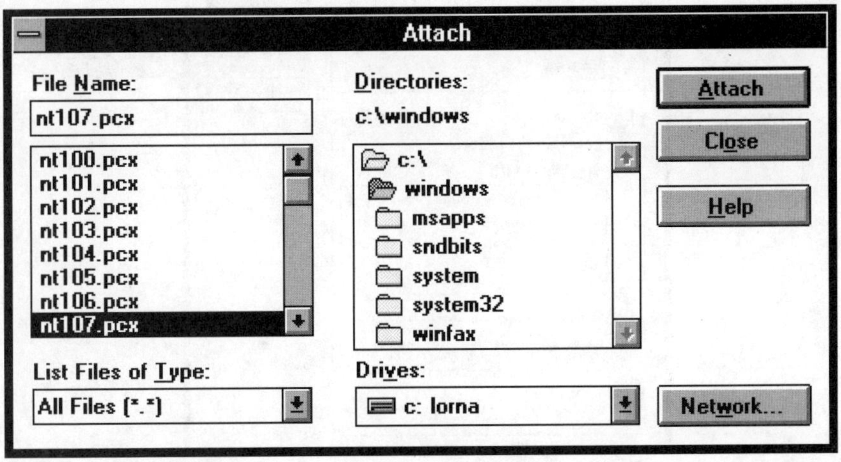

FIG. 17.14

New folders

To help you organize both your sent and received messages you can place them in folders. To do so drag the messages from the Inbox or Sent mail folders into your personalized ones. These can be either private or shared folders. A private folder is kept on your local hard disk while a shared folder is held in the postoffice directory on your mail server. Shared folders can be seen by other postoffice users. And depending upon the permissions you set other users can read and delete your messages in shared folders. If you grant write privileges to other users then they can add messages to the shared folder. This is useful if you wish to build a collection of related topics for future reference. To create a new folder:

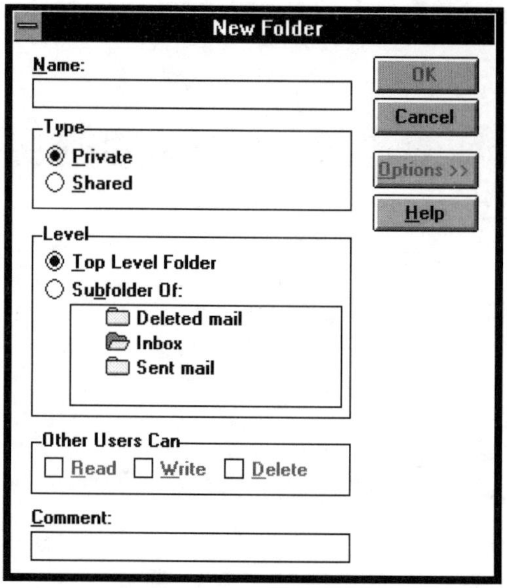

FIG. 17.15

Workgroup applications

1   Click File, New Folder to open the New Folder dialog (see FIG. 17.15).

2   In this dialog enter a name for the new folder and select the appropriate option button for a private or a shared folder.

3   In the Level section of the dialog you decide how the folder is to fit into the existing folder structure. A folder structure is identical to a directory structure. If you can't see the Level section click the Options button to expand the New Folder dialog.

4   In the Other Users Can section you set the permissions for other postoffice users. Click OK when you're finished.

You can alter the permissions on one of your own shared folders by first selecting the folder and then clicking File, Folder Properties.

Options

Clicking Mail, Options opens an Options dialog (see FIG. 17.16). You can set various parameters here that control how Mail works. Most of the options are self-explanatory. The Add recipients to Personal Address Book check box is for automatically appending recipients which you select from all the postoffice users into your own personalized address book. You can use this address book to quickly insert an addressee when sending mail. This saves you from finding the addressee in a sometimes lengthy list of all postoffice users. When you've read received messages in your Inbox folder you might want to file them in special private or

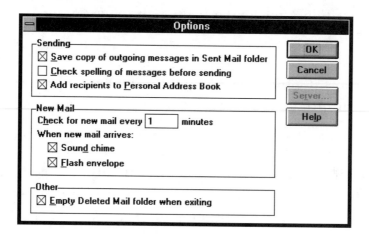

FIG. 17.16

shared folders. If the message is not important you can drag it into the Deleted mail folder. When you exit Mail you can have the Deleted mail folder purged by turning on the Empty Deleted Mail folder when exiting check box.

Personal address book and groups

When you send email and click the Address button in the Send Note window you are first presented with a list of all users with accounts at the postoffice. This is called the Postoffice List. The disadvantage of this list is that it includes all users who have accounts at the postoffice – you may have to find your addressee in a list containing many names, some of which you never send mail to. You can extract just those names that interest you and add them to your own Personal Address Book. Then in the Address dialog (accessed by clicking the Address button in the Send

Workgroup applications

Note window) you can switch to your own personalized list for convenience. In addition, you can place groups in the list. This means that if you choose a group for the To box the message is automatically sent to all members of the group.

There are at least three ways to add a name to your Personal Address Book. One, you turn on the Add recipients to Personal Address Book check box in the Options dialog (through Mail, Options). This is on by default and results in a Personal Address Book being constructed from the recipients you choose from the Postoffice List. Over a period of time the Personal Address Book becomes filled with only those names that you send mail to. As it becomes full you'll find it easier to use the Personal Address Book rather than the Postoffice List. The second method is to click the Add Names button in the Address dialog (see FIG. 17.17). This is the button to the left of the Details button and it adds the currently selected user in the Postoffice List to your Personal Address Book. The third method involves clicking the New Address button – this is the lowest button in the group of four buttons at the top of the Address dialog.

You can also add names when the Send Note dialog is not showing. You go through Mail, Address Book. To create groups in your Personal Address Book go through Mail, Personal Groups. You can then name a group and add users to it. Once a group's established its name appears in your Personal Address Book and you can click it to place in the To box. This means the message is sent to all users in the group – this saves having to submit the message repeatedly to the individual members of a target group.

FIG. 17.17

To switch between the Postoffice List and your Personal Address Book in the Address dialog click the Directory button (the one at the top). To show just the Personal Address Book click the Personal Address Book button (second from the top). The third button is the Find button and helps you to locate a particular user in a long list of names.

Finding messages

As you use the Mail system it's likely that you collect hundreds of messages on a large and busy workgroup. You can quickly find a stored message by clicking File, Message Finder and filling in the search criteria in the Message Finder dialog (see FIG. 17.18).

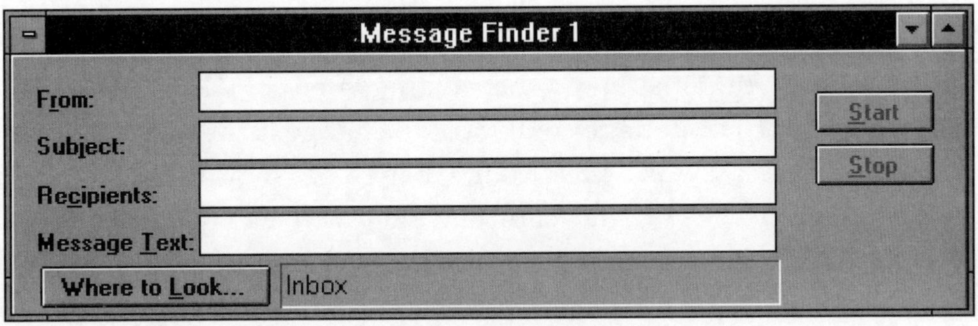

Workgroup applications

FIG. 17.18

Message templates

If you often send a message where only a few details change each time, you can store a template for the message. This is also helpful if you regularly send the message to many users – the template can store the addressees as well as the message text. To create a template double click the Send Note's Control menu without clicking the Send button. Answer yes when asked to save the message.

To use the template drag it to your Outbox if you want to send it 'as is'. If you want to add to or amend the template text select the message and click Mail, Forward.

Changing a password

You can change your mail password at any time. However, to change your password you must know the existing version. If you've forgotten it then the postoffice manager will have to change it for you (see above). To change your password click Mail, Change Password. Enter your old password (see FIG. 17.19) and your new one. You also need to verify the new password. The next time you sign in to Mail you'll need to use the new password.

Messages to text files

From time-to-time you may receive a message containing text you wish to work on in a word processor. You can export the received message to a text file and then import the text file version into your word processor. To convert a message to text click File, Save As. Of course, if there's only a small amount of text you might find Edit, Copy (or Edit, Select All) and Edit, Paste easier. Mail also allows you to use an existing text file in your message text – use Edit, Insert from File to do this.

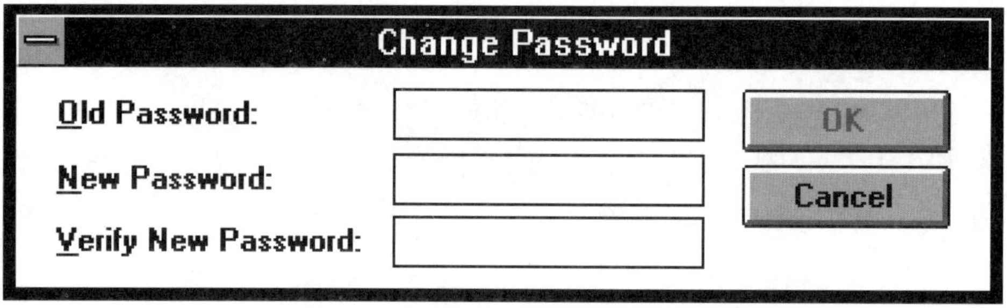

Change Password		
Old Password:		OK
New Password:		Cancel
Verify New Password:		

FIG. 17.19

Workgroup applications

Instead of transferring individual messages as text files you can export whole mail folders in Mail format. Later you can import these folders back into Mail. Use File, Export Folder and File, Import Folder to carry out these actions. Exporting a mail folder is a way of backing up your messages. You can also perform a more comprehensive backup by clicking Mail, Backup. You'll need a full backup on your portable if you want to work with Mail offline while away from the office.

Schedule+

Schedule+ (see FIG. 17.20) is a personal organizer that allows you to record appointments, tasks, and schedule meetings with other users. It replaces and surpasses Calendar which may be familiar to users of Windows for DOS and Windows for Workgroups. When you use

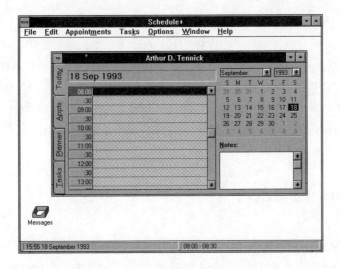

FIG. 17.20

Schedule+ you use the mailbox name and password that you set up in Mail. As a result if Mail is already running you're not prompted to sign in. You can also set reminders in Schedule+. However, to have the reminders work you don't need to keep Schedule+ running, but you must not sign out. You can quit Schedule+ by clicking File, Exit. This keeps your reminders functional and leaves Mail running if it's already open. On the other hand, clicking File, Exit and Sign Out also closes Mail (if it's open) and suppresses your reminders. The reminders become active again the next time you open Schedule+.

When you first open Schedule+ it displays your Appointments Book for today's date. You can change the day by using the month and year drop-down lists or by clicking in the calendar display. To return quickly to today simply click the Today tab at the left of the organizer. To redisplay the Appointments Book click the Appts tab. You can enter notes for the current day by typing in the Notes box.

The Appointments Book is where you record definite and tentative appointments. The Task list (click the Tasks tab) is for entering things-to-do, assigning priorities and organizing projects. The Planner (click the Planner tab) helps you to schedule meetings with other users when everyone is free. Let's look at the Appointments Book, Task list, and Planner in more detail.

Appointments Book

You use the Appointments Book to enter appointments. These appointments can be definite, tentative, or recurring. In addition, you can set reminders for appointments. Definite appointments appear as busy

Workgroup applications

slots when others view your schedule to try and arrange meetings – tentative appointments do not show to other users.

First to set up a definite appointment:

1   Open Schedule+ from your Main group. Go to the day you want to set an appointment for in the Appointments Book.

2   Click in a time slot to begin typing details of the appointment. If the appointment is going to spread over more than one time slot, drag over them.

3   Type in details of the appointment.

4   Press **Tab** when you finish typing.

The days for which you've set appointments appear in bold on the monthly calendar.

To invite another user to attend an appointment click Edit, Edit Appt and then click the Invite button in the ensuing Appointment dialog (see FIG. 17.21). This enables you to send a message inviting other users to the appointment using the Mail system. Inviting another user is not the same as scheduling a meeting. When you invite users you have no way of knowing if they're free until they reply to your invitation. To make sure that all potential attendees are free you should schedule a meeting in Planner. This is covered shortly.

To convert an existing appointment into a recurring appointment:

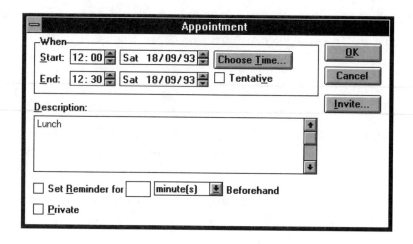

FIG. 17.21

1   Select an appointment and click Appointments, New Recurring Appt. This opens the Recurring Appointment dialog (see FIG. 17.22).

2   In this dialog click the Change button to see the Change Recurrence dialog (see FIG. 17.23). In this second dialog you can set the frequency of the appointment and the days of the week if the frequency is weekly.

3   Click OK twice to record the recurring appointment.

Later you can edit any recurring appointment by clicking Appointments, Edit Recurring Appts. You also create a recurring appointment not based on an existing one through Appointments, New Recurring Appt except that you should enter a description in the Recurring Appointment dialog.

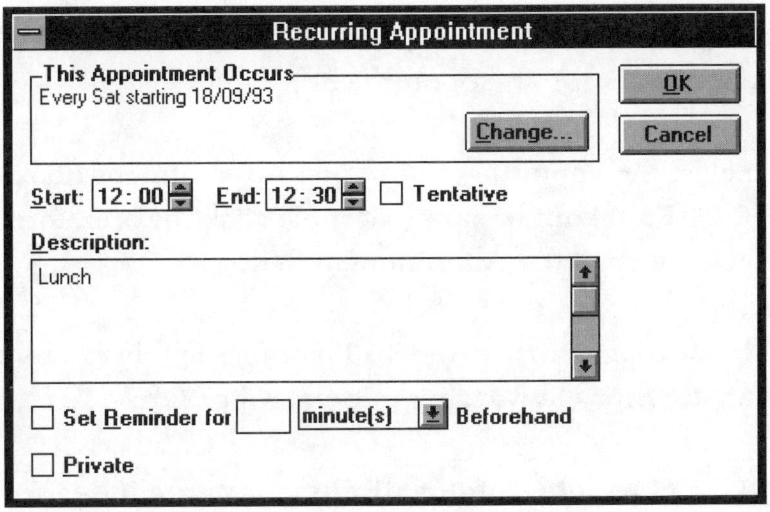

Workgroup applications

Recurring Appointment

This Appointment Occurs
Every Sat starting 18/09/93

Change...

OK

Cancel

Start: 12:00 End: 12:30 ☐ Tentative

Description:

Lunch

☐ Set Reminder for [   ] minute(s) ▼ Beforehand

☐ Private

FIG. 17.22

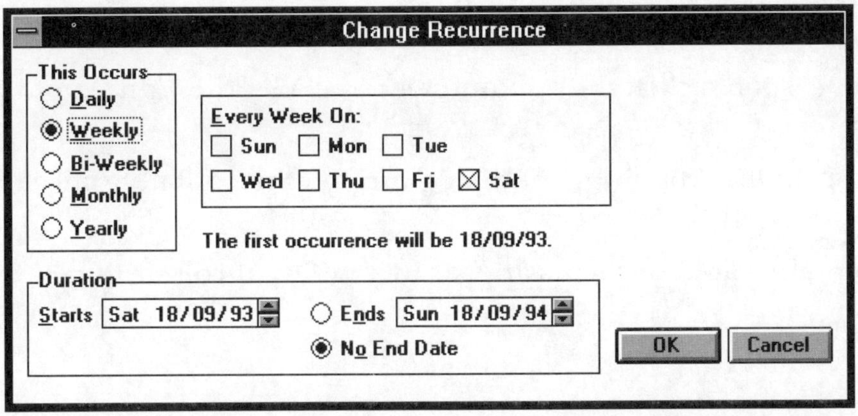

Change Recurrence

This Occurs
○ Daily
◉ Weekly
○ Bi-Weekly
○ Monthly
○ Yearly

Every Week On:
☐ Sun ☐ Mon ☐ Tue
☐ Wed ☐ Thu ☐ Fri ☒ Sat

The first occurrence will be 18/09/93.

Duration
Starts [Sat 18/09/93]   ○ Ends [Sun 18/09/94]
                        ◉ No End Date

OK   Cancel

FIG. 17.23

To set up a reminder for an appointment:

1   Select the appointment in your Appointment Book and click Edit, Edit Appt or simply double click the appointment. Both actions open the Appointment dialog.

2   In the dialog turn on the Set Reminder for check box and select an appropriate warning interval. Click OK.

You can have Schedule+ automatically set a reminder for all new appointments. To do this go through Options, General Options. To suppress all reminders click File, Turn Off Reminders. To turn them back on click File, Turn On Reminders. When a reminder is triggered (assuming you've not suppressed reminders) a dialog appears on screen. This shows the details of the appointment and you can set the reminder to trigger again. You click OK to remove the reminder dialog.

To make a tentative appointment:

1   Double click the appointment or click Edit, Edit Appt.

2   In the Appointment dialog turn on the Tentative check box.

Your tentative appointments appear in a different colour to the definite ones.

Workgroup applications

Task list

The Task list is where you enter a things-to-do list. You can assign priorities, due dates, and descriptions. You can also organize tasks into different projects. If you want to set a definite time to work on a things-to-do item you can add it to your Appointments Book.

To add a thing-to-do to the Task list:

1   Switch to the Task list (see FIG. 17.24) by clicking the Tasks tab.

2   Type a description of the task in the New Task box at the top and click the OK button.

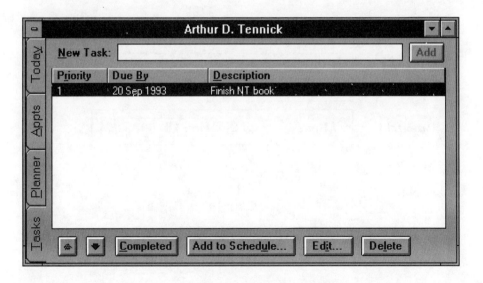

FIG. 17.24

You may want to edit the task to show a due date or change the priority. You edit the selected task by clicking the Edit button. This action opens the Task dialog (see FIG. 17.25). In this dialog you can assign the task to a project by selecting an existing project or entering a new project name in the Project drop-down list. Use the Due Date section to set a date by which the task should be completed (or none at all). In the Start Work section you select how long before the due date you should begin the task – turning on the Set Reminder check box means that you'll be prompted to begin work at the appropriate time. The Priority spin button is for assigning a priority to the task. Priority numbers are from 1 to 9, though you can type in letters instead. Letter priorities come after number priorities. Finally, turn on the Private check box if you want to hide the nature of the task from others viewing your Appointments Book – this is assuming you add your task to the Appointments Book in the first place.

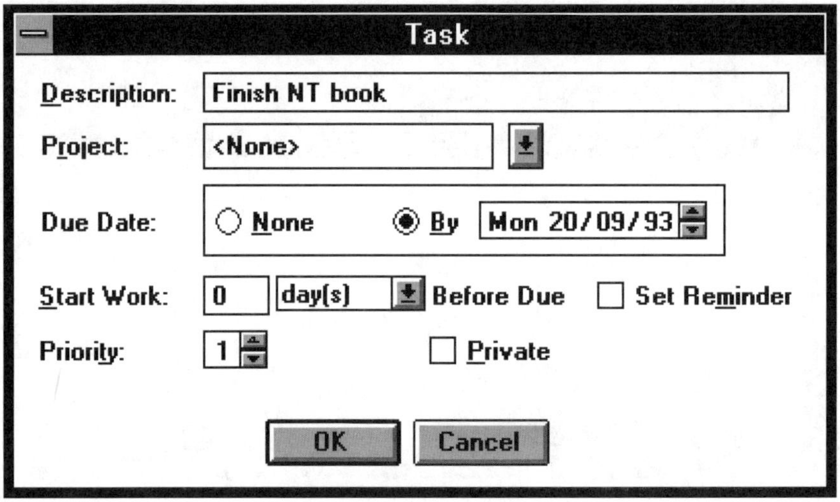

FIG. 17.25

Workgroup applications

You can delete a task or tell Schedule+ it's completed whenever you want. When you complete a task, select it and click the Completed button. To remove a task click the Delete button. To make sure that you have time to complete a task you might consider adding the task to a time slot in your Appointments Book. To place a task into the Appointments Book:

1   Select the task.

2   Click the Add to Schedule button. The Choose Time dialog (see FIG. 17.26) appears.

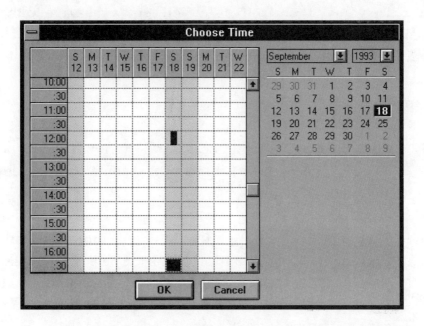

FIG. 17.26

3   In the Choose Time dialog select a time for the task and click OK.

By going through Tasks, New Recurring Task you can specify recurring tasks in a similar manner to recurring appointments.

Planner

A little earlier you read how to invite other users to an appointment. That method, which involved clicking the Invite button in the Appointments dialog, has one disadvantage – you can't tell in advance if the invitees are free at the time of the appointment. A better alternative is to use the Planner. This lets you see when both you and the potential attendees are all free. Once you've found a free slot you send a message to the others and make a provisional appointment. You can even have Schedule+ search for a mutually free time slot for you.

To arrange a meeting with other users:

1   Click the Planner tab, if necessary, to show your Planner (see FIG. 17.27). Note how your name is automatically entered as an attendee.

2   Click the Change button to add one or more extra attendees. Clicking the Change button opens the Select Attendees dialog (see FIG. 17.28) which is similar to the Address dialog in Mail.

Workgroup applications

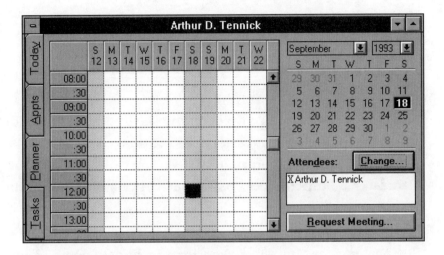

FIG. 17.27

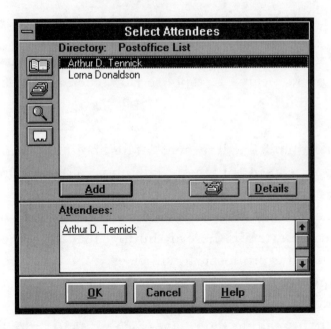

FIG. 17.28

3 In the Select Attendees dialog select one or more attendees by clicking the Add button. When you're finished click OK to close the dialog.

4 Back in your planner you can now see in which time slots you and the other potential attendees are busy. Select a time slot for the meeting that is completely free. You can have Planner move through all the free slots by repeatedly clicking Appointments, Auto-Pick.

5 When you or the Auto-Pick feature have selected a suitable time click the Request Meeting button. This opens a window where you can compose a message to all the other potential attendees.

6 Make sure the Ask for Responses check box is turned on if you want to receive a response from each attendee and click the Send button.

Each potential attendee will receive details about the proposed meeting. The message appears in both their Mail Inbox folder and in the Messages window (see FIG. 17.29) of their Schedule+. Each user can select the meeting request in the Messages window and click Read to see the details. When they read the details there are buttons that allow them to accept or decline the meeting proposal. In either case the reply appears in your Messages window. You can select replies and click Read to see if the replier has added an explanatory note. However, you can tell if they've accepted without reading the reply – a check mark appears against the entry in the Messages window. If another user has accepted then Schedule+

Workgroup applications

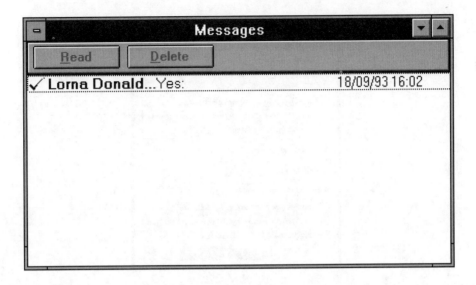

FIG. 17.29

makes an appointment for the time of the meeting in their Appointments Book.

Options menu

You can use the Options menu in to set a number of parameters. The choices available through Options, Display are self-explanatory and let you customize your screen. Options, General Options (see FIG. 17.30) contains a number of settings. For example, you can set or suppress automatic reminders for all appointments that are entered into your Appointments Book. Options, Set Access Privileges is for determining exactly how much information other users can see when they view your Schedule+ (through File, Open Other's Appt. Book).

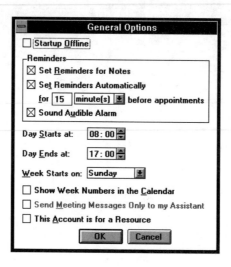

FIG. 17.30

User Manager

USER MANAGER

■ How to set up users and groups

■ How to create rights for groups

■ Audit policy

User Manager

User Manager (see FIG. 18.1) is in your Administrative Tools group in
Program Manager. It enables you to create and manage users and groups
of users, set audit policies, and assign rights to groups. Not all users can
use User Manager – and even if they can their scope of action depends
upon which group they belong to. This section details the actions that are
possible for a user who's a member of the Administrators group. This
gives the broadest scope – if you find you can't perform an action then log
back on as a member of that group.

When you create a new user then that user can log on to Windows NT,
with their own username and a password if one's required. You probably

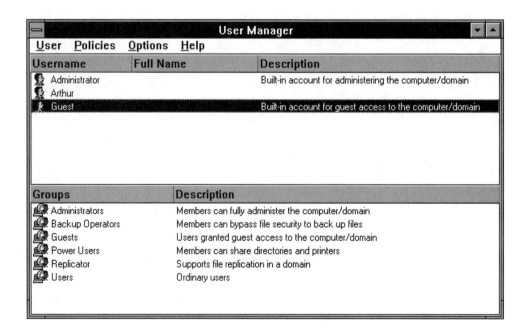

FIG. 18.1

User Manager

won't want all users to have identical scope. For example, you may not want them to have the ability to delete existing user accounts – you should reserve that ability for yourself and other trusted administrators. The easiest way to define the rights and permissions for users is to assign them to groups. By doing this the user inherits all the rights for the group. Creating or modifying rights for a group is far easier than creating or modifying rights for each individual user. So having created a new user account the first step is to place that user into one or more groups. If none of the existing groups have the rights you want for the user, you can also create new groups (or modify existing ones) with the required scope. This chapter on *User Manager* first discusses adding, modifying, and deleting user accounts and groups.

Existing users

When you first install Windows NT on a computer certain users exist by default. These users are members of default groups and there are further unpopulated groups, all with differing rights. Let's look briefly at these pre-defined users. There are, in fact, three default users – Administrator, Initial User (probably *you*), and Guest user. The Administrator and the Initial User are both members of the Administrators group while Guest is a member of the Guest user group. The Administrator account can never be deleted, though you can rename it if you wish – nor may the account be moved from the Administrators group to another group. If you know the password you can log on as the Administrator rather than under your normal username. The password for the Administrator is entered during the installation of Windows NT. The Initial User account is the account created during the installation process. Therefore, the name of the Initial User account is probably not Initial User, it's quite possibly the same as your username. However, this account is not created when installing on a computer that is part of an existing Windows NT domain – it's only created when adding the computer to a workgroup or if no network is specified.

Suppose your username is Hackenbush and your password is Groucho (passwords are case-sensitive) then when you log on as Hackenbush you are a member of the Administrators group. You could also log on as Administrator and you'd still be a member of the Administrators group. If you wanted to log on under another name, perhaps with fewer privileges, then create a new user account (and password) and add it to, say, the Power Users. You could then remove the Hackenbush account and perhaps rename the Administrator account. That way you have two accounts, both with different names and passwords – you could use the Power Users account for your day-to-day work and your Administrators account to give you maximum control over the workstation. For example, as a Power User you could still create new groups and users but not remove users and groups you didn't create. If you wanted to delete any user or group you would log on as Administrator.

The third default username is Guest which is a member of the Guests group. This is handy for casual users and has no password by default. However, the rights of Guest are quite restricted but they can generally create and delete their own data files in applications. The Guest account can be renamed but never deleted.

If there are other regular users of your workstation you might consider creating dedicated accounts and passwords for those users. You could then assign them to one of the default groups (for instance, Administrators,

Power Users, or Users), though you may not wish to assign them to the Administrators group. If none of the default groups provide the correct level of privileges for new users you can create new groups and add the users to the new groups.

Adding and modifying user accounts

Adding a new user account

To add an account for a new user:

1 Start User Manager from the Administrative Tools group in Program Manager.

2 Click User, New User to see the New User dialog (see FIG. 18.2). It's from this dialog that you set all the parameters for the new user.

3 Type a username (maximum of twenty characters) in the Username box. This entry is mandatory.

4 Type a fuller name for the user in the Full Name box. This entry is optional.

5 Type a description of the user in the Description box. This too is optional.

6 Type a password (maximum of fourteen characters) in the Password box. Remember that passwords are case-sensitive.

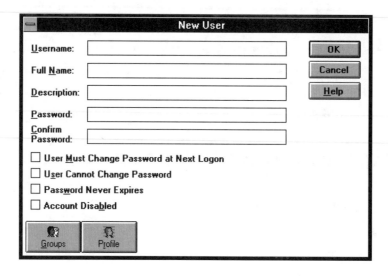

FIG. 18.2

You have to type the same password in the Confirm Password box.

7 Turn on (or off) the four check boxes at the bottom of the dialog. Let's work through these in order:

■ User Must Change Password at Next Logon

Enabling this check box forces the user to change the initial password you specify in the New User dialog as soon as they log on.

■ User Cannot Change Password

User Manager

The user must always use the password you specify. The only way to change the password is for an Administrator to modify the user account (see below).

■   Password Never Expires

You set the life of passwords in the Account Policy dialog (see below). When the life of the password is nearly over, Windows NT prompts the user for a new password. If you want a password to remain in force indefinitely then select this check box. You can also set an eternal password in the Account Policy dialog.

■   Account Disabled

If you turn on this check box it stops the user from actually using the account and logging on. This is handy if you're setting up a template user account to be copied to accounts for individual users. By setting up an inactive template you can set a number of parameters which can make creating an account for a 'real' user much easier.

The next step is to add the user to an existing group. This is discussed next so leave the New User dialog open – you add a user to a group from this dialog.

Adding a new user to a group

To add the new user to a group:

1   Click the Groups button in the New User dialog. This opens the Group Memberships dialog (see FIG. 18.3).

2   Select one or more groups in the Not Member of list in the Group Memberships dialog and click the Add button. To remove a group you added inadvertently select the group in the Member of list and click the Remove button.

3   Click OK to return to the New User dialog.

The next (optional) step is to create a profile for the user. This is covered next – once again you define the profile from the New User dialog so don't close that dialog just yet.

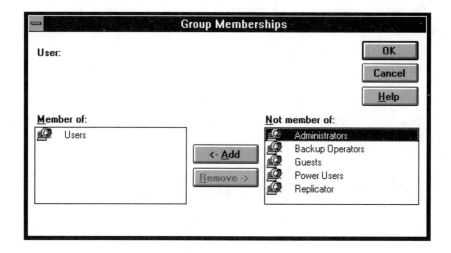

FIG. 18.3

User Manager

Setting up a profile

Setting up a user profile is optional. The profile can contain a logon script reference and a home directory for the user. A logon script runs every time the user logs on. Typically, a logon script will be a batch file (with a BAT or CMD extension) though you could also use an EXE executable. The logon script file should be created in the NT directory and it can help to set up a dedicated working environment for a particular user.

The home directory is the default directory for the user. This means that actions like File, Open and File, Save in applications will use that directory by default – although this is overridden if you've set a working directory in Program Manager or PIF Editor. It's also the directory on which the command prompt opens. If the directory you specify doesn't exist, then in most circumstances User Manager creates it for you. When a home directory is set up User Manager automatically creates the correct permissions for the directory – the user will have Full Control permission over the directory. If you don't establish a home directory then users will be using the USERS\DEFAULT directory.

You can employ the %username% placeholder when specifying the home directory. User Manager will replace the placeholder with a directory name based upon the username. For example, for a user called JohnS, a home directory of C:\USERS\%USERNAME% translates as C:\USERS\JOHNS. In a FAT partition long directory names are not supported so %username% does not work for long usernames.

To set up the user profile:

1   Click the Profile button in the New User dialog to access the User Environment Profile dialog (see FIG. 18.4).

2   If you want to define a logon script type the filename in the Logon Script Name box.

3   If you want to define a home directory enter the path in the Local Path box. In the home directory is to be on a network drive select a drive letter in the Connect box and enter a network path in the To box.

4   Click OK to return to the New User dialog. Click OK again to register the new user account and close the New User dialog.

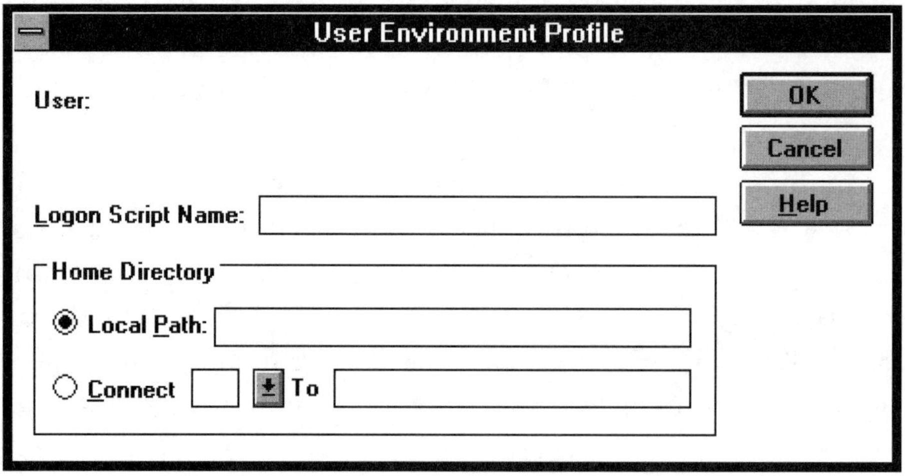

FIG. 18.4

Copying an existing user

Rather than create a user account from scratch you can copy an existing one. This has the advantage of preserving generic details like group memberships yet dropping specific details like username and password. You could set up a template user, with the account disabled, and copy from that. Then simply fill in the specific details like username and password. If the template has a home directory %username% in the user profile then the placeholder is replaced by a directory name based upon the username – provided it's not a long username in a FAT-based system. To copy an existing user account:

1   Select the user account to copy in the top half of User Manager.

2   Click User, Copy.

3   Fill in specific details for the new user and click OK. The procedures used are the same as for creating a new user (see above).

Modifying an account

You can change any user account details at any time. You can also change details for multiple accounts simultaneously. In the latter case you can't modify the username, full name, or password but you may modify the groups the users belong to.

To modify a user account:

1   For a single account select the user in User Manager and click User, Properties or double click the user account. To modify multiple accounts select the accounts and click User, Properties.

2   Make any changes in the User Properties dialog (see FIG. 18.5). You can also change group assignments and profiles through the Groups and Profile buttons. Note that if you enter a description for multiple accounts the description will apply to each single account selected. The settings are the same as those encountered when creating a new user account (see above). However, the Group Memberships dialog is slightly different for multiple users – instead of the Member of and Not member

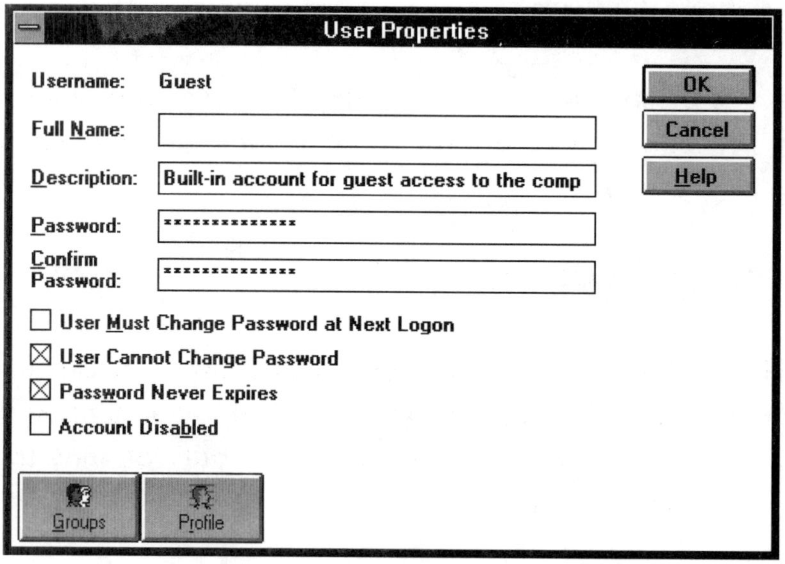

FIG. 18.5

of lists you see the All are Members of and Not all are Members of lists. To make sure that all the selected users are members of a particular group add that group to the All are Members of list. To ensure that none of the user accounts are members of a group add the group to the All are Members of list and then remove it to the Not all are Members of list.

3 Click OK in the User Properties dialog when finished.

Disabling and enabling user accounts

As already mentioned you can disable a user account. Disabling an account is a valid alternative when a user won't be joining the workgroup for a while or will be away for a protracted period. You would also want to disable any account that you use as a template for other accounts. When you copy the template to create a new user account the disabled setting is automatically dropped. To disable a user account:

1 Select one or more user accounts in the top half of the User Manager window.

2 Click User, Properties. If only one account is to be disabled you can simply double click the account. In either case the User Properties dialog appears.

3 Turn on the Account Disabled check box.

4 Click OK to confirm the change.

Deleting user accounts

You can delete a user account when you're convinced that the user won't require access to Windows NT in the future. You may also periodically wish to purge long-disabled accounts in the same way. To delete one or more accounts:

1   Select the accounts in the User Manager window.

2   Click User, Delete.

3   Answer in the affirmative to any confirmation messages.

Renaming user accounts

If you want to alter a username it's often better to rename it directly rather than deleting the original account and then creating a new one. Renaming directly has the advantage of retaining all the other details such as group memberships and rights. You can only rename accounts for one account at a time:

1   Select the account in User Manager.

2   Click User, Rename.

3   Enter a new username (maximum twenty characters) in the Rename dialog (see FIG. 18.6).

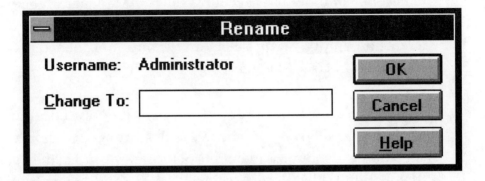

FIG. 18.6

4   Click OK to confirm the new username.

Adding and modifying groups

In the previous discussions for adding and modifying user accounts it was assumed that the available groups were adequate. However, you may want to create a customized group that has differing rights and permissions from any of the existing groups. You can define a new group before creating the user accounts that are to belong to the group. Alternatively, you can create a group retrospectively and modify the user accounts so they are made members of the group where appropriate.

Adding a new group

You can create an empty group or one that already has members:

1   Select one or more user accounts in User Manager if you want the new group to be populated with selected accounts. To create an empty group select any group (and hence no user accounts) in User Manager.

2   Click User, New Local Group. This opens the New Local Group dialog (see FIG. 18.7). If you selected accounts in the previous step they are shown as members of the new group in the dialog. If you didn't select accounts then it's easy to add them from the dialog and to do so later. There are two ways to alter the members of a group at a later date. One, you can modify the group (see below). Two, you can modify user accounts (see above) and change the group memberships there. Adopt whichever approach is easiest under the circumstances.

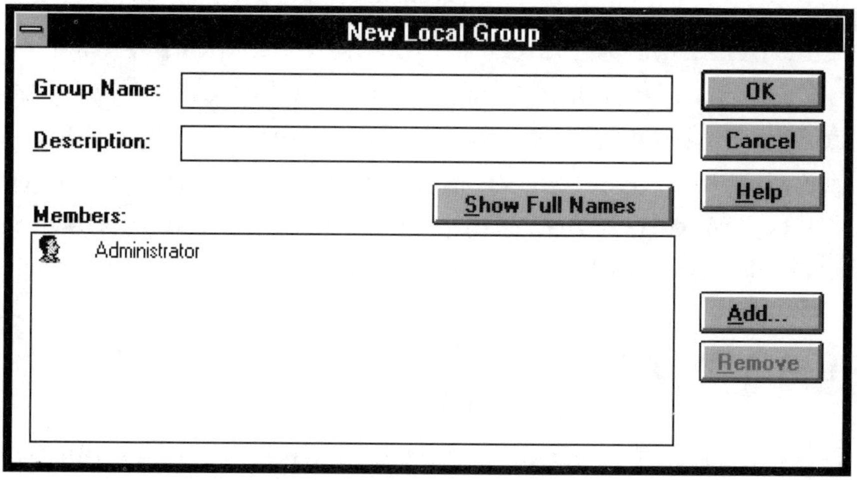

FIG. 18.7

3   Type a name for the new group in the Group Name box.

4   Type a description for the new group in the Description box.

5   To add new members to the group now click the Add button. This opens the Add Users and Groups dialog. The Add Users and Groups dialog is discussed in detail in Chapter 9 on *File Manager*. When you've finished adding users click OK to return to the New Local Group dialog.

6   To remove any members listed in the New Local Group dialog select them and click the Remove button.

7   Click OK when finished defining the new group.

When you've created the new group don't forget to assign it the necessary permissions in File Manager and Print Manager. You are referred back to the chapters on *File Manager* and *Print Manager* to see how to do this. You also need to grant rights to the group. This is covered later in this chapter.

Copying an existing group

Rather than creating a group from scratch you can copy an existing group. This has the advantage of copying all the existing members into the new group. However, any permissions or rights are not copied from the existing group to the new copy. You must establish its rights and permissions yourself. To copy an existing group:

1   Select a group in the User Manager window.

2   Click User, Copy.

3   Enter a new name for the copied group.

4   Continue, as in the previous section for adding new groups, to set up the group.

5   Click OK.

Modifying a group

Modifying a group is helpful when you want to change the group members. You can also change the description of the group but not the group name. To rename a group you must first delete the group and recreate it afresh. To modify a group:

1   Select the group from the lower half of the User Manager window and click User, Properties. Alternatively, you can simply double click the group.

2   In the subsequent Local Group Properties dialog (see FIG. 18.8) add and/or remove members as appropriate. You can change the description in the Description box.

3   Click OK to finish.

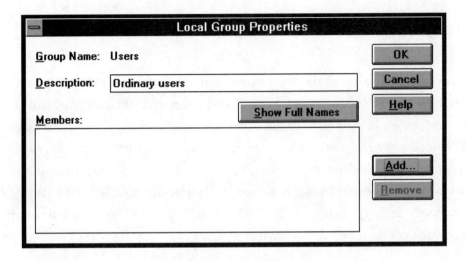

FIG. 18.8

Deleting a group

Think carefully before deleting a customized group. If you need a similar group in the future you need to define it from scratch, and this includes assigning members, rights, and permissions. User Manager does not allow you to remove any of the default groups. Deleting a group only removes the group together with its rights and permissions. It does not remove user accounts that are members of the group. To delete a group:

1   Select the group to be deleted in the lower half of the User Manager window.

2   Click User, Delete.

3   Answer in the affirmative to any warning messages.

Security

As well as maintaining user accounts and groups you should be aware of security issues. Needless to say, all of the security issues are important – however, even if you ignore account and audit policy you must get your rights policy worked out. The latter determines whether the user accounts and groups you define are actually capable of carrying out any meaningful actions, and it determines the scope of those actions. Security issues (that is account policy, rights policy, and audit policy) are discussed in the remaining sections of this chapter.

Account policy

The account policy determines how user account passwords are handled. The account policy is global and effects all user accounts identically – you can't set a different account policy for a particular user. To set your account policy:

1   Click Policies, Account.

2   Make your choices in the Account Policy dialog (see FIG. 18.9). For example, you can establish the minimum and maximum life-spans of passwords. Most of the options are self-explanatory. The Password Uniqueness section is perhaps the only one that requires amplification. In this section turn on the option button for Do Not Keep Password History if you want users to be able to reuse old passwords without restriction. For a more secure environment you might want to force brand new passwords when users change passwords – to do this turn on

User Manager

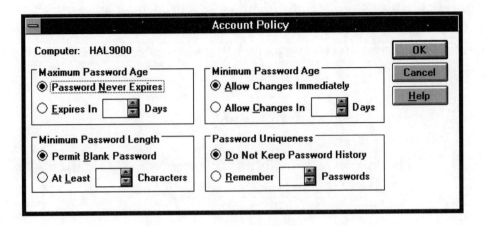

FIG. 18.9

the Remember Passwords option button and enter a high figure in the corresponding box.

3 Click OK to confirm your password settings.

Rights policy

Rights are not the same as permissions. Rights are global or system wide while permissions are local and relate to particular objects. For instance, you set permissions on files, directories (in File Manager), printers (in Print Manager), and ClipBook pages (in ClipBook Viewer). In general, rights override permissions. Suppose you're a member of the Backup Operators group. This is one of the default groups and one of its default rights is to perform backups and restore backups. However, the owner of a directory may not have given permission for the Backup Operators group to read from or write to the directory. This could mean that the files in that directory can't be backed up or restored by a Backup Operator member. But the precedence of rights over permissions gives a backup operator the authority to perform a backup or restore on the closed directory.

To establish or check on your rights policy:

1 Click Policies, User Rights. This opens the User Rights Policy dialog (see FIG. 18.10).

2 Select a right from the drop-down list. The Grant To list shows the groups and user accounts that have the current right.

3 To stop an individual or group from having that right select the account or group from the list and click the Remove button.

4 To give the right to an account or group click the Add button. This opens the Add Users and Groups dialog. Make the appropriate choices there and click OK to return to the User Rights Policy dialog.

5 Click OK to keep any changes.

As a reference here's a list of the rights you can assign or remove in the User Rights Policy dialog:

■ Access this computer from the network

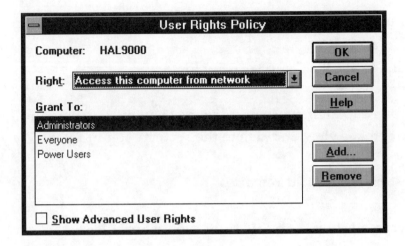

FIG. 18.10

Allows connection to the computer over the network.

■   Back up files and directories

Allows any member of the group to back up files.

■   Change the system time

Enables the user to alter the system clock.

■   Force shutdown from a remote system

Not currently supported.

■   Log on locally

Lets the user log on directly to the workstation.

■ Manage auditing and security log

Enables a group member to decide which events are to be audited. It also lets the member view and delete the security log in Event Viewer.

■ Restore files and directories

Any user in a group with this right can restore files.

■ Shutdown the system

Allows the user to shutdown the system. All users can log off but only users in groups with this right can shutdown Windows NT.

■ Take ownership of files and other objects

Lets the user take ownership of files and other objects.

Audit policy

Your audit policy determines which events are recorded in the security log, which you can view in Event Viewer. When setting up the audit policy you can decide not only the events to track but whether to record successful and/or failed events. In addition, you can have the system shutdown automatically when the security log is full. This is handy as someone trying to break into the system will generate a lot of events and

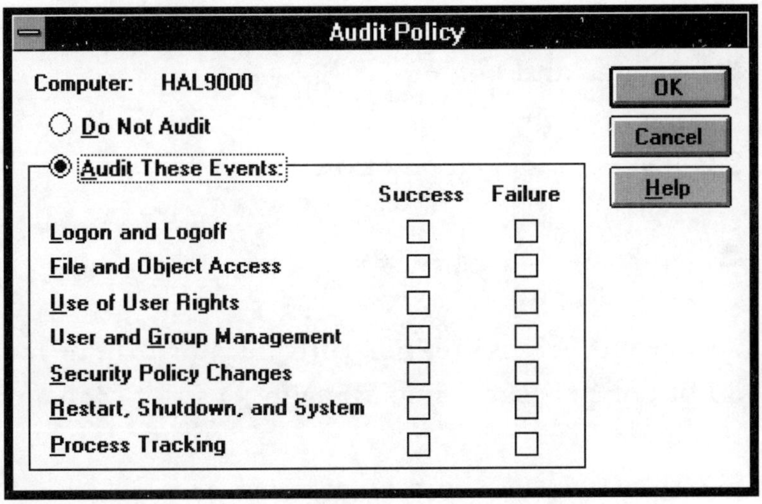

FIG. 18.11

you may want to shutdown before they are successful. The size of the security log is set in Event Viewer.

To set up the audit policy:

1   Click Policies, Audit to open the Audit Policy dialog (see FIG. 18.11).

2   Turn on the Do Not Audit option button if you don't want events to be audited.

3   If you do want to track events turn on the Audit These Events option button. Then enable or disable the appropriate check boxes. For specific events you can choose to record successful and/or failed events. The events are as follows:

■   Logon and Logoff

Someone has logged on or off.

■   File and Object Access

A user has accessed a file, directory, or printer for which an audit policy is set in File Manager or Print Manager.

■   Use of User Rights

A user carried out an action that is a right (see above for a list of rights). The exception to this is logging on or off.

■   User and Group Management

A user has accessed User Manager to make changes to user accounts or groups.

■   Security Policy Changes

A user has made changes to rights policy (see above) or audit policy.

■   Restart, Shutdown, and System

A user shuts down or restarts Windows NT. This option also records events that affect system security.

■   Process Tracking

Records processes, for example, starting an application.

4   Optionally, enable the Halt System when Security Event Log is Full check box. Turn this check box on with caution – it can make the computer unusable until the system administrator clears the security log.

5   Click OK to preserve your changes.

Event Viewer

EVENT VIEWER

- How to log system and security events

- Finding and viewing events in logs

- Creating log archives

Whenever you start Windows NT many of the events which occur are recorded in the event log. You can determine, to some extent, which events are recorded in the log through your audit policy. However, some events are always recorded. Some events generate dialogs on screen as well as being recorded in the event log. The event log has three components: the system log, the application log, and the security log. The system log logs events such a driver failing to start correctly and other system events. The application log records application events. The security log logs security events. The events that are recorded depend upon your audit policy.

You use Event Viewer (see FIG. 19.1) to view and filter events. You can also save logs to archives and clear logs. In addition, you can set a maximum size for each of the three log files. By default, when a log is full the oldest events are dropped from the log to make room for new ones. The exception to this is when you've set the system to shutdown when the security log is full (see the section on *Audit policy* in Chapter 18 on *User Manager*).

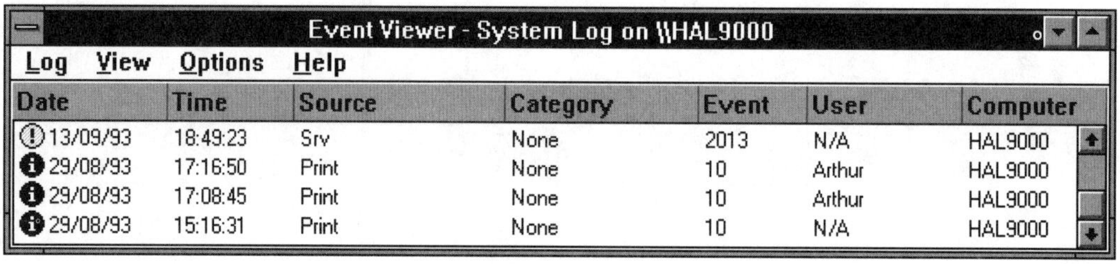

Event Viewer - System Log on \\HAL9000							
Log View Options Help							
Date	Time	Source	Category	Event	User	Computer	
ⓘ 13/09/93	18:49:23	Srv	None	2013	N/A	HAL9000	
ⓘ 29/08/93	17:16:50	Print	None	10	Arthur	HAL9000	
ⓘ 29/08/93	17:08:45	Print	None	10	Arthur	HAL9000	
ⓘ 29/08/93	15:16:31	Print	None	10	N/A	HAL9000	

FIG. 19.1

Event Viewer

You start Event Viewer by double clicking its icon in the Administrative Tools group in Program Manager. The first time you open Event Viewer it displays the system log. To quit Event Viewer when you finish click Log, Exit. To switch between the three types of logs click Log followed by System, Application, or Security (though you must be a member of the Administrators group to view the security log). To update the viewed log to show events since you opened the log click View, Refresh. If you want to see the logs for other workstations click Log, Select Computer and select a computer. To clear a log click Log, Clear All Events. This action gives you the opportunity to save the log to an archive before it's cleared. Archiving logs (see later) is handy if you want to keep a permanent log of all events.

You can also set various logging options. To set options:

1   Click Log, Log Settings to see the Event Log Settings dialog (see FIG. 19.2).

2   In this dialog you can set options for any of the three logs. You select a log from the drop-down list at the top of the dialog.

3   If you want you alter the maximum size for the log in the Maximum Log Size box.

4   Select one of the option buttons in the Event Log Wrapping section. The options are explained here:

■   Overwrite Events as Needed

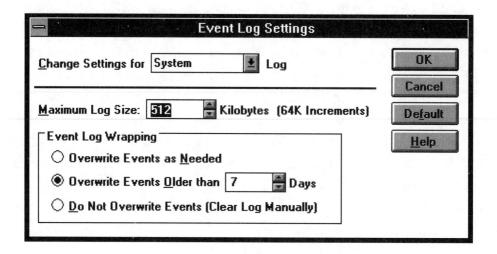

FIG. 19.2

When the selected log is full each new event that's added causes the oldest event to be dropped.

■ Overwrite Events Older than

Keeps events for the specified number of days before they get overwritten by new events.

■ Do Not Overwrite Events

With this option selected you must clear the log manually from time-to-time.

5 Click OK to keep your changes. You can revert to the default settings first by clicking the Default button.

When viewing one of the three logs in Event Viewer you can sort and filter the log, search for particular events, or view further information about an event. To sort the log chronologically click either View, Newest First or View, Oldest First. To view further details about an event click View, Detail with the event selected or double click the event. In the ensuing Event Detail dialog (see FIG. 19.3) you use the Previous and Next buttons to scroll through details about other events.

Filtering events

When you view the system, application, or security log you can see all the events recorded. If, however, you want to concentrate upon specific

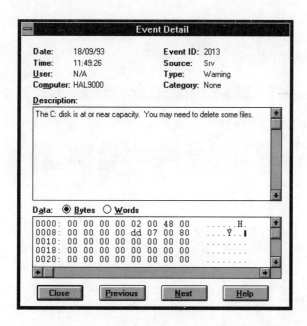

FIG. 19.3

events (you may be trying to diagnose a problem) you set a filter. A filter displays only those events that match your criteria. The other events are still there and still being recorded, they're merely temporarily suppressed in the display. You impose a filter by setting criteria in the Filter dialog which you access by clicking View, Filter Events. To turn off the filter click View, All Events. Let's take a look at the Filter dialog:

1	Click View, Filter Events to see the Filter dialog (see FIG. 19.4).

2	Enter or select the criteria for the filter. Here's a list of the possibilities available:

■	View From

View right from the oldest event in the log or from a date and time you specify.

FIG. 19.4

■ View Through

View through to the latest event in the log or to a date and time you specify. Dates and times correspond to the Date and Time columns in the log window.

■ Types

View events belonging to different types. Error events are the most serious. Warning events are less severe but may give rise to potential problems. Information events are successful events. Success Audit and Failure Audit events correspond to the events marked in your Audit Policy dialog (see the earlier chapter on *User Manager*). These types correspond to the icon column in the log window.

■ Source

View events generated by a particular source. Corresponds to the Source column.

■ Category

View events belonging to a particular category of the selected source. Corresponds to the Category column.

■ User

View events generated by a particular user. Corresponds to the User column.

■   Computer

View events generated by a particular computer. Corresponds to the Computer column.

■   Event ID

View a specific event. To work out the event number to enter find one occurrence in the log window first. Corresponds to the Event column.

3   Click OK to impose the filter.

The filter stays in force until you set differing criteria, or click View, All Events or you exit Event Viewer. If you checked Options, Save Settings on Exit then the filter in force when you exited is reimposed when you next start Event Viewer. If you want to return to the initial, default criteria click the Clear button in the Filter dialog.

Searching for events

Rather than setting a filter to view certain events you can search for particular events one at a time. To do so you set the criteria in the Find dialog (click View, Find). To return to the initial, default criteria click the Clear button in the Find dialog. To continue a search you can press **F3** –

this bypasses the Find dialog and uses the current search criteria. To implement a search:

1 Click View, Find.

2 In the Find dialog (see FIG. 19.5) specify your search criteria. The entries you make are similar to those discussed in the previous section on filters. You use the Description box to enter any part of an event record description.

3 Turn on the Up or the Down option button.

4 Click the Find Next button when the criteria are in place.

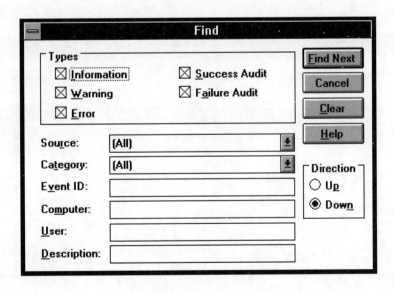

FIG. 19.5

Archiving events

As your logs are going to get overwritten or cleared sooner or later you might want to save your log files as archives. You can then view these archives at any time in Event Viewer or save them as text or delimited files for analysis in word processors, spreadsheets, or databases. If you don't archive a log then the events it records are lost when those events are overwritten by newer events or cleared from the log. To archive a log:

1   Click Log, Save As.

2   Enter a filename for the log (see FIG. 19.6). There's no need to enter an extension, Event Viewer adds the appropriate one automatically.

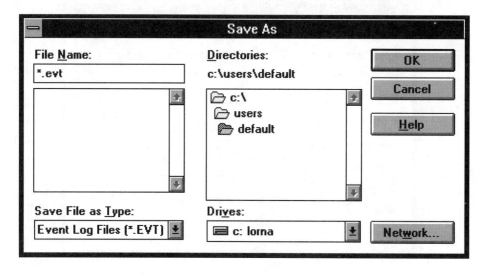

FIG. 19.6

3   In the Save File as Type box select a file type. If you choose a log file format Event Viewer adds an EVT extension to the filename and you can reopen the archive in Event Viewer at a later date. If you choose a text or a delimited format Event Viewer adds a TXT extension. This choice means you can't reopen the log in Event Viewer but you can import it into your word processor, spreadsheet, or database for further analysis. It also means you can concatenate more than one log to produce exhaustive reports on system performance. This may help you to identify security threats, hardware and software problems, potential hardware bottlenecks, threats to data integrity, and so on.

4   Click OK.

Once you've successfully archived a log file you may want to clear the log in Event Viewer through Log, Clear All Events. Before doing so make sure that the EVT or TXT file contains the correct information. To check an EVT file you must load the archive back into Event Viewer – but it has no effect on any of the current three logs which continue to record in the background. To view an EVT archived log:

1   Click Log, Open.

2   Select the log to view in the ensuing dialog and click OK.

3   In the subsequent Open File Type dialog select the type of log for the archive (system, application, or security) and click OK.

Backup

BACKUP

- How to back up files and directories

- How to restore files and directories

- Looking after your tapes

Backup

Backup (see FIG. 20.1) is in the Administrative Tools group of Program Manager. As the name suggests it provides backup and restore facilities which will appear quite sophisticated to DOS and Windows for DOS users. However, you must have a tape drive in order to use it at all. If, like me, you don't have a tape system you have to employ backup or xcopy at the command prompt – or if you can be bothered to juggle files to fit on floppies you can drag-copy files from File Manager. In addition, you can only have Backup back up files from directories over which you have the necessary privileges, unless you are a member of the Administrators or Backup Operators groups.

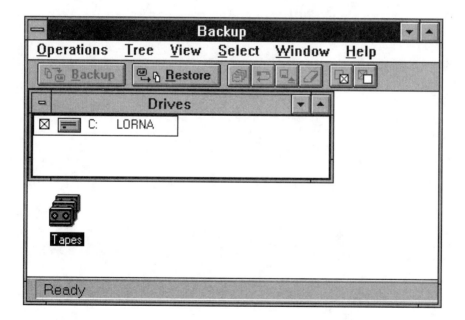

FIG. 20.1

Backup

Backing up

Selecting files for backup is similar to selecting files and directories in File Manager except you turn on a check box next to the directory or file icon. When Backup opens make sure the Drives window is visible. If you want to back up a complete drive turn on the check box next to the drive. If you want to select specific directories and files on a drive double click the drive icon in the Drives window to open a directory and files window. In this latter window turn on the check boxes next to the directories and/or files you wish to back up. You can expand and collapse directories the same as you would in File Manager. If you don't have a mouse then go through Select, Check and Select, Uncheck to turn check boxes on and off. Once you've selected the required drives, directories, and/or files you begin the backup process. To back up selected drives, directories, and/or files:

1   Click Operations, Backup or the Backup button on the toolbar. This opens the Backup Information dialog.

2   Make relevant selections and entries in this dialog and click OK to proceed. The entries and selections to be made in the Backup Information dialog are discussed presently.

3   The next dialog is the Backup Status dialog. This displays the status of the backup. Click OK when the backup is complete. You can click Abort to end the backup process at any time, but this means any remaining files will not be backed up. During the backup process you may see extra dialogs asking you to insert new tapes as each tape becomes full.

But let's return to the selections and entries you make in the Backup Information dialog:

■   Tape Name

Enter the name for the tape (maximum thirty-two characters) or rename an existing tape name.

■   Verify After Backup

Verifies the backed up files against the originals on disk.

■   Backup Local Registry

Includes Windows NT Registry files in the backup.

■   Restrict Access to Owner or Administrator

Stops other users (apart from the owner, or members of the Administrators or Backup Operators group) from reading, writing to, or erasing the tape.

■   Append

Adds the backup files to the tape after any existing backup set.

■   Replace

Replaces any existing backup set on the tape.

■   Backup Type

Use this drop-down list to select the nature of the backup. The choices are Normal, Copy, Incremental, Differential, and Daily. Normal is the same as a full backup and marks the original files once they're backed up. Copy is the same as Normal except the original files are not marked as having been backed up. Incremental backs up and marks only those files that have been modified since the last backup. Differential is the same as Incremental except the files are not marked as having been backed up. Daily backs up, but does not mark, only the files that have been modified on the current day.

■   Log File

Enter the name of a log file to record the progress of the backup operation.

■   Full Detail

Logs all information to the log file.

■   Summary Only

Logs selected information to the log file.

■   Don't Log

Does not log any information to the log file.

Restoring

Restoring is backup in reverse. You select the tapes, backup sets, or individual files to restore in the same manner as you select items to back up – only you do so in the Tapes window. But before you can make a selection you must load the tape's catalog to see its contents. To see an overall catalog of the backup sets on a tape double click the tape's icon (or click Operations, Catalog). To see a detailed catalog of a particular backup set double click the set's icon (or click Operations, Catalog). To make sure you can select all items on a tape you should open the overall catalog first. To begin restoring after you've made a selection:

1   Click Operations, Restore or click the Restore button on the toolbar. This opens the Restore Information dialog.

2   Make the necessary entries and selections in this dialog and click OK. A discussion of the entries and selections follows shortly.

3   The next dialog is the Restore Status dialog. When the restore process is complete click OK in this dialog. Clicking Abort ends the restore process prematurely. If the backup set extends across further tapes you'll be asked to insert a new tape. If a more recent copy of a file you're restoring already exists on disk you'll be asked to confirm replacement of the disk copy.

Now let's take a look at the entries and selections in the Restore Information dialog:

■   Restore to Drive

Specify the drive you wish to restore to.

■   Alternate Path

Enter a path (if you wish) that's different from the one backed up. This enables you to compare the restored files with the originals.

■   Verify After Restore

Verifies the restored files on disk against the backed up versions on tape.

■   Restore File Permissions

Gives the original permissions to the restored files. If you don't turn on this check box the restored files inherit the permissions of the directory into which they're restored – these permissions may have changed from the original directory permissions.

■   Restore Local Registry

This restores Registry files if they were originally backed up to the tape.

■   Log File

Specify a name for a log file.

■   Full Detail

Logs all the information about the restore process.

■   Summary Only

Logs only selected information about the restore process.

■   Don't Log

Doesn't log any information at all.

Looking after your tapes

You can use Backup to erase (Erase Tape) your tapes. Both a quick erase and a secure erase are available. With a quick erase only the tape header is deleted. With a secure erase the entire contents of the tape are deleted – this option can take quite a bit of time.

Some tapes may require retensioning (Retension Tape) from time-to-time. Retensioning causes the tape to fast forward and then to rewind. This operation picks up any slack in the tape and means it passes the tape head more smoothly in future.

Disk Administrator

DISK ADMINISTRATOR

■ Viewing disk partitions and volumes

■ Creating partitions

■ How to set up volume and stripe sets

Disk Administrator (see FIG. 21.1) is in the Administrative Tools group of Program Manager. You use Disk Administrator to partition hard disks and create volume sets. You are not encouraged to experiment with Disk Administrator – this section assumes you are happy with the concepts of partitions, primary partition, and extended partitions. Using Disk Administrator without a full understanding of these concepts can make your computer unusable.

When you open Disk Administrator the Disk Administrator window appears. This window shows all the hard disks on your system, free space on those disks, and how the partitions are organized. You are referred to the colour-coded legend at the foot of the Disk Administrator window. To close the Disk Administrator window click Partition, Exit. Let's work through some of the possibilities.

To create a primary partition (NT supports up to four per disk) on a disk:

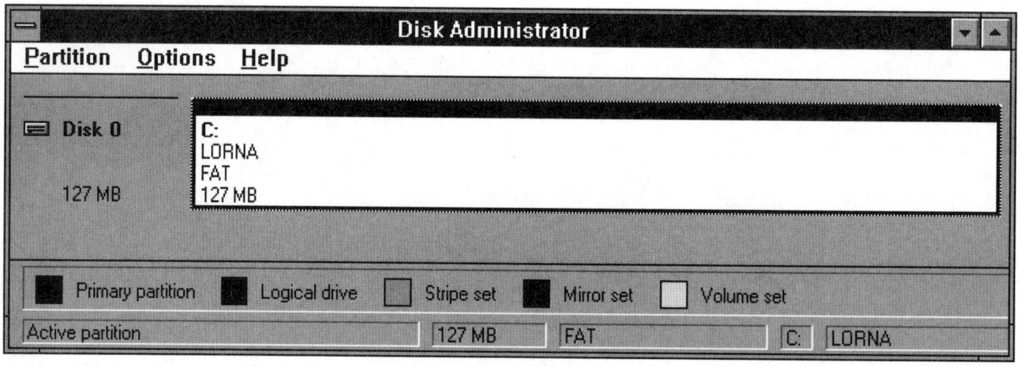

FIG. 21.1

Disk Administrator

1   Select a free area on a disk.

2   Click Partition, Create.

3   In the Create Primary Partition dialog enter a size for the partition and click OK.

To make a primary partition into the active partition:

1   Select the primary partition you wish to make active.

2   Click Partition, Mark Active.

3   Click OK in the dialog that appears. Active partitions are marked with an asterisk in the Disk Administrator window.

To create an extended partition:

1   Select some free space on the disk.

2   Click Partition, Create Extended.

3   Enter the size for the extended partition in the Create Extended Partition dialog.

4   Click OK.

Once you have an extended partition you can create logical drives within the partition:

1   Select some free space within an extended partition.

2   Click Partition, Create.

3   Enter a size for the logical drive in the Create Logical Drive dialog.

4   Click OK.

To assign drive letters to a partition or logical drive:

1   Select the partition or logical drive.

2   Click Partition, Drive Letter.

3   From the Assign Drive Letter dialog (see FIG. 21.2) select a letter for the drive.

4   Click OK.

Before you can use a partition with a particular operating system it must first be formatted. The DOS and Windows NT command is format. Please use this with extreme caution as formatting removes any existing files in the partition. You are referred to your operating system documentation to see how to format a disk. In NT you can type **format /?** at the command prompt for further guidance. You may also want to set or change the volume label. You can use File Manager or label at the command prompt to do this.

You can delete existing partitions, logical drives, and volumes from Disk Administrator. To do so (again use caution as data may be lost):

1   Select the partition, logical drive, or volume.

2   Click Partition, Delete.

3   Click Yes in the warning dialog.

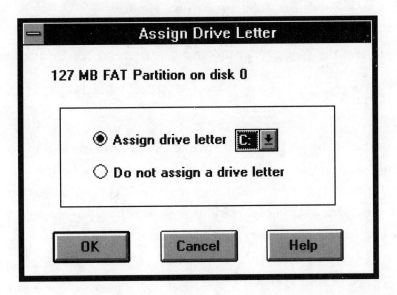

FIG. 21.2

You can save and restore details about your current disk organization. Before saving information you should ensure that it's updated first – exit Disk Administrator, restart the computer, and open Disk Administrator again. To save your disk configuration:

1 Click Partition, Configuration, Save.

2 Insert your Windows NT Emergency Repair Disk or a blank floppy.

3 Click OK.

To re-establish a saved configuration:

1 Click Partition, Configuration, Restore.

2 Insert the floppy containing your saved configuration.

3 Click OK.

A volume set is a single partition spread across multiple hard disks. The component parts of the single partition do not have to be the same size on each disk. You can spread a volume set for one partition across a maximum of thirty-two disks, and you can include more than one area of free space from an individual disk. To create a volume set:

1 Select a free space on one disk.

2 Hold down **Ctrl** and select free space on one or more other disks.

3 Click Partition, Create Volume Set.

4 Enter the total size of the volume set in the Create Volume Set dialog. If the size is less than the combined total of all of the free space then Disk Administrator tries to spread the set as evenly as possible across each disk – it does this by attempting to make the volume set components equal in size on each disk.

5 Click OK.

You can extend the size of an existing volume or volume set at any time, provided you have free space on one of your hard disks:

1 Select the volume or volume set and an area of free space.

2 Click Partition, Extend Volume Set.

3 Enter a size for the extended set in the Create Extended Volume Set dialog.

4 Click OK.

You can also delete an existing volume set. Once more, you should approach this action with caution as data loss may result. The procedure is the same as for deleting a partition, logical drive, or volume discussed earlier.

Stripe sets are similar to volume sets. The difference lies in the fact that a stripe set can only include one area of free space on each disk. Further, Disk Administrator always tries to make the components equal in size, and data input and output may show performance gains. Like volume sets, stripe sets are not recognised by DOS so if you boot into DOS (on a dual-boot system) the stripe set won't be available. To set up a stripe set:

1   Select an area of free space on the first disk.

2   Hold down **Ctrl** and click one area of free space on the other disks you want in the stripe set.

3   Click Partition, Create Stripe Set.

4   Enter the size of the stripe set in the Create Stripe Set dialog.

5   Click OK.

Deleting a stripe set is the same as deleting a volume set. All data in the stripe set is lost if it's deleted.

Odds and ends

ODDS AND ENDS

- A quick look at Terminal

- A quick look at Performance Monitor

- Character Map and multimedia applets

It's always difficult to know exactly what to include (and what to leave out) in a book of this nature. Space considerations prevent a fully-comprehensive coverage of every single aspect of Windows NT. Hopefully, what has been discussed is the most relevant for most readers. Unfortunately, though, a few topics had to be missed out. In particular, there is nothing on Terminal, Performance Monitor, and the various multimedia applets. I've taken the view that many users of modems are fairly technical people anyway, and that Terminal should appear quite straightforward after other communications applications. Performance Monitor is quite complex – however, it's probably of interest mostly to power users and system administrators. Once again, these tend to be people with a technical background and should soon get to grips with Performance Monitor. The multimedia applets have been ignored as it's still a minority who have multimedia hardware – the applets are quite easy to use anyway, you can work out what they do without having to read a book for the information. Apologies to those readers who feel otherwise – but then there's no pleasing all the people all of the time...

This section is a kind of mopping-up operation – it tries to mention, at least in passing, what has not been mentioned before. Let's begin with one aspect of Task List which is new to Windows for DOS users.

Task List

Task List in Windows NT differs in one respect from Task List in Windows for DOS – it has a New Task box. To run an application quickly press **Ctrl-Esc** to show Task List (see FIG. 22.1), or double click the desktop background if it's not obscured. Enter the name (and the path if

Odds and ends

FIG. 22.1

necessary) of the application in the New Task box and click the Run button.

This is handy if you don't want to root around in Program Manager groups to find an icon or search through File Manager directories. Of course, if the application does have a Program Manager icon you can assign a shortcut key – this is probably even more convenient than using Run in Task List.

Administrative Tools group

Performance Monitor

Performance Monitor lets you view various performance levels on your system. You do this by charting or logging activities. You can also have it create reports on performance and to alert you if certain things happen (or fail to happen). Specific performance limits can be set to trigger programs and you can save logs and view them later. The latter is helpful if you're concerned about system bottlenecks.

All I want to do here is to give a simple example of charting the amount of processor time taken by Performance Monitor itself and another application:

1 Open Performance Monitor (see FIG. 22.2) from the Administrative Tools group.

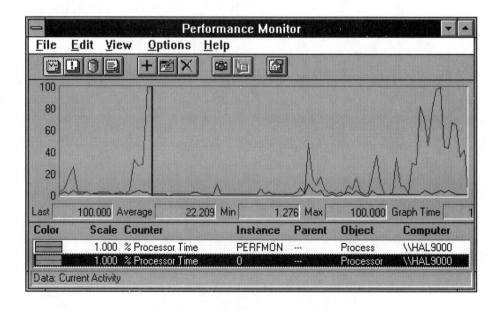

FIG. 22.2

Odds and ends

2 Click Edit, Add to Chart. This opens the Add to Chart dialog (see FIG. 22.3). Note that if Edit, Add to Chart is not available you're not in chart view. To make sure you're in chart view click View, Chart.

3 Select Process (not Processor) from the Object drop-down list.

4 Select PERFMON (that is, Performance Monitor) from the Instance list.

5 Select %Processor Time from the Control list.

6 Click Add. This will place a colour-coded line on the final chart to show the amount of processor time taken by Performance Monitor itself.

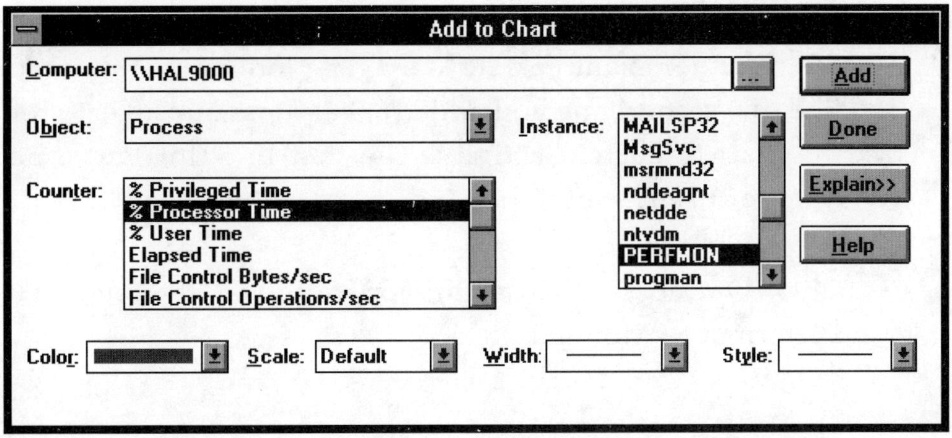

FIG. 22.3

7 Now to add another line to the chart. Select Processor (not Process this time) from the Object drop-down list.

8 Select %Processor Time from the Control list and click Add. The resulting line will show the amount of processor time taken by all running processes.

9 Click Done to close the Add to Chart dialog.

10 Click Options, Always On Top. This means you'll be able to see Performance Monitor at all times. Drag the Performance Monitor window to one side so you can start applications from Program Monitor.

11 Let the chart settle down for a few seconds – you might want to wait until it starts charting from the left-hand side again.

12 Open and close one or more applications from Program Manager, for example, File Manager. Notice how the coloured line (the second one you added) peaks and subsides to reflect the level of current activity. The first line (for Performance Monitor itself) should be much more stable.

13 Click Options, Always On Top followed by File, Exit in Performance Monitor.

Odds and ends

Accessories group

Terminal

Terminal is a communications application. You use Terminal in conjunction with a modem to log on to bulletin boards and conferencing systems. For example, if you have a username and password you can log on to Phone Base in the UK to search for telephone numbers by name, town, and county. Terminal also enables you to download and upload both text and binary files. Here's a basic example (it assumes you have a modem, that you're dialling from the UK, and you're prepared to pay the telephone bill!):

1 Open Terminal (see FIG. 22.4) from the Accessories group in Program Manager.

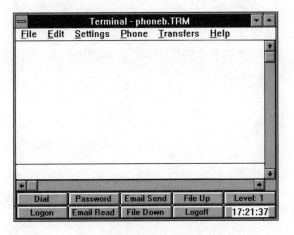

FIG. 22.4

2   Click Settings, Communications to open the Communications dialog (see FIG. 22.5).

3   In this dialog try the following settings and click OK:

Baud Rate   2400
Data Bits   7
Stop Bits   1
Flow Control   Xon/Xoff
Connector   COM2: or whatever serial port is used by your modem

4   Click Phone, Dial. Type **0734 270065** and click OK.

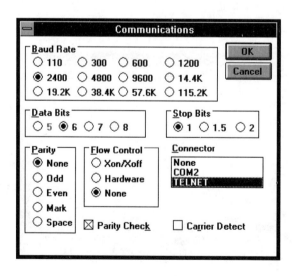

FIG. 22.5

Odds and ends

5 When you're connected enter **new** to log on as a new user. You've just joined the Microsoft Bulletin Board!

6 When you want to end the connection press **x** to log off.

7 When you are logged out click Phone, Hangup.

The number given in the preceding example is correct at the time of writing. I can make no guarantee that this number will hold in the future or that Microsoft continues to offer its Bulletin Board service. Also, at the time of writing, there are no connect charges, so all you pay for is the cost of the telephone call to Reading. To dial from outside the UK use +44 734 270065. Please note that some modems may need further configuration in order to work with the example given.

CD Player

CD Player, as you might expect, is for playing audio CDs. However, you must have an NT-compatible CD-ROM or a CD player linked to your computer. A CD-ROM that is compatible with DOS is not necessarily compatible with Windows NT. If you do have a compatible CD-ROM, place an audio CD in the drive and away you go. You control CD-ROM drivers through the Drivers icon in Control Panel.

Media Player

Media Player is for playing an assortment of multimedia devices. Such devices must be MCI-compatible.

Odds and ends

Volume Control

If you have an NT-compatible sound card use Volume Control to control output and input volumes.

Character Map

This is quite a handy little accessory (see FIG. 22.6) used to insert special characters into a document. Examples might include copyright or trademark symbols. In Character Map select a font (Wingdings is worth investigating) and click on a character and the Select button. The character appears in the Characters to Copy text box. When the desired characters are shown in this box click Copy to place the characters on the Clipboard. In the destination accessory or Windows application switch to the same font and click Edit, Paste to place the special characters in your document.

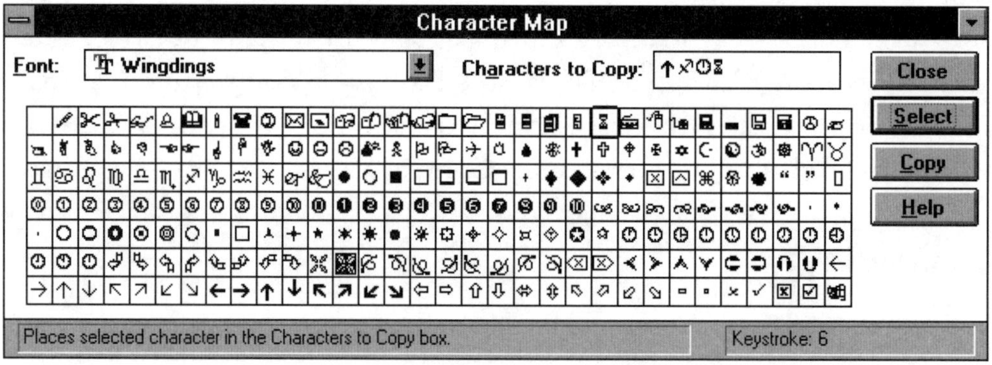

FIG. 22.6

Odds and ends

Clock

When you start Clock, the Settings menu allows you to switch between a digital and an analog clock. A minimized Clock can keep ticking away at the bottom of the screen, should you need to see the time. Further configuration is possible including size, font, hiding the title bar, and keeping on top.

Sound Recorder

Sound Recorder is for recording, editing, and playing sound files. These must have WAV format. There are two ways in which to use sound. First, you can attach sounds to Windows events, for example when Windows NT starts up. To do this use the Sound icon in Control Panel and not Sound Recorder. Second, you can place sound objects into documents. Here you use Sound Recorder as an OLE server. Once again, you must have the right hardware to exploit multimedia.

Games group

Solitaire

Also called Patience in the UK. Click to deal from pack and drag to place in playing area. Drag, or double click, to build up the discard piles.

Odds and ends

Minesweeper

Click to clear a free square, but watch the numbers exposed. Right click to mark suspected mines. You must clear all squares or mark them correctly as mines to win.

Freecell

Totally addictive! If you're a system administrator you might want to hide this before end users discover it's there. It's a lot like Solitaire (Patience) but requires more skill. You can transfer cards from column to column in the playing area, as you would in Solitaire – only click rather than drag. Unlike Solitaire you can place any card in an empty column. You can also place a maximum of four cards in the temporary holding area (free cells) at the top left. You can also move cards back down into the playing area. To move cards first select then click on the destination. The area at the top right is for your discard suits, as in Solitaire. Good luck!

Installing Windows NT

INSTALLING WINDOWS NT

- How to install from floppy disks

- How to install from CD-ROM

- Choosing a disk partition

Before you begin to install Windows NT you have to make a couple of decisions. First, do you want NT to be your sole operating system or do you want a dual-boot system? Second, do you want to create an NTFS partition or stick with existing FAT or HPFS partitions? You must also decide whether to install from floppies or from CD-ROM. This section begins by looking at these choices.

Let's consider a typical case, indeed the situation that the vast majority of readers will find themselves in. Suppose you've had DOS as your operating system and maybe run Windows for DOS as well. It's likely that you have a large number of DOS and Windows for DOS applications. And it's certain that you have a FAT disk partition. To keep DOS as an alternative operating system you must preserve the FAT partition. This enables you to boot into DOS and to run Windows for DOS. This, of course, allows you to continue running all your DOS and 16-bit Windows applications. Having said that, Windows NT is quite happy to run DOS and Windows for DOS applications. However, you may have an important application that just won't run satisfactorily or you may have some hardware devices that are not yet supported by NT. Then it makes sense to keep DOS in a FAT partition. You may also find that if security is not a problem that Windows for DOS is actually more convenient to use for a number of tasks. You may also want to keep DOS until NT has proved itself to you. If you change your mind later then you can drop DOS altogether by converting its FAT partition into an NTFS one. Incidentally, the same arguments apply to OS/2 users with an HPFS partition.

An NTFS partition provides a number of important benefits. It supports the setting of file and directory permissions (FAT only supports permissions on shared directories), and is better for system security generally. In addition, you can have file and directory names with a

Installing Windows NT

maximum of 256 characters. And when you run DOS and Windows for DOS applications under NT they can access files and directories with such lengthy names. The drawbacks to an NTFS partition include the inability of another operating system to access files and directories in the partition. Should you format drive C as an NTFS partition then you can't even boot into another operating system. If you want the best of both worlds you may want to have both a FAT and an NTFS partition. Having drive C as the FAT partition means you can boot into DOS (or NT) and run Windows for DOS. A second NTFS partition means you can exploit long filenames and the ability to set file and directory permissions. With a FAT/NTFS partitioned disk you can place NT into either of the partitions. However, if your hard disk already has a single FAT partition then creating the second partition results in all files in the FAT partition being lost – you must reinstall DOS and Windows for DOS. But you can convert a single FAT partition into a single NTFS partition without the loss of files. You should think about the alternatives carefully before beginning to install NT.

You also need to decide whether to install from floppies or from CD-ROM. The former can be quite tedious and involves quite a lot of disk swapping. On the other hand, you may have to stick with floppies if your CD-ROM is not supported. There are two levels of CD-ROM support, Windows NT support and DOS support. To see if your CD-ROM is directly supported by Windows NT then it's probably listed in the hardware compatibility list in your NT documentation. If it's not directly supported by NT you may still be able to use your CD-ROM for installation if it's supported by DOS. Your CD-ROM is DOS-supported if you can use it from DOS or Windows for DOS.

You should also think about the installation process itself. There are two basic processes: Express Setup and Custom Setup. Express Setup does most of the work for you and is recommended unless you have good reason not to use it. Custom Setup is for advanced users and it allows you to make a few choices during installation. This might be a viable alternative if you know that Windows NT doesn't detect your hardware correctly. It might also be an option if Express Setup fails for any reason. Most of the choices made for you by Express Setup (or the choices you make during Custom Setup) can be changed after installation – usually through Control Panel, Windows NT Setup, and Print Manager. The final thing to do before starting installation is to have a blank floppy to hand. This does not have to be formatted and is used during the installation to create the Emergency Repair Disk. The instructions that follow are for Intel-based PCs – the instructions for RISC-based machines differ slightly in some respects. You are referred to your NT documentation and your RISC computer documentation.

To install Windows NT from floppies:

1   Switch off your computer.

2   Insert the Windows NT Disk 1 - Setup Disk for Floppy Disk in drive A: – your computer must be capable of booting from floppy.

3   Turn on the computer.

4   Respond to directions and enter options appropriately during the setup process.

Installing Windows NT

To install Windows NT from an NT-supported CD-ROM:

1   Switch off the computer.

2   Insert the Windows NT Setup Disk for CD-ROM Installation in drive A:.

3   Switch on the computer.

4   Follow the instructions on screen and insert the Windows NT compact disc when prompted.

5   Respond to directions and enter options appropriately during the setup process.

You can also install from a DOS-supported CD-ROM. Here you'll need a second blank floppy which must be formatted – this is in addition to the floppy used as an Emergency Repair Disk. You also need 85 megabytes of free disk space. Once installed Windows NT takes up about 75 megabytes – the reclaimed 10 megabytes are for temporary installation files. To install Windows NT from a DOS-supported CD-ROM:

1   Insert the Windows NT compact disc in your CD-ROM drive.

2   From the DOS prompt log on to your CD-ROM. For example if the CD-ROM is drive E: enter **E:**.

3   Change to the I386 directory on the compact disc – type **cd \i386** and press **Enter**.

4   At the DOS prompt enter **winnt**. This starts WINNT.EXE which is also used for installing across a network. In that case start WINNT from a network drive and not from your local CD-ROM. Press **Enter** to accept the path for the installation files.

5   Insert a blank *formatted* floppy in drive A: when requested. This is used to create a special Setup disk which you are prompted for later.

6   Respond to directions and enter options appropriately during the setup process.

Once you begin the installation process as outlined above there are a number of choices to be made and actions to be taken. The exact nature of these choices and actions can vary from system to system. Here are the ones you are most likely to see, and it's best to be prepared:

■   Express versus Custom Setup

As already indicated, in the vast majority of cases it's better to go for Express Setup. Custom Setup involves making a few more choices. For example, you can set the size of your paging file.

■   Windows NT directory

Again it's usually better to accept the default. If Windows for DOS, or Windows for Workgroups, is detected you can install NT into your Windows for DOS directory. This is recommended if you want to work with both versions of Windows.

Installing Windows NT

■   Name and company

This is for registration purposes and the name entered does not have to be the same as your username.

■   Disk partitions and file systems

Hopefully, the discussion earlier helps you to make the right choices here. You won't be asked about file systems if you're installing into a Windows for DOS or Windows for Workgroups directory.

■   Printers

You are given the opportunity to install a printer. You should be aware of the type of printer you want to use, or one that's closely compatible. You can always delay this choice until after installation – then use Print Manager to install and configure printers. The Printer Name you enter does not have to match the full name of your printer. Enter something that is recognisable later – for example, Main Laser Printer.

■   Network card

NT detects most network cards automatically. Normally you should accept the defaults. You can change your mind later through the Network icon in Control Panel.

■   Joining a workgroup or domain

If it's appropriate you can join a workgroup or domain. The default workgroup is called WORKGROUP. You are also asked to provide a computer name, a username, and a password. Use these to log on for the first time. You are also asked to provide a password for the Administrator user.

■   Locality and time

Choose the options that are appropriate to your country.

■   Emergency Repair Disk

The installation process creates an Emergency Repair Disk on a blank floppy.

When installation is complete restart the computer and log on. If you open File Manager in the Main group you can see your NT directory. This is probably, though not necessarily, WINNT or WINDOWS\SYSTEM32 if you're installing to a Windows for DOS system. Also using File Manager you can see some new files in your root directory on an Intel-based PC. These files include BOOT.INI, NTLDR, and NTDETECT.COM – all of these are essential for starting NT and BOOT.INI is essential for starting DOS on a dual-boot system. There's also possibly a file called PAGEFILE.SYS – this is your swap file or virtual memory. If you do have a dual-boot system (for example, you've kept DOS in a FAT partition) then BOOTSECT.DOS is in your root – never delete this file. If you have a SCSI disk you'll also find NTBOOTDD.SYS.

Installing Windows NT

When you keep DOS and Windows for DOS (or Windows for Workgroups) in a FAT partition you can boot into DOS (and correspondingly Windows for DOS and Windows for Workgroups) or Windows NT. That way you can work with any version of Windows. It's easy to customize Windows NT so it resembles your existing Windows for DOS or Windows for Workgroups. Or if you prefer, you can migrate settings to NT when you log on. For example, you can have Windows NT recreate your Windows for DOS (or Windows for Workgroups) groups. Then you have a consistent and recognisable interface no matter which version of Windows you decide to run.

Index

Index

Index

Index

Index

Index

Index

F

Index

Index

Index

Index

Index

Index

Index

Index